LATIN AMERICAN REVOLUTIONARIES AND

THE ARAB WORLD

For Claudia Mejía and Sofía Vélez

Latin American Revolutionaries and the Arab World

From the Suez Canal to the Arab Spring

FEDERICO VÉLEZ
Zayed University, UAE

ASHGATE

Published by
Ashgate Publishing Limited
Wey Court East
Union Road
Farnham
Surrey, GU9 7PT
England

Ashgate Publishing Company
110 Cherry Street
Suite 3-1
Burlington, VT 05401-3818
USA

www.ashgate.com

British Library Cataloguing in Publication Data
A catalogue record for this book is available from the British Library.

The Library of Congress has cataloged the printed edition as follows:
Vélez, Federico.
  Latin American revolutionaries and the Arab world : from the Suez Canal to the Arab spring / by Federico Vélez.
      pages cm
  Includes bibliographical references and index.
  ISBN 978-1-4724-6721-8 (hardback : alk. paper) -- ISBN 978-1-4724-6722-5 (ebook) -- ISBN 978-1-4724-6723-2 (epub) 1. Arab countries--Foreign relations--Latin America. 2. Latin America--Foreign relations--Arab countries. 3. Revolutions--Arab countries--History--20th century. 4. Revolutions--Arab countries--History--21st century. 5. Revolutions--Latin America--History--20th century. I. Title.
  DS63.2.L29V45 2015
  909'.09749270825--dc23

                                                                                          2015019122

ISBN 9781472467218 (hbk)
ISBN 9781472467225 (ebk – PDF)
ISBN 9781472467232 (ebk – ePUB)

MIX
Paper from responsible sources
FSC
www.fsc.org   FSC® C013985

Printed in the United Kingdom by Henry Ling Limited, at the Dorset Press, Dorchester, DT1 1HD

Contents

List of Figures

Preface

My friend Andy Klatt inspired me to write this book with an anecdote he told me long ago in Medford, Massachusetts. His generous internationalist spirit and his commitment to global justice had taken him to Nicaragua in the 1980s. His government, the United States (US) government, had declared Nicaragua to be a threat both to its own security and to that of the region. Therefore, Washington was financing a group of counterrevolutionaries created to destroy the Nicaraguan government in the hands of the *Frente Sandinista para la Liberación Nacional* (also known as the Sandinistas) since 1979. Andy had gone to help collect the coffee yield, as peasants had been drafted by the Sandinista government and sent to the front lines to fight the counterrevolutionaries, also known as *la contra*. On a road waiting for a truck that would take him to the coffee fields, he had a brief exchange with some young Nicaraguans, who told him that they had been trained in Lebanon by a Palestinian group. Despite my insistent request for more details, Andy had no more information to share with me. "We took different paths, and I never saw them again," he said. That was the end of my conversation with Andy that day, but it was the first day for this book.

I wanted to understand the reasons behind an encounter between revolutionaries from Latin America, Nicaraguans in this case, and Palestinian guerrillas, as well as the articulation and international implications of the encounter. My initial research led me to explore declarations from both the Sandinistas and the Palestinian Liberation Organization (PLO), as both organizations publicly acknowledged in the 1980s that they had years of revolutionary solidarity in the past. The US archives also contained documentation from the Ronald Reagan administration (1981–1989) on the Sandinista-Palestinian relationship, which Washington interpreted as being part of a major international strategy coordinated by Moscow to expand its influence in the region. Within the framework of Cold War rationale, the evidence available was cited as justification for the diplomatic and military campaign the US was waging in Central America in the 1980s against Nicaragua. My initial approach was to study this Palestinian-Sandinista encounter as another case in the global confrontation between the Soviet Union and the United States.

As my investigation progressed, I began to find other episodes of encounters between Arab and Latin American revolutionaries that predated those of the Sandinistas and the Palestinians. Thanks to the work of Piero Gleijeses, I found out that more than two decades before the triumph of the Sandinistas in Nicaragua, Cuban revolutionaries had initiated what they heralded as a close political and military alliance with the government of Algeria and its leader, Ahmed Ben Bella. Fidel Castro and the other leaders of the Cuban revolution were convinced that Algeria and Cuba were "sister revolutions"—the product of the same injustices committed by colonial powers on two different continents over the centuries and two nations destined to work together to spread revolutions throughout the world, particularly in Africa and Latin America. Castro also pursued the recognition of Cuba as a nation inscribed in the nascent Afro-Asian bloc of nations of which Egyptian President Gamal Abdel Nasser was its indisputable leader by the early 1960s. The Cuban government felt connected to the wider global trend of nationalist revolutionaries constructing for themselves a new space in the world that extended beyond the framework of the Cold War.

Even before the Cuban revolution, nationalist intellectuals were closely following the political events occurring in Egypt in the 1950s. Egypt's political and social revolution and Nasser's assertive foreign policy captivated their imagination. The mystique surrounding Nasser's personality and his revolution would irradiate throughout Latin America. Dissatisfied with what they saw as the betrayal of the democratic model during the early years of the Cold War, Latin American intellectuals would turn to the 'other south' in search of inspiration.

Parallel to my historical research, current events were revealing the attraction that the Arab world continued to have for Latin American revolutionaries. At the beginning of the twenty-first century, the new president of Venezuela, Hugo Chavez, proclaimed himself "another Arab" and declared the region an essential partner in what he thought was an emerging front against the changing world order after the Cold War. He identified himself as part of a revolutionary continuum that emerged in the twentieth century in both Latin America and the Arab World with Nasser in Egypt, followed by Fidel Castro in Cuba, Qaddafi in Libya, culminating in his Bolivarian revolution in Venezuela.

This book tells the story of the encounters between Latin American revolutionaries and the Arab world: the story of what Latin American revolutionaries saw, and what they wanted to see, in the Arab world in the last 60 years.

Federico Vélez

Acknowledgments

Andy Klatt inspired me to write this book after telling me of an episode of his life as an internationalist working to help Nicaraguans survive the covert war unleashed by the United States against Nicaragua in the 1980s. Parts of this book come from my doctoral dissertation at the Fletcher School of Law and Diplomacy. Leila Fawaz helped me put together the modern history of the Arab World; and Peter Winn that of modern Latin America. Tony Smith helped me with the theoretical discussion of politics during the Cold War. These are incredible mentors and friends. I want to thank the Al-Husaini family for their hospitality during my stay in Ramallah. Yamila Al-Husaini, in particular, helped me to navigate the intricacies of Palestinian politics. In Managua, Nicaragua, Julián Gómez opened up his home to me, a generous act that allowed me to do much of my research in that country.

The University of Mostaganem made my encounter with President Ahmed Ben Bella possible in October, 2005. Finally, Zayed University's Office of the Provost allowed me to have a semester of sabbatical leave that helped me finish my investigation on Venezuela.

Claudia Mejía's love, support, and encouragement made this book possible, and Sofía Vélez, born and raised between Latin America and the Arab World, has helped me to better understand both regions through her inquisitive and lovely eyes.

Introduction

This book has two purposes. The first is to articulate the story of a series of encounters between Latin American and Arab revolutionaries as part of the broader global history of the twentieth century and beyond. The second purpose is to contribute to the debate regarding the ideological and political autonomy of those actors on the periphery of the international system by arguing that these actors have been far more independent in their actions and political convictions than we had previously assumed.

The first purpose requires the study of more than 60 years of encounters between Latin American revolutionaries and the Arab World. The book begins by tracing the influence of the Egyptian leader Gamal Abdel Nasser in Latin America within the framework of increasing nationalist demands in the region as well as the global emergence of the decolonization movement, the Third World, and the Cold War. The story continues with the Cuban revolution and the Cubans' pursuit of Nasser's diplomatic recognition as part of the efforts to inscribe the revolution within the nascent Afro-Asian bloc of newly independent, anticolonial nations. Inscribing Cuba in the growing Afro-Asian movement would be fundamental in defining the international character of the revolution, but the realities of the limited concrete diplomatic or military support that Cuba could receive from Egypt, or from any other nation of the Afro-Asian front, became evident as US aggression increased and as the revolution became increasingly radicalized. Algeria and Cuba, the "sister revolutions," would collaborate in what Cubans understood as a common commitment to revolution, social progress, and Afro-Asian liberation. Their strong alliance lasted only until 1965 when the Algerian leader Ahmed Ben Bella was deposed, depriving Cuba of its most important ally in the Middle East. Nicaragua's Sandinista National Liberation Front (FSLN) would receive military training from different Palestinian groups in Jordan and Lebanon in 1970. Once in power, the Sandinista government would be the strongest supporter of the Palestinian cause in Latin America. Finally, as the century ended, the new president of Venezuela, Hugo Chávez Frías, declared himself to be an ideological descendant of Gamal Abdel Nasser while launching a diplomatic offensive against the US both in Latin America and the Arab World.

Throughout these years, Latin American revolutionaries firmly believed that they were bound to the Arab World by a common colonialist experience and the firm determination to fight against the injustices of the world order. This conviction would obscure their understanding of cultural differences, the complexity of regional and local politics, and the acceptance of fundamental deficiencies of political legitimacy amongst their Arab counterparts.

The book's second purpose is to explore the nature of relations between the periphery and the core during the Cold War. The encounter between Arab and Latin American revolutionaries would occur primarily during the Cold War, a period of ideological, economic, military, and political competition between the Soviet Union and the United States. The conflict, which began shortly after the Second World War, created a world divided between two camps, with each side composed of countries aligned with each superpower. The further development of nuclear arsenals on both sides and the capacity to respond to such an attack with another of the same kind prevented the superpowers from escalating their conflicts to a nuclear confrontation. Early scholarship on the Cold War would argue that superpowers then used proxies across the world to advance their strategic interests. Proxies were not ideologically independent and had a limited capacity for action, especially if they were on the periphery of the global system.

This book argues that the encounters between Latin American revolutionaries and their Arab counterparts reflects the quite the opposite. Regardless of the importance of Moscow to their own survival, Latin American revolutionaries pursued relations with Arab regimes despite the alternating views of indifference and at times clear opposition of the Soviet Union.

The first encounters between Cuban revolutionaries and Egypt predated relations with the Soviet Union. In Havana, Egypt was perceived to be a natural ally of their nationalist revolution, and Cairo's neutrality in the conflict between the United States and the Soviet Union was considered a possible diplomatic option in the early days of the revolution. As Havana's nationalist revolution also became socialist, the Soviet Union had greater economic and military influence in Cuba, but it did not diminish Cuba's interest in the Arab World. The origins of the support for the Algerian revolution also predated a stronger relationship with Moscow, but the zenith of Cuba's alliance with Ahmed Ben Bella's revolution came precisely when relations with the Soviet Union reached their lowest levels after the Cuban Missile Crisis of 1962. The Sandinistas in Nicaragua had to explore other sources of support beyond Cuba in the early 1970s, and they alone found this support in the Palestinian movement. Palestinians would support the Sandinistas at a time when the Soviet Union, and Cuba itself, could not be of much help.

Even after the Cold War and the further implosion of the Soviet Union in 1991, the Arab world continued to be a referent for Latin American revolutionaries. Since 1999, Caracas has viewed Latin America and the Arab world as regions united in challenging the forces of neoliberalism and the military expansion of a sole world power. From the invasion of Iraq in 2003 to the Israeli military incursions in Lebanon and Gaza and the popular uprisings that shook the Arab world from 2010 onward Caracas saw the hands of the United States, and its allies, behind every military or social development in the region.

As a door to the new world of independent and neutral Afro-Asian nations, partners in their global revolutionary projects and wars of national liberation, and perceived allies in their fight against a social world order that they denounced as unfair, the Arab world has been a point of reference for Latin American revolutionaries for more than 60 years. This book narrates that story.

Chapter 1
Gamal Abdel Nasser in Latin America[1]

In 1966, Juan Pablo Pérez Alfonzo, a prominent Venezuelan intellectual and founding member of the Organization of Petroleum Exporting Countries (OPEC), reminded Latin Americans of the powerful lesson the Egyptian leader Gamal Abdel Nasser gave to the region. Egypt, according to Pérez Alfonzo, stood firmly against the war of aggression unleashed by the United Kingdom, France, and Israel three months after Nasser ordered the nationalization of the Suez Canal Company in July 1956. By successfully confronting the tripartite attack in October of that year, Egypt showed the world that it was possible for countries on the periphery of the system to claim for themselves the rightful ownership of their natural resources and to administer these resources in the most efficient manner. Pérez Alfonzo argued that Egypt had shown the world that "human solidarity could confront blatant injustices" and that small nations could find the necessary qualified manpower to operate large enterprises such as the Suez Canal.[2] He urged his readers in Latin America to see Egypt as a nation "successful in her fight for development, and economic liberation," a nation focused on helping herself and other nations.[3]

It appeared that Egypt had succeeded where Latin America failed. Less than four years after coming to power following a coup d'état against the old regime in 1952, Nasser had transformed his country. Egypt, in the eyes of the world, had achieved a true place in international affairs by pursuing an assertive nationalism and had demonstrated that it was not only willing, but also capable, of taking control of its own destiny. In contrast, by the 1950s fears of a communist expansion had put an end to the social changes that had taken place across the Latin America in the last decade. Reversals in democracy and political participation, and the almost unanimous acceptance of the United States' leadership in world affairs, were the new reality of the region. By 1952, the Colombian historian Germán Arciniegas denounced the unfolding of what

---

1 A version of this chapter has been published by the journal *Varia Historia*, 31.55, January–April 2015.

2 Juan Pablo Pérez Alfonzo, "Organización de Países Exportadores de Petróleo (OPEP)," *Política: Ideas para una América Nueva*, 45, January (1966), 8–9.

3 Pérez Alfonzo, "Organización de Países Exportadores de Petróleo," 9.

he described as a "vast conspiracy against democracy, liberty, and respect for human rights that has been set in motion in Latin America." The "forces of totalitarianism," Arciniegas maintained, were in a "life-and-death struggle" against the forces of democracy.[4]

Latin America at the Time of Nasser

The New World Order in Latin America (1945–1948)

The triumph of the allies in the Second World War represented the triumph of democracy not just in Europe but across the world.[5] In Latin America, where democratic regimes had been rather exceptional occurrences, students, intellectuals, union leaders, and a new generation of politicians demanded a political transition toward open societies and democratic political systems. In making their demands, they counted on the unrestricted support of the United States government, which was committed to being a force for democratic transition across Latin America.[6] By the end of the war, there was already a noticeable move toward democracy across the region. Although non-democratic sectors remained powerful, they became sidetracked under the mounting pressure for political change. Over a short period of time, new governments came to power through general elections that were, for the most part, open and free from major corruption.[7] Democracy continued in countries with a previous democratic tradition, such as Uruguay, Chile, Colombia, and Costa Rica.[8] In other countries, however, these events were largely a novel experience. In Ecuador, for example, a coalition of political forces deposed the dictator Carlos Arroyo del Rio and installed the progressive regime of José María Velasco Ibarra.[9] Around the same time, Cuban strongman Fulgencio Batista permitted

---

4 Germán Arciniegas, *The State of Latin America* (London: Cassell & Co., 1953), xi.

5 For a comprehensive study of this period, on which this segment is based, see Leslie Bethell and Ian Roxborough, *Latin America Between the Second World War and the Cold War 1944–1948* (Cambridge: Cambridge University Press, 1992).

6 Samuel Huntington, *The Third Way: Democratization in the late Twentieth Century* (Oklahoma, OK: Oklahoma University Press, 1991), 18; and Bethell and Roxborough, *Latin America*, 8.

7 "South America's Rising Cry: 'Democracia'," *New York Times*, January 13, 1946, SM7.

8 "Chilean Disavows One Party Regime," *New York Times*, November 3, 1946, 47.

9 "Candidate A Red, Ecuadorians Say: Foes Assail former Interior Chief and a Top Presidential Aspirant Free Elections Promised," *New York Times*, March 31, 1956, 4.

partially free elections. Multiparty elections were also allowed in Peru,[10] whereas Venezuela experienced the first democratically elected government in its history when the progressive regime of Rómulo Betancourt came to power.[11] In Guatemala, the thirteen-year dictatorship of General Jorge Ubico ended in October 1944, and a new progressive regime was elected under José Arévalo. In Brazil, Getúlio Vargas, who had been in power since 1930, allowed open elections for the first time in December 1945.[12] In short, by the end of the war, only the smallest and most backward regimes of Central America and the Caribbean had not experienced significant changes in their political structures.[13]

As the Americas emerged with a stronger commitment to democratic systems, the progressive sectors that had made the transition possible were demanding and working toward the achievement of more inclusive societies. Across the region, new political actors articulated a new range of social demands to set in motion the transformation of their societies. As beneficiaries of Soviet participation in the war on the side of the Allies, many countries allowed socialist and communist parties to participate in the political process of the moment—although their popular appeal remained low, perhaps with Chile as the only exception.[14] In this progressive environment, the United States helped to broker the establishment of diplomatic relations between several Latin American countries and the Union of Soviet Socialist Republics (USSR).[15]

---

10 In Peru, the leading candidates promised a "peaceful revolution," and all pledged to address the historical inequalities of the country. "All Parties Vote on Peru President," *New York Times*, June 10, 1945, 16.

11 "Betancourt Wins Latin Recognition," *New York Times*, October 26, 1945, 8.

12 "President Dutra of Brazil," *New York Times*, December 12, 1945, 25.

13 "Nicaragua Ruled by One-Man Regime," *New York Times*, May 26, 1952, 12; "Dominicans Thrive at the Cost of Liberty," *New York Times*, March 28, 1953, 7; on transitions around the region and a comprehensive study of the changes taking place, see Bethell and Roxborough, *Latin America*, 5.

14 "Chilean Reds Seek Key Cabinet Posts; Despite Setbacks in "Broken" Strikes, Party is Strong—It Now Condemns the U.S.," *New York Times*, April 10, 1946, 12.

15 "Latins Urged to Accept Russia; US and Mexico Striving to Persuade 13 Republics to Recognize Ally Formally," *New York Times*, February 25, 1945, 14. FRUS, "Informal Good Offices of the United States in the Establishment of Diplomatic Representation Between the Soviet Union and Certain of the American Republics," in FRUS, vol. IX, 1945, *The American Republics* (Washington, DC, 1969), 223–230. "Argentina, Soviet Enter Relations; 28 Year Nonrecognition Ends as Peron Beams," June 7, 1946. Also, Bethell and Roxborough, *Latin America*, 10–11.

*The Onset of the Cold War—the Collapse of the
Democratic Experiment*

The alliance between the Soviet Union and the United States proved to be short-lived. Two years after the end of the Second World War, suspicion over each other's policies across Europe signalled the beginning of a 40-year conflict that soon extended across the globe. In order to prevent the expansion of communism in the Americas and firmly settle the region within the American orbit, the Rio Conference of 1947 crafted an inter-American treaty of reciprocal defense that expanded the definition of security to include attacks of a nonmilitary nature and to include the protection of American states in cases in which

> the sovereignty or political independence of any American State should be affected by an aggression which is not an armed attack or by an extra-continental or intra-continental conflict, or by any other fact or situation might endanger the peace of America.[16]

Latin American reactionary sectors previously displaced by progressive social forces took note of the changes that were taking place across the Atlantic and promptly began to play into the security anxieties of the United States to reverse recent social and political changes.[17]

Progressive sectors of society soon began to be seen and portrayed by reactionary forces as potential instruments of international Soviet-style communism. The first victims of this conservative backlash were labor unions, followed by Communist parties, culminating in the severance of diplomatic relations with the Soviet Union by several Latin American countries.[18]

---

16 Pan American Union, Inter-American Treaty of reciprocal assistance signed at the Inter-American Conference for the Maintenance of Continental Peace and Security, Rio de Janeiro, August 15–September 2, 1947, (Washington, DC: Pan American Union, General Secretariat, Organization of American States), Inter-American Treaty of Reciprocal Assistance, Art. 6; "Text of Marshall and Vanderberg Talks on Rio Treaty," New York Times, September 5, 1947, 4.

17 This analysis of the collapse of democracy after the Second World War draws mainly from the ideas expressed by Bethell and Roxborough, "The Postwar Conjuncture in Latin America: Democracy, Labor and the Left," in Bethell and Roxborough, eds., *Latin America*, 16–32.

18 "Brazil is on Guard after Ban on Reds: President is Expected to Issue Decree Barring Reorganizing of the Communist Party." *New York Times*, May 9, 1947; "Brazil and the U.S.S.R.," *New York Times*, October 22, 1947; "Chile Seizes Communist Chiefs; Army Controls in Four Provinces," *New York Times*, October 23, 1947. 1. Bethell and Roxborough, *Latin America*, 16.

By the 1950s, Latin Americans were living in less democratic and less inclusive societies. Juan Domingo Perón was deposed in Argentina. In Venezuela, a military coup in 1948 against President Romulo Gallegos put an end to one of the most progressive regimes in the region. Gallegos had refused to ban the Communist Party of Venezuela (PCV), and his administration had continued to deny diplomatic recognition to the dictatorships of the Caribbean and Central America in an effort to force a democratic transition in the region. A coalition of conservative forces, with the support of the United States, supported the ten-year dictatorship of General Marcos Pérez Jiménez after its coup in November 1948. Venezuela under Pérez Jiménez was described by the American press as "completely friendly," and a country with "the best of intentions." In Venezuela, the western world can keep its fingers crossed and hope for the best.[19] In Guatemala, an experiment in social justice brought about by President Jacobo Arbenz ended with a coup d'état organized by the Central Intelligence Agency of the United States in 1954 acting on the suspicion that a nationalist movement could be used by communism to advance its interests in the region. Arbenz had dared to enact a land reform that went against the interests of the largest landlord in the country, the American United Fruit Company.

Panamanian Nationalism and Nasser

With these political changes, Latin America closed into itself from the social and political changes taking place in newly independent countries emerging from the collapse of old colonial empires. Panama was probably one of the few exceptions. Fifty-three years before the events in Suez, the United States had carved out a country from Colombia to build an interoceanic canal after the Colombian Congress refused to accept the conditions initially agreed upon by both governments. Structured as an American protectorate, the country, which was given the same name as its isthmus—Panama—granted the United States the right to build an interoceanic canal together with the use, occupation, and control of a five-mile zone on each side of the waterway, also known as the Canal Zone. The concessions stipulated in the first diplomatic treaty between the new republic and the United States were in perpetuity, with the possibility of unilateral territorial expansion and the acceptance of a military intervention in the Canal Zone and across the country, should it become necessary to facilitate the operation or defense of the canal.

Over the years, Panamanian nationalism turned against the American presence and against American influence over local and international politics, its control

---

19 Steve Ellner, "Venezuela," in Bethell and Roxborough, *Latin America*, 167–169; "Venezuela's role is Vital to the West," *New York Times*, April 28, 1951, 5.

of the labor market in the most important economic sector of the country, the expansion of Anglo-Saxon culture in the Canal Zone, and its monopoly over the canal and the business infrastructure that supported its activities. This growing discontent, which included a wide sector of society from the poor unskilled labor force to the more affluent middle class, forced the Panamanian government throughout much of the 1930s to seek the renegotiation of the 1903 founding Hay-Bunau-Varilla Treaty. This attempt culminated in the nominal ending of the protectorate status in 1939 and minor concessions that did not alter the nature of Panama's demands against the American presence.[20] Although nationalist claims receded during the Second World War as Panama, like most Latin American countries, set aside past grievances against the United States and lent its support to the Allied cause, demands for the renegotiation of the conditions resurfaced in 1947. In that year, Panama's foreign minister, Ricardo Alfaro, resigned in protest over his government's consideration of a proposal to extend the leases of thirteen military bases outside the Canal Zone. Under the threat of a national strike and constant pressure from a mob outside threatening to lynch any member who voted in favor of the agreement, the National Assembly rejected the extension of the leases for American bases outside the Canal Zone. The United States then decided to confine the defense of the canal exclusively to the Canal Zone. However, nationalist demands increased throughout the early 1950s, and the National Assembly unanimously called for the Panamanian government to urge Washington to further negotiate the 1903 treaty.[21]

Gamal Abdel Nasser's challenge to the remnants of British colonialism began to appear as an issue in the negotiations between the US and Panama. As early as 1954, a new round of demands from Panama forced the US to return to the negotiating table and to accept a recalculation of royalties and an improvement in the labor and economic situation of Panamanians working in the American Zone.

The following year, when the United States asked the government of Panama for two hilltop sites for military radar systems under U.S. jurisdiction outside the main Canal Zone, the government of Panama not only rejected the request but again raised objections regarding the labor conditions in the Canal Zone and the amount of contraband coming from the Canal Zone into Panama, which was cheating the country of vital customs revenues.[22] President Eisenhower

---

20 For an account of this growing nationalism and the first renegotiation of the 1903 Hay-Bunau-Varilla Treaty, see Lester D. Langley, "Negotiating New Treaties with Panama: 1936," *The Hispanic American Historical Review*, 48.2 (May 1968), 220–233.

21 Harding Earl, *The Untold Story of Panama* (New York: Athene Press Inc., 1959), 110.

22 FRUS, "Political and Military Relations of the United States and Panama: Impact of the Suez Canal Crisis," in FRUS vol. VII, 1945, *The American Republics* (Washington,

met with Panamanian President Ricardo Arias in Panama and promised him that the United States would do everything possible to help his government.[23] Shortly after, President Eisenhower asked his Secretary of Defense to seek an agreement with the Panamanian government that would leave the Panamanians satisfied because the local population could be easily manipulated by Panamanian Politicians. According to Eisenhower, "local politics can feed on resentments brought by real or imagined injustices to the native population." The United States, the President argued, should attempt to meet the Panamanians "half-way," but, "without incurring the risk of divided control or beclouding our clear title to ownership."[24] In short, Eisenhower emphasized to his representatives to reach an agreement having in mind that that every concession should be made to ensure that "future years do not bring about for us, in Panama, the situation that Britain has to face in the Suez."[25]

It was already too late. The nationalization of the Suez Canal Company by the Egyptian leader Gamal Abdel Nasser on July 26, 1956, rekindled Panama's nationalist demands. Nasser's decision reignited demands and aspirations in the isthmus. The diplomatic correspondence between Panama and the United States provided clear notice of the change. The Acting Officer in charge of Central American and Panamanian Affairs, in a memo to the Deputy Assistant Secretary of State of Inter-American Affairs, explained the situation to his superiors in Washington:

> The Panamanians, unable or unwilling to see beyond the superficial analogies between the two situations, have made no secret of the fact that they follow with keen interest the developments of the Suez. The Government of Panama unquestionably looks to the day when it will be able in one way or another to emulate the recent action of Egypt. There is quiet talk from time to time in even responsible circles in Panama of eventual nationalization or internationalization of the Panama Canal. Within the last few months an ex-Foreign Minister, who has always shown himself to be friendly toward the United States, remarked to our Ambassador that "Now Egypt has her canal and we shall someday have ours."[26]

DC: United States Government Printing Office, 1987), 274–275.

23 FRUS, "Political and Military Relations of the United States and Panama," in FRUS, vol. VII, 1945, *The American Republics*, 277–280.

24 FRUS, "Political and Military Relations of the United States and Panama," in FRUS vol. VII, 1945, *The American Republics*, 281.

25 FRUS, "Political and Military Relations of the United States and Panama," in FRUS vol. VII, 1945, *The American Republics*, 281.

26 FRUS, "Political and Military Relations of the United States and Panama," in FRUS vol. VII, 1945, *The American Republics*, 284, 285.

Panamanian overtures in support of Egypt's policies went from private to public in Panama City.[27] The United States wanted to make it clear to the Panamanians that emulating Nasser, even if only at the level of his nationalist discourse, would bring consequences to Panama. On August 9, 1956, the US ambassador to Panama, Julian Harriman, and Assistant Secretary of State Henry Holland, met with President Arias, the Panamanian Minister of Foreign Affairs, and the Chairman of the Panamanian Council of Foreign Relations in Panama City. Holland unambiguously warned President Arias about Panama's interest in Nasser and the consequences it would have for Panama's position in world affairs. In unambiguous terms, Holland told his audience,

> I had, in my thinking, attempted to put myself in the place of a Panamanian and determine what would be the best course for my country. This, of course, depended upon what my objective with respect to the Panama Canal might be.
>
> I knew that some Panamanians favored eventual nationalization or internationalization of the Canal. If I belonged to this group I would see two possible courses. The first would be to try to intervene in the Suez problem, to identify Panama with Egypt and to draw analogies between the two canals. The second course would be to avoid any participation in the Suez problem and to await a more favorable time to pursue my objective.
>
> Of these two courses, the second seemed to me the better. The first would necessitate the immediate sacrifice of some exceedingly valuable short-term assets of Panama. These are the present good will of the United States people and Government and the intention of the administration to urge favorable action by the next Congress on the legislation appropriating funds to construct the bridge across the Canal, the legislation regarding equal pay rates in the Zone and the legislation transferring to Panama certain lands and other assets covered by the recent treaty amendment. Likewise, the first course would necessitate Panama's identifying herself with the enemy of the United States and of Panama, since it is probable that Soviet Russia will align herself with Egypt.[28]

The United States wanted to raise the stakes by warning Panama of the consequences of these overtures to Egypt.

---

27 FRUS, "Continued U.S. Consideration of the Suez Situation; United States Diplomatic Activity Prior to the Suez Canal Conference, August 3–15," in FRUS, vol. XVI, *Suez Crisis July 26–December 31, 1956* (Washington, DC: United States Government Printing Office, 1990), 163. A Questao de Suez," *O Estado de São Paulo* (Sao Pãulo), September 19, 1956, 1.

28 FRUS, "Political and Military relations of the United States and Panama; impact of the Suez Canal Crisis," in FRUS, vol. VII, 1945, *The American Republics: Central and South America*, 292.

This interest in the events in Egypt had brought Panama to a political crossroads. According to Washington, it was time for Panama to make a decision. The Ambassador was clear, Panama needed to decide between either continuing its alliance with the United States or going down the Egyptian-Soviet path. If it decided to follow Egypt's pro-Soviet policies, "the present peculiar relationship between Panama and the United States would, of course, come to an end."[29] Holland placed the blame on "local communists, the local sector which favors nationalization of the Panama Canal and the local opposition to the existing Government" and accused them of pressuring the President to follow the Egyptian example. "Expressing some interest on the situation in Egypt," the Ambassador continued, "might not have been a bad decision after all, but it was now time to close and file this episode." It was now time for Panama to "desist from further statements on the subject; otherwise, it might find itself unwillingly embroiled in a problem that could only prejudice the interests of Panama."[30]

Diplomatic communication between Egypt and Panama was also discouraged by the United States. When Acting Foreign Minister Molino informed Holland that the Panamanian government had instructed its ambassador in Rome to travel to Egypt to learn about the Suez situation, Holland said

> that this might prove to be a mistake, and that it might be better for him to advise his Ambassador to stay away from Cairo. This would prevent the possibility of Egypt's managing to draw Panama into the dispute in some way.[31]

If the Panamanians seemed attentive to the admonitions coming from the Assistant Secretary, in public they acted differently. The government continued its support for the Egyptian decision and, in an act of defiance, invited Cairo to send a delegation to the inauguration of the new Panamanian president on October 1, 1956.

Eisenhower, however, was losing patience with the Panamanians and their infatuation with Egypt. A diplomatic plot was hatched to "bring the Panamanians to their senses." The State Department began to circulate the idea of contacting the government of Nicaragua to explore the construction of a new interoceanic canal in that country. Panamanian fear of the United States constructing a new canal would

---

29   FRUS, "Political and Military Relations of the United States and Panama," in FRUS, vol. VII, , 1945, *The American Republics*, 294.

30   FRUS, "Political and Military Relations of the United States and Panama," in FRUS, vol. VII, , 1945, *The American Republics*, 294.

31   FRUS, "Political and Military Relations of the United States and Panama," in FRUS, vol. VII, 1945, *The American Republics*, 295.

discourage possible moves by Panama, inspired by developments at Suez, to challenge our treaty rights in the Canal Zone, [and] also to bring about a more reasonable attitude on the part of Panama on Canal Zone problems. Its effectiveness would depend upon the degree to which we could impress the Panamanians that we are in earnest.[32]

If the Americans had to leave, an impatient Eisenhower vowed, we "would take the locks with us."[33]

Nationalist demands were articulated by the Panamanian government because of their own interests in the events in Egypt, but also because they were feeling the pressure from different sectors of society that were closely following the events in the Middle East. The events in Suez had awakened different sectors of society to the realities of the Middle East in general and Egypt in particular. A survey conducted by the University of Michigan among law students in Panama City found that an overwhelming majority thought that the nationalization of the Suez Canal "was a great thing" and that Nasser's Egypt was a primary foreign model to Panama.[34] In support of Nasser, university students in Panama City called for a General Assembly in September 1956. They demanded that the Panamanian government abolish the 1903 treaty and lend its full support to the cause in Egypt. Nasser, according to the Panamanian students, had acted within "the legitimate exercise of its sovereign rights."[35] By the late 1950s, organized groups of students began a series of peaceful protests against the American presence in the Canal Zone. On May 2, 1958, university students entered the Zone, planting 75 Panamanian flags across the Zone in demand of a renegotiation of all bilateral agreements. The following year, on November 3, 1959, two members of the National Assembly led a group of Panamanians on a "sovereignty" rally to demand the presence of the Panamanian flag in the Zone, which ended with skirmishes between American and Panamanian forces and the expulsion of the students from the Canal Zone.[36]

---

32 FRUS, "Political and Military Relations of the United States and Panama," in FRUS, vol. VII, , 1945, *The American Republics*, 305–306.

33 FRUS, "Political and Military Relations of the United States and Panama," in FRUS, vol. VII, 1945, *The American Republics*, editorial note, 291.

34 Daniel Goldrich, *Radical Nationalism: the Political Orientations of Panamanian Law Students*, Bureau of Social and Political Research (East Lansing, MI: Michigan State University1962), 16, 21.

35 Harding, *The Untold Story of Panama*, 125.

36 The video at Proyecto Nuevo 87, https://www.youtube.com/watch?v=rjcJrvLo_ME depicts these events.

In 1960, the University of Panama organized the first international conference on interoceanic channels in Panama City. The conference gathered scholars from other Central American countries and Mexico and served as the forum for the first legal and political comparative studies between Egypt and Panama canals. There was a general interest in studying both the legal arrangements imposed by the owners of the waterways and the national aspirations of both countries. Among those studying Panama's nationalist demands from a comparative perspective was the Panamanian jurist Professor Eloy Benedetti, who provided the first academic study of the legal framework governing the two waterways based on a fact-finding mission he undertook in Egypt. Comparing both countries, Benedetti found that Panama was in a more precarious situation than Egypt before Nasser's nationalization in terms of its national rights over the Canal Zone. He lamented the encroachment of the United States on Panama's sovereign rights over the Panama Canal materialized in the granting of consular representations to third countries, holding a monopoly over the toll system, using the Zone as the army's largest military base south of the United States, and being the place that other American agencies used to extend Washington's control over the rest of the continent. Benedetti decried the administrative inefficiencies caused by the United States' control over all functions in the Zone and argued that Egyptians were far more efficient in the administration of their canal than Americans were of the Panama Canal.[37] Egypt, Benedetti urged, was the only country that could serve as a referent for Panama's unique circumstances. There was much to coordinate in the future between the two governments, so he advised the government of Panama to "keep close and cordial relations with the government in Cairo."[38]

Panamanian demands continued unabated throughout the 1960s, inspired by the Egyptian example and the successful installation of the first nationalist revolution in Cuba in 1959.[39] Demands erupted again on January 9, 1964, when a group of Panamanian students demanded that their country's flag be raised in one of the Canal Zone's secondary schools in response to the refusal by American students to accept a previous agreement allowing the Panamanian flag on their campus alongside the U.S. flag. American students surrounded the Panamanian students, chanting the American national anthem and tearing up the Panamanian flag. The reaction was a general uprising against the American

---

37 Eloy Benedetti, *Tres Ensayos sobre El Canal de Panama* (Panamá: Ministerio de Educación, 1965), 60, 68, and 69.

38 Benedetti, *Tres Ensayos*, 103. For a valuable comparative study, see the work of another intellectual, the Costa Rican Vicente Saenz, "Los Canales Internacionales," *Cuadernos Americanos*, 16, May–June (1957): 13–16.

39 "Panama—Storm Center of Hemisphere Frictions; Crisis Reflects Bitter History Outbreaks Stir Deep Concern," *New York Times*, January 12, 1964, E4.

presence in the Canal Zone that resulted in the destruction of American property and twenty deaths, events that led President Roberto Chiari to break diplomatic relations with the United States until Washington accepted the full revision of the treaties governing the US presence in the isthmus.[40]

Both countries resumed diplomatic relations later in the year, and the United States allowed Panamanians to raise their flag alongside the American flag in the Canal Zone. The events of 1964 eventually led to a comprehensive treaty in the following decade between the United States and Panama. By 1968, General Omar Torrijos had taken the armed forces to power and installed a populist regime branded by friends and foes as a "Nasserist" regime, both for its military origins and for its commitment to neutralism and social progress.[41] Torrijos successfully negotiated a final agreement with the United States in 1977 that abrogated the Hay-Bunau-Varilla Treaty of 1903, returning sovereignty and, ultimately, full control of the canal and the Canal Zone to Panama in the year 2000.

"Military Nasserism": Clamoring for a Latin American Nasser

Egyptian nationalism also had an echo beyond Panama, although governments were more cautious in their official positions, favoring the mediation of the United Nations instead of supporting Egypt directly. Nonetheless, the nationalization of the Suez Canal and Egypt's response to the French, British, and Israeli invasion of October 29, 1956 were widely supported by different sectors, especially in countries with a considerable Arab population.

The night of the tripartite invasion of Egypt, the Argentinean local press reported that as news of the military attack reached Buenos Aires, supporters gathered in front of the Egyptian Embassy and presented the ambassador with a note of support signed by an ad hoc commission created to gather national support for Egypt's cause—the Commission in Solidarity with Egypt. Supporters of Egypt chanted slogans in favor of Nasser and against Israel, France, and Britain. At some point, the police had to intervene to restore order, but the protesters disobeyed the police orders, which required police reinforcements. Failing to disperse the crowds, police used tear gas in an effort

---

40 "Gunfire Flares; Relations Severed Till Pacts Are Altered, Chiari Asserts Panama Moves to Scrap Canal Treaties. Embassy Evacuated; 20 Die in Riots Oder Restored But Zone is Tense Troops Bar New Clashes—Panama Officials Bitter Over Army Firing," *New York Times*, January 11, 1964, 1

41 Howard J. Wiarda, "The Latin American Development Process and the New Developmental Alternatives: Military 'Nasserism' and 'Dictatorship with Popular Support'," *The Western Political Quarterly*, 25 (1972), 472.

to end the demonstration and surrounded the Egyptian embassy. With access to the embassy blocked, protesters moved to the Syrian embassy, where they were also met with tear gas and forced to disperse.[42] As news of the protests spread around the city, a new group of protesters gathered in the streets connecting the embassies. They chanted pro-Egypt slogans and were broken up by the police, who were about to confront a new group of 300 people in Calle Corrientes. These and other groups began to chant "Argentina with Egypt" and "Death to Israel." A third group of approximately 100 people formed in Corrientes Street after the two previous groups were dissolved. Most, mainly Argentineans of Arab descent and several Syrians, ended up in jail that night, accused of disorderly behavior.[43]

In Rio de Janeiro, Brazil, protesters gathered around the Egyptian embassy, and more than a dozen students declared their willingness to go to Egypt and fight in the Egyptian army.[44] By mid-November, students in different schools in São Paulo and Rio de Janeiro mounted protests against the invasion of Egypt. A student communiqué rejected the tripartite attack on the small nation and derided "futile" actions against "all of those who are fighting, as the Brazilian people are, for the consolidation of national sovereignty and the political and economic independence of their country from any world power."[45] Brazilian students at the Egyptian embassy also called on President Juscelino Kubitschek to oppose the hostile actions against Egypt at the United Nations and through all other available diplomatic channels.[46]

The left saw an opportunity to bring Nasser's Egypt to national politics when, on November 8, 1956, Kubitschek's government asked the Brazilian Congress for approval to send a military detachment as part of an Emergency Force created by the UN General Assembly to guarantee the separation of forces and the end of hostilities. Throughout the crisis, Brazil had decided to remain neutral while actively attempting to find a solution to the conflict through the United Nations. Macedo Soarez, Brazil's Minister of Foreign Relations, announced that the country believed "the Suez Canal belongs to Egypt, but its use constitutes an international service,"[47] and problems relating

---

42 "Los Diplomáticos Argentinos saldrán de El Cairo y Budapest," *La Prensa* (Buenos Aires) November 3, 1956, 4.

43 "Los Diplomáticos Argentinos saldrán de El Cairo y Budapest," *La Prensa*, 4.

44 "Uma Ficcao Criada Pelo Imperialismo e Inimizade entre Israel e o Egito," *Impresa Popular* (Rio de Janeiro) November 1, 1956, 1, 2.

45 "Contrarios a Agressao que atingiu o Egito," *Impresa Popular* (Rio de Janeiro), November 2, 1956, 4.

46 "Contrarios a Agressao que atingiu o Egito," *Impresa Popular*, 4.

47 "A Posicao do Itamarati na crise de Suez," *O Estado de São Paulo* (São Paulo) September 20, 1956, 1.

to it should be discussed and resolved within the United Nations.[48] Yet the left wanted to record its support for Nasser. During the debate, Senator Kerginaldo Cavalti, leader of the Popular Socialist Party (PSP), defended Egypt and its uncompromising nationalism. Cavalti warned other members that Brazil might someday face the same situation as Egypt. The senator warned that the invasion of Egypt could be the first in a series of attacks against the national interests of other countries such as Brazil. According to Cavalti,

> [A]s they intervene today in Egypt, in order to take the Suez Canal, tomorrow either England or the United States could intervene in Brazil in order to fulfill their interests. They might want us to subordinate our interests in our national oil industry "Petrobras" [Brazilian Petroleum Company] to their whims.[49]

Arab-Brazilians lauded the decision to send troops to Egypt as Brazil's entry onto the international stage as "a leader against tyranny." They asserted that his stance would have the support of "the nations of the Americas, Arab countries, and those who loved peace."[50]

Soon, support for Nasser's policies evolved into a general call for the emergence of a nationalist leader within the armed forces of Latin America, to follow the steps of Egypt and lead his country to a meaningful political and economic independence from foreign interests while launching his nation onto a path of solid economic development and social progress.

The left was not alone in its attempts to create an image of Nasser in Latin America, and it faced competition from other sides. Parallel to demonstrations supporting Egypt, Latin American Jewish communities began to organize to support Israel against Nasser's rising influence. Jewish newspapers in Portuguese and Spanish constantly criticized Nasser and lobbied for their own governments' solidarity with Israel. In Chile, Argentina, and Brazil, the three Latin American countries with the largest Jewish communities, there was an organized campaign to influence public opinion against the Egyptian leader. The editorial pages of the Jewish newspaper *Mundo Judío* analyzed the efforts of the Jewish community in Chile to support Israel and concluded that although at "the beginning of the conflict between Israel and Egypt Chilean public opinion seemed to side with the Egyptians," the work done by their community

---

48 Argentina also decided not to take an official position and work through a UN solution. See "Posición de la América Latina ante la Grave Crisis en el Cercano Oriente," *La Prensa* (Buenos Aires) November 8, 1956, 3.

49 "Protesto no Senado Contra a Brutal Agressao ao Egito," *Impresa Popular* (Rio de Janeiro) November 7, 1956, 2.

50 K. Mossadeque, "Caravana," *Impresa Popular* (Rio de Janeiro) November 11, 1956, 3.

among politicians in the Chamber of Deputies, at press conferences, and in presentations to the public had an effect; now, the newspaper claimed, "public opinion has turned to support the truth."[51]

His opponents presented Nasser not as a threat to the existence of Israel alone but as an eventual threat to Latin American culture in general. "I do not understand how writers and journalists in the Americas are in support of Nasser's advances in the region," one editorialist in *Mundo Judío* wrote, continuing,

> Nasser is not fighting against imperialism, he dreams of having full hegemony over the Mediterranean. This is no other thing but the old Saracen ambitions, which our cultural forefathers fought against for centuries. A well-armed Arab confederation, as it is in its way of being, will threaten Greece, Italy, France, and Spain, all the countries of the Latin seas. Arabs instead of moving forward have been moving backward and are at the doorsteps of being a semi-barbaric people to the point that, nowadays, they cannot demonstrate any major cultural advance. The way Nasser acts is a clear manifestation of their rudimentary state. An empire is always an undesirable thing, but an uncultured empire is a double disgrace.[52]

The Jewish community in Rio de Janeiro also mobilized in support of Israel and against Nasser. On December 13, 1956, more than 1,500 people attended a rally organized by the Federação das Sociedades Israelitas do Rio de Janeiro (Federation of Israeli Societies of Rio de Janeiro) in the Carlos Gomes Theater. Important members of the political class were invited to the theater to support Israel and reject Nasser.[53] The Jewish newspaper *Jornal Israelita* justified the Israeli invasion of Suez[54] and warned its readers that Nasser was yet another totalitarian leader building a political system "without a clear political orientation but with a cheap anti-westernism, anti-Israelism, militarism, and a vacuous idea of greatness."[55] If Nasser was left unchecked, they argued, the world would witness a rerun of the events of Munich in 1938, when the European powers were unable or unwilling to confront Hitler's defiance of the international system. In another editorial, this newspaper concluded that Israel was engaged in

---

51 "Esclarecimiento," *Mundo Judío* (Santiago) November 29, 1956, 3.

52 Ciro Alegría, "Los Sueños de Gamal A. Nasser y nosotros los Lationamericanos," *Mundo Judío* (Santiago) September 5, 1956, 4.

53 "Protesta a Comunidade Israelita Contra As Perseguicoes No Egito," *Jornal Israelita* (Rio de Janeiro) December 23, 1956, 1.

54 "Porque Israel Invadiu o Egito," *Jornal Israelita* (Rio de Janeiro) November 18, 1956, 1.

55 "O regime Totalitario do Coronel Nasser no Egito," *Jornal Israelita* (Rio de Janeiro) October 2, 1957, 2.

self-defense and that France and England were merely upholding international law.[56] Farther north, in Venezuela, the pro-American dictator General Marcos Pérez Jiménez blamed the Suez crisis squarely on Nasser, a leader he considered "a very dangerous element in the world picture today."[57]

Despite the opposition, support for Egypt among Latin America's left evolved not only as support for Nasser but also as a call for the emergence in Latin America of a member of the armed forces who would be capable of duplicating his charisma, leadership, and commitment to social justice and national independence from foreign and local interests. In other words, they argued that, what Latin America needed was the emergence in the region of a Latin American Nasser.[58]

The Brazilian congressman and prominent intellectual leader of the left, José Guimarães Neiva Moreira, a founding member of the Partido Democratico Trabalhista (Brazil's Workers' Party), argued in favor of a Nasserist regime and prescribed the conditions under which a Latin American Nasserist regime would appear. Neiva Moreiva argued that Nasserism might not be an unknown phenomenon in Latin America because the region had been governed by the military throughout history, with civilian rule being the exception. Members of the armed forces have historically been defined as protectors of foreign and local interests and custodians of the social status quo. When those men in arms are the protagonists of a process of political liberation or help to transform old political institutions, they deserve the name of "the people in uniform" (pueblo uniformado).[59] In modern times, the emergence of a leader of this type would only be possible if close attention were paid to three fundamental changes in the Egyptian armed forces and were replicated in Latin America. Neiva Moreiva argued that under Nasser, the Egyptian armed forces broke with the counterrevolutionary role that the colonial powers had assigned to military institutions in the Third World. As such, these armed forces broke with their historical design because they had been created or transformed into custodians of social immobility and of the socio-political order subordinated to foreign interests and local oligarchies. Furthermore, Nasser assigned the Egyptian armed forces to the vanguard of a people's revolutionary nationalism. Finally, revolutionary nationalism had to be both anti-capitalist and geared toward

---

56 "A Crise do Oriente Medio," Jornal Israelita (Rio de Janeiro) November 11, 1956, 2.

57 FRUS, "581. Memorandum of a Conversation, The White House, Washington, November 23, 1956, in FRUS 1955–1957, vol. VII, The American Republics, Central and South America, 1148.

58 Wiarda, "The Latin American Development Process," 472.

59 Neiva Moreira, El Nasserismo y la Revolución del Tercer Mundo (Montevideo: Ediciones de la Banda Oriental, 1971), 186.

a special type of socialism adapted to the realities of an Arab society and determined to clash with the structures of the old regime.[60] Independence from foreign and local interests would clear a path toward full development under the guidance of a military leader with the same qualities as Gamal Abdel Nasser.

The Secretary General of the Socialist Party of Uruguay, Vivían Trías, took Moreira's argument further and argued, disregarding both the history of Egypt and that of Latin America, that the armed forces, if ideologically grounded in the ideas of Nasser, could serve as the vehicle to lead the masses into a revolutionary process. "*Nasserist*" could apply to any officer who was "nationalist, progressive or inclined towards socialism."[61] With the exception of Chile, the Communist Party throughout Latin America had been decimated by years of repression, and it was clear by the 1960s that the weakened party could not bring about a communist revolution without the support of the armed forces. Oblivious to the fact that Nasser had persecuted and incarcerated Egyptian communists by the thousands, several Latin American Marxists saw the "Egyptian Revolution of 1952" as a model to emulate.[62]

In the 1960s, when a new military wave took power in Latin America (in countries such as Peru and Panama) claiming to have the key to national development, social progress, and independence from foreign and local interests, such military groups were branded by scholars and supporters as part of a new generation of *Nasserists*: leaders opposing the old elite.[63] Even dictators who had previously been toppled were rebranded as Nasserists by their supporters with the expectation that, at some point in history, they or their disciples would make a messianic return. Juan Domingo Perón, deposed in 1955 in Argentina, was a case in point. In 1961, the journalist Raúl Jassen called for a "Nasserist" regime that would restore authority in the country by placing Argentina under the command of a nationalist leader from the armed forces. Jassan called on a tradition of military leadership prevalent in his country to be the source of future "Nassers" who would eliminate internal corruption and Argentinian servitude to foreign interests. Like the servile regime of King Faruq, eliminated by Nasser in the revolution of 1952, the "mercantilist and liberal republic" of President Frondizi in Argentina, which was servile to the "interest of imperialism[,] would be eliminated" by a dominant figure who

---

60 Moreira, *El Nasserismo*, 199, 200.

61 Vivian Trias, "Marxismo y Caudillismo," in Neiva Moreira, *El Nasserismo y la Revolución del Tercer Mundo* (Montevideo: Ediciones de la Banda Oriental, 1971), 239.

62 Trias, "Marxismo y Caudillismo," 240–254.

63 Wiarda, "The Latin American Development Process," 473.

would "rescue the fatherland … return its lost dignity, and make the National Revolution happen."[64]

Such a person was nowhere to be found in Latin America. The whole idea wold have to wait at least 40 years until finally, in Venezuela, an army officer would proclaim himself to be both a follower of, and heir to, Gamal Abdel Nasser.

---

64 Jassen Raúl, *Nasser: Soldado de la Revolución Nacional* (Buenos Aires: A. Peña, 1961), 8–10.

Chapter 2
The Cuban Revolution and Egypt: Defining the Limits of the Third World Alliance

In no other Latin American country would the legacy of Gamal Abdel Nasser and his generation be as important, and at times controversial, as it would become in Cuba. If Nasser rekindled a nationalist movement in Panama, in Cuba he would be regarded as a revolutionary in his own right and the man who would open the Afro-Asian world to Cuba. The young revolutionaries who triumphantly entered Havana on January 9, 1959 were conscious of the significance the new order emerging in Africa, the Middle East and Asia could have in shaping the future of international events and of Egypt's role in shaping the world. Immediately after taking power, in an effort to free itself from the United States' historical economic and political control over the island since the island independence from Spain in 1898. The new Cuban government identified their revolution with the anti-colonial struggles occurring across the Atlantic in Asia, Africa and in particular in the Middle East. The Cuban government wanted the new world that was emerging from the decolonization struggles of the 1950s to embrace the Cuban revolution as one of its own. In particular, it struggled to gain the recognition and support of Nasser's Egypt. These efforts to obtain recognition from Egypt would not only be characterized by moments of profound identification but also at times a clear realization that the two countries' revolutionary processes were very different.

The Cuban Revolution: Finding a Place in the World

The young revolutionaries who took power on the island of Cuba in 1959 harbored deep admiration for the Egyptian leader, Gamal Abdel Nasser. While still in the mountains of Cuba, they had followed Nasser's agrarian reforms with intense interest; while fighting a guerrilla war against the dictatorship of Fulgencio Batista, they had closely watched Nasser's successful confrontation with Great Britain over the Suez Canal and his policy of neutrality in the Cold War. "It could not be otherwise," concluded Armando Entralgo, a leading academic and longtime Cuban diplomat to Africa:

Figure 2.1   Cairo, Egypt: Egypt's President Nasser gestures to a crowd, as visiting Cuban Industry Minister Ernesto Guevara, (L), looks on admiringly

Source: © Bettmann/CORBIS 1959

Nowadays, [after the collapse of the Soviet Union and the Socialist regimes in Eastern Europe] we place a lot of emphasis on the uniqueness of each revolutionary experience, and rightly so, but in those days we felt very much part of a universal movement Nasser had begun, and we believed that there were clear parallels between our [Egypt and Cuba's] own recent histories, and our own revolutionary movements.[1]

Two months after the triumph of the revolution Fidel Castro began to speak of adopting a neutralist stance in world affairs. His announcement came in response to a speech given in Havana by a friend of the revolution, the ex-President of Costa Rica, José Figueres, who warned Cuba not to forget that it was a Western country and should not side with any foreign power.[2] Castro, present at the event, responded to Figueres by asserting that he envisioned a neutral Cuba: "Why should Latin America be with either side? Why could we not proclaim our right to live, even if we are killed at the end?" But it was clear that this neutrality would be an assertive neutrality critical of the historical role of the United States. In a clear reference to the American government and its abandonment of Cuba after the Second World War, Castro continued, arguing that "the people of Cuba has always been called to support 'their' cause, yet after the wars are over Cuba was always left without its sugar quota, and has been left humiliated."[3] Castro further responded to his guest by declaring that the problems Cuba faced did not come from other continents but from the Americas.[4]

Despite this early hint that his revolution might embrace neutrality, Castro established no contacts with Egypt or any other leader of the nonaligned movement and decided to soften the tone of his neutralist discourse, at least in the early days of the revolution. The United States still controlled much of Cuba's economy, and Castro needed to exercise caution while dealing with Washington.

The Eisenhower administration was also cautious. Before considering the use of force like in Guatemala in 1954, the administration opted to have an

---

1 Armando Entralgo (1935–2004), Director of the Center for the Studies of Africa and the Middle East CEAMO and former Cuban Ambassador to Ghana, interview with the author, Havana, December 30, 2001.

2 "Calurosa acogida a Don José Figueres," *Revolución* (Havana), March 21, 1959. His remarks appeared in the same newspaper on March 23, 1959, 25.

3 "Calurosa acogida a Don José Figueres," *Revolución* 25.

4 R. Hart Phillips, "Castro Bars Pledge to Join the US in War," *New York Times*, March 23, 1959, 1, 4.

influence in the new government.[5] In April 1959, Castro was invited to the United States for an unofficial visit. The visit allowed him to tour several cities and increased the visibility of his revolution in America while at the same time provided Castro with breathing room before the further radicalization of his revolution.[6] Without providing many details regarding his future foreign policy, Castro essentially told the American public what they wanted to hear. He announced that Cuba would to stand behind the Rio Treaty and the Organization of American States and there would be elections on the island in the near future.[7] President Eisenhower declined to meet with him, but Castro met with Vice-President Richard Nixon and US Secretary of State Christian Herter in Washington, and both concluded that, despite initial fears, Castro did not pose a significant danger to American interests.[8] Others within the State Department were less convinced of Castro's malleability. "On balance," reads an unattributed State Department memorandum to President Eisenhower, "despite Castro's apparent simplicity, sincerity and eagerness to reassure the United States public, there is little probability that Castro has altered the essentially radical course of his revolution."[9]

Those who feared Castro received a premonitory warning when during his trip he rejected the first US attempts to exercise oversight over the revolution. In Washington, Castro was offered assurances that the United States would assist Cuba in obtaining economic aid from the International Monetary Fund (IMF) and other organizations, provided that his government was willing to follow their economic prescriptions.[10] To their surprise, Castro announced that he was not interested in asking the US for loans and only sought good relations and fair play based on mutual respect and understanding.[11]

---

5 FRUS, "Telegram from the Embassy in Cuba to the Department of State 14 April 1959," in FRUS vol. VI, 1958–1960, *Cuba* (Washington, DC: United States Government Printing Office, 1991), 456–457.

6 Jorge I. Domínguez, *To Make the World Safe for Revolution: Cuba's Foreign Policy* (Cambridge, MA: Harvard University Press, 1989), 18.

7 Dana Adams Schmidt, "Castro Rules out Role as Neutral; Opposes the Reds," *New York Times*, April 20, 1959, 1, 5.

8 FRUS, "Visit to the United States by Prime Minister Castro, April 1959," in FRUS vol. VI, 1958–1960, *Cuba*, 476.

9 FRUS, "Visit to the United States by Prime Minister Castro, April 1959," in FRUS vol. VI, 1958–1960, *Cuba*, 482.

10 E.W. Kenworthy, "Cuba's problems Pose test for US policy: Castro 'unofficial' raises a flurry of official interests," *New York Times*, April 26, 1959, E7.

11 Domínguez, *To Make the World Safe for Revolution*, 18; see also FRUS, "Memorandum of a Conversation, Department of State, Washington, April 16, 1959," in FRUS vol. VI, 1958–1960, *Cuba*, 471–472.

Upon Castro's return from the United States, the radicalization of the revolution began apace. This sharp veer to the left led to a rapid deterioration in relations between Cuba and the US. The most radical members of Castro's inner circle began to displace moderates from positions of power. In June 1960, five moderate ministers were expelled from the government, an action that was later to be followed by the expulsion of the anticommunist President Manuel Urrutia – who was replaced by the trusted Osvaldo Dorticós. Three months later Raúl Castro, Fidel's brother and a longtime member of the Communist Party in his youth, assumed full control of the Armed Forces.[12] The exodus continued, and within a matter of weeks, two more former leaders of the revolution departed: the chief of the Revolutionary Air Force, Pedro Luis Lanz, who defected to the US, while the military commander of Camaguey province, Huber Matos, landed in jail accused of being a counterrevolutionary.[13] In November 1959, the final remaining anticommunist ministers were forced to resign, while the more radical Ernesto Guevara – also known as "El Che" – became president of the Cuban Central Bank.

The leeway the United States government was prepared to grant the Cuban revolution was rapidly coming to an end. The land reform law that came into effect in June 1959 affected several American landowners. When the US government announced that it supported the Cuban government's agrarian reform plans, as long as the owners were promptly, adequately, and fairly compensated, the Cuban government replied that it could not postpone the implementation of the land reform until it had the cash to compensate the owners. Landowners were forced to accept Cuban long-term bonds.[14] By October 1959 the US ambassador to Cuba, Philip Bonsal, was protesting to President Dorticós the "continuous and deliberate efforts in Cuba to substitute the traditional friendship between the American and the Cuban peoples with mistrust and hostility," and although Bonsal gave assurances that his government was not supporting efforts to topple the revolution, he warned them that communism "could never be compatible with the principles that are the foundations of the American Republics, and other nations."[15]

---

12 *Revolución* (Havana), October 21, 1959, 1.

13 Domínguez, *To Make the World Safe for Revolution*, 19.

14 FRUS, "The Cuban Government's Promulgation of an Agrarian Reform law, and the Question of Asylum for Batista, May–October 1959," in FRUS vol. VI, 1958–1960, *Cuba*, 529.

15 "Rechaza Cuba 'Nota' de E.U.," *Revolución* (Havana), October 28, 1959, 1, 19.

Egypt: The Portal to Neutralism and the Afro-Asian Bloc

The radicalization of Cuba's government and society was running parallel to the vertiginous changes in its foreign policy.[16] The new government promptly sponsored amateurish guerrilla groups seeking to topple Caribbean and Central American dictators. Groups were sent to Nicaragua, Panama, Haiti, and the Dominican Republic, and were defeated by the governments of those countries without much difficulty.[17] Despite their failure, it was clear that the Cuban revolution had awakened a revolutionary ethos in Latin America that began to trouble governments throughout the region.[18] With the exception of Mexico, which maintained a distant friendship with Cuba, relations with other Latin Americans countries deteriorated progressively. Conservative Latin American regimes began to fear that Castro was taking the revolution too far to the left and was overly antagonistic towards the United States. Moreover, they feared that Castro could inspire the progressive sectors within their own societies, which they had displaced from power since the beginning of the Cold War, to begin a revolutionary process modeled on the Cuban experience.

In part as a response to the growing isolation of the Cubans within the inter-American system, but equally in response to the ideological drive of the government itself, Cubans began exploring relations with the emerging bloc of Afro-Asian nations. Momentarily set aside during Castro's visit to the United States, the notion of detaching Cuba from the United States and allying it with the nations adopting a neutralist stance in the Cold War began to reappear after April 1959. There was a growing sense among Cuban leaders that their country's colonial past and revolutionary present were closely connected with the ongoing struggle against colonialism and imperialism occurring in Africa, the Middle East, and Asia. Cuba's poor—primarily mulattos and Afro-Cubans—became the direct beneficiaries of their Government's new social policies and core supporters of a revolution and a country that would subsequently proudly proclaim itself "Afro-Latin."

By June 1959, Castro had decided to begin exploring how to inscribe the Cuban revolution within the Afro-Asian bloc. The first and most important mission dispatched by the new Cuban revolutionary movement departed to Egypt under Ernesto Guevara. The delegation arrived in Cairo on June 12, 1959. As the seat of the Egyptian Government, Cairo had been transformed into an obligatory pilgrimage site for all of the national liberation movements and new governments born out of the growing wave of national liberation

---

16 Domínguez, *To Make the World Safe for Revolution*, 20.

17 "Panama" *Revolución* (Havana), June 19, 1959, 10.

18 "Según despachos de Managua Somoza aplastó la rebelión," *Revolución* (Havana), June 15, 1959, 20.

throughout Africa and Asia. The Cubans knew that they needed Egyptian diplomatic support, and the visit appeared to be geared towards achieving Nasser's endorsement of the Caribbean revolution.

Guevara had the opportunity for a long conversation with Nasser. Despite the Cubans' best intentions, the only witness to that conversation, Nasser's friend Mohamed Heikal, does not recall the first encounter being a great success for the Cubans. According to Heikal, the Cubans tried to impress Nasser, with Guevara telling him that,

> in 1956, when things were going badly for Castro fighting his war up in the Cuban hills, he used to be encouraged by the way Egypt had overcome the attack by Britain, France and Israel. Nasser was a source of moral strength for them.[19]

Nasser, apparently, was nevertheless unimpressed with the Cuban revolutionaries. According to Heikal, since the Cuban revolution's triumph in January of 1959, Nasser had tended to dismiss these young insurgents as "theatrical brigands, but not true revolutionaries."[20] Unsurprisingly, Heikal concluded, Nasser was wary of the warm welcome Castro had received in Washington in March and remembered the events in Guatemala in 1954—where the nationalist government of Jacobo Arbenz was deposed by a CIA-financed military coup—too well to harbor any hopes that a truly revolutionary government could be installed so close to the United States.[21]

It was up to Guevara to prove the revolutionary credentials of the Cuban revolution to Nasser, and it appears that in his efforts to demonstrate the seriousness of their social and political programs, Guevara showed less deference than might have been expected by a senior political figure such as Nasser. In the midst of the conversation, Heikal recalls that Guevara begun inquiring after the effects of Egypt's agrarian reforms and the social dislocation caused by the overall process. Heikal recounts that Guevara asked Nasser: "How many refugees had the agrarian reform caused?" The question apparently took Nasser by surprise. He told Guevara that "there were not many—and they were mainly "white Egyptians, men of other nationalities who had become Egyptianized." On hearing this, Guevara took the opportunity to further challenge Nasser: "That means," Guevara replied, "nothing much happened in your Revolution." Guevara was quick to tell Nasser how he judged a revolution: "I measure the depth of the social transformation by the number of people who are affected by it and feel that they have no place in the new society." An astonished Nasser

---

19 Mohammed Heikal, *The Cairo Documents* (New York: Doubleday & Company, 1973), 344.

20 Heikal, *The Cairo Documents*, 343.

21 Heikal, *The Cairo Documents*, 343.

countered that his revolution had one objective, "Liquidating the privileges of a class but no individuals of that class." Nasser explained that his reforms left former landowners without power while "allowing them to become useful members of that society."[22]

It is reasonable to conclude that despite Cuban admiration for Nasser's foreign policy legacy, following this early encounter the Cuban leaders began to realize that their Caribbean revolution was a more radical project than that of Egypt. Clear differences between the Egyptian and Cuban models would soon become evident. One should not forget that "Nasserism" was devoid of any particular ideology beyond its commitment to nationalism, despite a discourse embedded in socialist jargon, while the Cuban revolutionaries were soon seriously converted to Marxist-Leninist dictates. "Nasserism" never developed into a comprehensive or articulated prescription for a new society; it was, as one historian of this time would put it, "not an ideology but an attitude of mind."[23] As in Cuba, the pressing land problem was one of the first issues that Nasser addressed after gaining power. Nasser expropriated large estates in what he termed the beginning of a "'socialist, democratic, co-operative" policy to ameliorate the conditions of the rural peasants.[24] Large landowners disappeared as a powerful social group in Egypt, yet the poor peasants did not see their share of land ownership increase significantly. When the first land reform was enacted in 1952, poor landowning peasants constituted 94 percent of all owners and controlled 35 percent of the cultivable land; nearly ten years later—and after a second land reform in 1961—they still constituted 94 percent of all owners, but the land they controlled only amounted to an unimpressive 52 percent. The land reform was more a political tool to castigate enemies whose property was sequestered and whose political rights were denied because they were publicly branded "reactionary capitalists," than a universal program applied throughout the country. Moreover, it would take Nasser nearly ten years to begin a redistributive process in the industry and service sectors, and this was more of a reaction to economic conditions in Egypt—and the rest of the Third World—than the product of his ideological commitments. Moreover, as a nationalist calling for the political unification of the Arab World, Nasser despised the concept of class-warfare, and insisted upon the necessity of harmonizing class interests. Communists would have no place in such a revolution and would be met with suspicion or even outright persecution. Furthermore, the extent of social reforms in Egypt was far from impressive when compared to the achievements of the more ideologically committed

---

22 Heikal, *The Cairo Documents*, 343.

23 Albert Hourani, *Arabic Thought in the Liberal Age 1798–1939* (Cambridge: Cambridge University Press, 1983), 358.

24 Hourani, *Arabic Thought*, 358.

Cuban government over the next decade. If we take the efforts to combat illiteracy and advance the state of women in society, two of the hallmarks of the socialist revolutions in the second part of the twentieth century. As examples, by 1962, a massive educational program had been instituted that would nearly eradicate illiteracy in Cuba, as thousands of teachers were sent throughout the countryside. While the rest of Latin America would continue to have high levels of illiteracy, Cuba would achieve levels of literacy equal to, or superior to, those of many developed countries. In contrast, Egypt's revolution reduced illiteracy from 71 percent in 1960 to an unimpressive 57 percent in 1970, with female illiteracy—virtually eliminated in Cuba—remaining at a high 71 percent.[25] Egyptian's women participation in the workforce would rise from 8 percent in 1937 to only 9.2 percent in 1976. In contrast, Cuban women were mobilized in the educational campaign against illiteracy and were then incorporated into universities and other centers of study; by the mid-1980s, the adult female workforce participation rate was 37 percent, an increase from a figure of 14 percent in 1953.[26]

Despite Nasser's initial coldness and the policy differences between the two regimes, Guevara's primary goal in Cairo was to obtain political support for the Cuban revolution, not policy advice, and this he achieved. The Egyptian leader recognized Cuba as the only anti-colonial, anti-imperialist nation in Latin America, and Cuba would use this recognition as a first step in building her case for the redefinition of Cuba as a nation within the emerging Afro-Asian bloc. In the last days of his two-week visit, Guevara met with Anwar al-Sadat, the Secretary General of the Islamic Congress and the Afro-Asian Congress, and received an unexpected invitation from the Egyptian government for Cuba to attend the next Afro-Asian Congress.[27]

With Guevara's visit, the Egyptians had the opportunity to obtain first-hand information about the Cuban revolution, while Guevara had the opportunity to tour Gaza and Damascus, as well as much of Egypt. In the Gaza Strip, the Palestinians received Guevara with placards that proclaimed Nasser and Castro their revolutionary leaders, while the Egyptian authorities in Gaza publicly recognized the significance of Castro and the Cuban revolution. The parallels between Cuba and Egypt began to emerge in the reports of the Cuban

---

25 Non-revolutionary regimes such as Turkey and Iran had lower levels of illiteracy than Egypt: 62 and 64 percent, respectively. See John Waterbury, "Reflections on the Extent of Egypt's Revolution: Socioeconomic Indicators," in Shimon Shamir, *Egypt from Monarchy to Republic: A Reassessment of Revolution and Change* (Boulder, CO: Westview Press, 1995), 62.

26 Louis A. Pérez, *Cuba: Between Reform and Revolution* (Oxford University Press, 2nd edn., 1995), 371.

27 "Invitada Cuba al Congreso Islámico," *Revolución* (Havana), June 27, 1959, 10.

press on Guevara's visit to Gaza. According to the Havana daily newspaper *Revolución* Palestinians in Gaza proclaimed that "As Nasser has become a symbol for the Arab people, Castro has become a symbol for the liberation of Latin America."[28] Pleased with the welcome, Guevara nevertheless rushed to qualify the identification of Cuba with Nasser's regime, in an attempt to at least assuage American and Latin American fears, telling the Egyptian audience that there were no calls—at least not at the time—for a pan-Latin American Union, in reference to Nasser's Pan-Arab movement. The Cuban revolution was only interested in "exporting ideas;" Guevara argued, each country was responsible for determining its own means of resolving its own history of underdevelopment and oppression.[29] At the very least, Guevara's trip had served to awaken the Egyptian government to the existence of the Cuban revolution and garner its support. This was sufficient to validate Cuba's new position in world affairs and the opening gambit of what would become a national foreign policy priority of breaking the growing isolation of their revolution in the Americas.[30]

Guevara was convinced that the future of the Cuban revolution lay with the Afro-Asian bloc. Thrilled by the Egyptian government's imminent inclusion of Cuba in the Afro-Asian conference, Guevara wrote in October 1959:

> Still surprised by their ability to dream of being free, Africa and Asia are beginning to see beyond the oceans … Could it not be that our brotherhood challenges the immensity of the seas, the barrier of different languages and the existence of cultural links to make us one as partners in this fight? … Cuba has been invited to the new Afro-Asian conference. An American country will expose to the Afro-Asian forum the truth about our own reality. Our going is no accident. We are going as part of an historical convergence of all the oppressed peoples in the world in this hour of their liberation. We will go there to tell them that Fidel Castro is a man, a popular hero, not a mythological abstraction, but we will also tell them that Cuba is just the first sign in the awakening of the Americas.[31]

---

28 "Entusiasta Recibimiento le tributan a Guevara en Gaza," *Revolución* (Havana), June 18, 1959, 10.

29 "Cuba no exporta revoluciones sino ideas: Dijo Dr. Guevara," *Revolución* (Havana), June 30, 1959, 10.

30 "Invitada Cuba al Congreso Islámico," *Revolución* (Havana), June 27, 1959, 10.

31 Ernesto Che Guevara, "Desde el Balcón Afro-Asiático," in E.C. Guevera, *Contexto Latinoamericano* No. 12/2010 Coyoacán, México, D.F. Mexico, 57–9. Available at http://www.oceansur.com/media/fb_uploads/contexto/contexto_latinoamericano_12.pdf.

Between Nasser and Khrushchev: Neutralism vs. Soviet Aid

In addition to establishing new links with Nasser and the Afro-Asian bloc, Guevara's trip to Egypt also provided him with an appreciation of the value of the Soviet Union as an ally. According to one of Guevara's biographers, the Mexican historian Jorge Castañeda: "The Suez Canal crisis of 1956 and Britain's boycott of Egyptian cotton made a strong impression on him."[32] During the boycott, the Soviet Union had been key to the survival of the Egyptian revolution by buying Egypt's cotton and supporting its development programs.[33] Guevara gleaned another significant piece of intelligence during his visit to Egypt and other countries; that it was possible to be neutral in the Cold War and still receive military and economic aid from the Soviet Union. The crucial question was how to walk the fine line between alignment and neutrality without compromising the independence of the Cuban revolution.

In Egypt, Guevara told reporters that Cuba did not have official relations with the Soviet Union at that time, "although on the basis of a future commercial agreement those relations might be established."[34] While trading with the USSR might have been anathema to Latin American nations, in his trips to other nations, such as India, Indonesia and Sri Lanka, Guevara learned that trade with the USSR was not just confined to Egypt; it was, in fact, common practice among members of the Afro-Asian bloc.[35]

The Cuban revolutionaries had had no contact with the Soviet Union before the triumph of the revolution, and despite the Soviet Union's early recognition of the new government in January 1959, Havana did not take any steps towards the Soviets until October of that year. On October 16, Alexander Alexeev met with Fidel Castro as an official representative of the Soviet information agency, TASS. The Soviets requested that Castro facilitate the opening of diplomatic relations between the two countries, but Castro simply replied that the time was not yet right for this step. The Soviets, however, were left with the impression that the new Cuban government would not be unwilling to engage in further contact. Castro suggested that the Soviet Prime Minister, Anastas Mikoyan, visit Cuba, and the visit was scheduled for February 1960.[36] The Soviets had already

32 Jorge Castañeda, *Compañero: The Life and Death of Che Guevara* (New York: Alfred Knopf), 1997, 161.

33 Castañeda, *Compañero*, 161.

34 "Cuba no exporta revoluciones sino ideas," 10.

35 "llego a Belgrado la delegación de Cuba," *Revolución* (Havana), August 13, 1959, 10.

36 This episode in the establishment of Cuban–Soviet relations is entirely based on Domínguez, *To Make the World Safe for Revolution*, 21 and passim. "Mikoyan Praises Cuba," *New York Times*, February 9, 1960, 7.

been assisting Cuba since August and September of 1959 by buying their sugar on the international market, and a formal trade agreement was signed in January 1960, when the Soviets pledged to purchase 100,000 tons of sugar from Cuba.[37] In February, during Mikoyan's visit to Cuba, the Soviets pledged to purchase 20 percent of all Cuba's sugar exports and lend the island $100 million in economic assistance. Soon the Cubans would negotiate similar treaties with Eastern European countries, and even with the People's Republic of China. Then, in April 1960, the Cubans upped the ante by asking the Soviet Union for arms. Three months later, the head of the Armed Forces, Raúl Castro, visited Moscow to formalize the purchase, and Soviet arms began to arrive in September of the same year.

Like their revolutionary predecessors in Africa and Asia, the Cubans had begun to exploit the implicit composition and power structure of the international system, particularly to safeguard the survival of their revolution. Some members of the Soviet hierarchy might have retained doubts regarding Castro's spontaneous friendship and his revolutionary commitments; but at that point, no one in the Soviet Union was prepared or willing to question the leader of a revolution so near the United States.[38]

As efforts towards the establishment of full diplomatic relations with the Soviet Union continued to gain speed, the revolution increasingly distanced itself from the United States. The American government's apprehension was on the rise, but in August 1959, in a desperate attempt to exercise some control over the Cuban revolution, the Department of Agriculture—the institution responsible for establishing the annual quota of sugar that the United States purchased from abroad—agreed to increase the amount of sugar Cuba was allowed to sell to the United States. As the new decade began, Washington sent a final signal to the Cubans that it would not intervene in the internal affairs of the revolution. The Eisenhower administration pledged to recognize the "right of the Cuban government and people ... to undertake those social, economic and political reforms which, with due regard for their obligations under international law, they may think desirable."[39] Moreover, the US made efforts to smooth relations between the two governments and asked the Argentinean ambassador to Cuba, Julio Amoedo, to mediate between them. However, as Amoedo later concluded, the Cubans were more interested in exploiting the mediation to buy time until they could gauge the degree of commitment they could expect from the Soviet Union.[40] Once Prime Minister Mikoyan arrived

---

37 Dominguez, *To Make the World Safe*, 22.

38 Dominguez, *To Make the World Safe*, 22.

39 Dominguez, *To Make the World Safe*, 23.

40 Dominguez, *To Make the World Safe*, 23. "Go-Between of '60 in Havana Named." *New York Times*, April 14, 1964, 26; "Castro Called Red by Own Free Will," *New York*

from Moscow and the two governments signed the Cuban-Soviet pact on February 13, 1960, the Cubans dropped any pretense of interest in reaching a compromise with the United States.[41]

On March 1, 1960, Eisenhower asked Congress to grant him the authority to adjust the sugar quotas of foreign countries. The Cubans denounced the measure as "Economic aggression against Cuba."[42] Just three days later, a Belgian ship, *La Coubre*, loaded with arms and ammunition for the Cuban government, exploded in Havana harbor. Castro blamed the explosion on United States sabotage. Relations were on the verge of collapse. In June, the Cuban Petroleum Institute (ICP) sent 20,000 barrels of Soviet crude oil for processing to the Texaco refinery in Cuba, which under the terms of its concession was required to refine crude oil owned by the Cuban government. Texaco refused to process the oil, and the Cuban government responded by seizing the refinery. This sequence of events was repeated with the Shell and Standard Oil refineries. On July 5, the Cuban Cabinet authorized the expropriation of all property belonging to US citizens or firms, and on July 6, President Eisenhower cut Cuba's sugar quota by 95 percent for the remainder of 1960. The Soviet Union announced that it would purchase the Cuban sugar that the US refused to buy. The Soviets used the visit of the Cuban Armed Forces Minister, Raúl Castro, to Moscow to issue a clear warning to the Americans:

> The Soviet Union will use all means at its disposal to prevent an armed intervention by the United States against Cuba ... the Socialist countries ... can fully take care of supplying Cuba ... with all the necessary merchandise which is now denied to it by the United States and other capitalist states.[43]

As the second anniversary of the revolution approached, the United States had fewer instruments of control and influence over Cuba, because the island was now less dependent on the United States as a market for its products. The support that the Egyptians and, most importantly the Soviets gave the island had successfully prevented Cuba's isolation in the international community.

The Soviet Union had certainly gone a long way towards demonstrating that it could be a reliable partner, and the Cubans for their part were greatly relieved to find new markets and new sources of economic aid. Yet the Cubans were still far from committing themselves to the Soviet Union in any respect. Despite the sympathies of some members of the Cuban government for the Soviet Union,

---

Times, April 21, 1964, 43.

41   Dominguez, *To Make the World Safe*, 23.

42   Dominguez, *To Make the World Safe*, 24.

43   Dominguez, *To Make the World Safe*, 25. "Raul Castro Talks in Moscow," *New York Times*, July 21, 1960, 2.

and the growing influence of the communist party in the revolution, the Cubans did not wish to give the Soviets the impression that there was any likelihood that Cuba would become a satellite like some of the Eastern European states.[44]

A Further Call to the Afro-Asian Bloc

This drive towards a break with the United States also implied a new foreign policy detached from the inter-American system. In December 1959 Walterio Carbonell, a Cuban intellectual and at some point ambassador to Tunis, called for the development of a Cuban foreign policy fully committed to the creation of an American-Afro-Asian bloc. The logic for this, according to Carbonell, was that

> Since the Afro-Asian bloc emerged, France has not been able to prevent the discussion of the Algerian question at the United Nations.[45]

A unique opportunity had emerged for Cuba, Carbonell argued, as these regions could act now as a bloc protecting their interests in a genuine independent organization—far from the Baghdad Pact or the OAS. Carbonell argued that the burden was now on Cuba's shoulders. Carbonell argued,

> The historical merit of uniting Africa, and Latin America and Asia, corresponds to the mission of the Revolutionary government of Cuba. If Cuba achieved this union, it would have a preeminent role at the United Nations.[46]

Months later, the Cuban government would begin to implement an activist policy, what many began to call the "Carbonell theory," in Africa when it began to aid the Algerian revolutionaries.[47]

Castro's ultimate confrontation with the United States, and doubtless Guevara's earlier trip to Egypt, contributed to the Egyptian leader's increasing interest in the Cuban revolutionaries. The Cubans, for their part, were never reticent in demonstrating to Nasser their readiness to establish an alliance with

---

44   *Revolución*, especially in 1959, closely followed events in Egypt. In March of that year, the campaign against communists was noted on its front page. See also "Nasser," *Revolución* (Havana), March 23, 1959, 1.

45   Walterio Carbonell, "Congreso mundial de países subdesarrollados," *Revolución* (Havana), December 5, 1959, 2.

46   Carbonell, "Congreso mundial de países subdesarrollados," 2.

47   Carlos Moore, *Castro, the Blacks, and Africa* (Los Angeles, CA: Center for Afro-American Studies, University of California, 1988).

the Afro-Asian bloc in whatever shape or form it could be constructed, be it a diplomatic force within the United Nations or even a military alliance. This all hinged on whether Egypt would fully commit to the formation of this new entity. Raúl Castro provided a further manifestation of Cuba's revolutionary drive while visiting Alexandria, Egypt in July 1960 as the leader of a Cuban delegation invited to attend the celebration of the eighth anniversary of the Nasserite revolution. One of the objectives of his visit was to again stress to the Egyptians the similarities of their two revolutions and to intensify relations between the two nations. According to the Cuban newspaper *Revolución*, Raúl told the audience at a celebration gathered at the municipal stadium in Alexandria: "monopolists have united their forces and have tried to smash our revolution exactly as they tried with Egypt when this country decided to nationalize the Suez Canal."[48] He called upon the Egyptian people to form a united front to "fight against imperialism in Asia, Africa, and Latin America."[49] Castro assured his hosts that the Cubans had strongly supported Egypt during the events of 1956 and four years later were prepared to "unite our forces with our Arab brothers."[50] Nasser responded in the same vein, telling Castro: "We also passed through difficult times during which we were exposed to intimidation and pressure. We persisted and won."[51]

It was clear that Raúl Castro obtained what he wanted from the Egyptian leader when Nasser told his countrymen, "we, the people of the United Arab Republic, fully support the cause of liberty throughout the world; we support the cause of liberty in Cuba; we support the fight put up by Fidel Castro."[52] Little more than a year after Guevara's first trip to Egypt, the Cuban revolutionaries were convinced that a new relationship was emerging between them and the leader of the Afro-Asian bloc. The limits of Egypt's commitment to the Cuban revolution would subsequently be revealed, but for the moment the Egyptian rhetorical commitment seemed more than promissory. In August 1960, a correspondent for *The Times* captured the prevailing feeling among Cubans in regards to Nasser and the Egyptian revolution.

> In spite of all that has been said and done, the majority of Cubans still believe that the Castro revolution is a noble expression of nationalism and the search for social justice. The resignations from the Cuban diplomatic corps, the defections

---

48 "La Revolución Cubana no retrocederá jamás," *Revolución* (Havana), July 28, 1960, 1, 6.

49 "La Revolución Cubana no retrocederá jamás," 1, 6.

50 "Entrevista de Raúl Castro con Nasser," *Revolución* (Havana), July 27, 1960, 9.

51 Gamal Abdel Nasser, speech delivered at the Municipality Stadium in Alexandria. *President Gamal Abdel Nasser Speeches and Press Interviews*, Cairo, July–September 1960, 55.

52 Nasser, speech delivered at the Municipality Stadium in Alexandria.

of Cuban airline pilots, the stifled protests of professors at the University of Havana, the tentative opposition of the Roman Catholic Church, and the steady efflux of depressed, fearful, or unemployed Cubans to Miami—none of this has persuaded the majority that their revolution has been betrayed by communism.

Nor is anything less likely to convince them than the loud American argument that Cuba has become simply a Russian satellite. "Yes," said a young Cuban secretary the other day, "that's just like the Americans. They think you're a commie if you nationalize the telephone company!" The reproach can too easily be supported; and this alleged failure of the American imagination about the emotional context of the Cuban revolution inevitably brings to mind Britain's relations with the Arabs.

"Nasser is our father", one youth told me—and some of the parallels are indeed close. The Cuban revolution promised escape from a regime that was more single-mindedly corrupt even than Farouk's Egypt. It offered social justice to the underemployed and landless peasantry through land reform, education and housing; and it promoted that nebulous, but magic, virtue of national dignity—best interpreted, in Latin America, as the ability to cock a snook at the ubiquitous American boss..[53]

The United Nations General Assembly: Castro's Bandung

Fidel Castro announced his decision to attend the opening session of the fifteenth General Assembly of the United Nations in September 1960. From Havana, he intimated that he not only intended to speak for Cuba, "but for the peoples of all under-developed nations."[54] Castro was prepared to reframe the history of Cuba alongside that of the emerging progressive countries of Africa and the Middle East and simultaneously denounce the United States in the world's largest forum. The United States responded to Castro's visit to New York with hostility. The Cuban government was informed that Castro's movements would be restricted to Manhattan while he was in New York.[55] The Cuban delegation arrived at the Shelburne hotel on the East Side of Manhattan amidst a crowd of supporters shouting "Viva Fidel" and calling for his appearance. Despite the welcoming crowds, the hotel's management received the Cuban delegation with hostility; they consistently seemed to be short of space to accommodate the Cubans' needs and demanded to be paid cash in

---

53 "Cuba and the Cold War," *The Times*, August 9, 1960, 9.

54 "Havana Protests," *New York Times*, September 15, 1960, 12.

55 The Cubans responded by restricting the American ambassador to the Vedado residential district in Havana while Castro attended the New York gathering. See "Cuba Restricts US Ambassador," *New York Times*, September 17, 1960, 1.

advance. Castro protested to the United Nations regarding the treatment his delegation was receiving from the hotel management and the New York Police, ultimately accepting the invitation to move the Cuban delegation to the heart of black New York: the Hotel Theresa in Harlem. Moving the delegation to the Theresa proved a substantial publicity coup for the Cubans. Castro gained the friendship and support of the Afro-American community while using the opportunity to tell them, as the *New York Times* reported, that

> he understood that United States Negroes were not as "brainwashed" as whites by official propaganda about Cuba, and had more sympathy for his Government, which he added, had wiped out race discrimination. He was said to have asserted that Cubans, Africans and United States Negroes all were in the same boat.[56]

Castro's visit to the United Nations had begun favorably. It seemed that New York would do for Castro what Bandung had done for Nasser. It was his entrance onto the main stage of international affairs. If the United States and the rest of the Americas were turning their backs on Cuba, world leaders wanted to meet him. Gamal Abdel Nasser met with him at the Hotel Theresa before his marathon speech at the General Assembly. Nasser and Castro discussed the similarities in their countries' histories, revolutions, and one-crop economies. As Chou-En-Lai had advised Nasser to seek the aid of the Communist world in Bandung, now it was Nasser who took the opportunity to discuss the possibility of Cuba trading sugar to the communist bloc for long-term credits, technical assistance, and Soviet arms.[57] Nasser was exhibiting a greater interest in the Cuban revolution than ever before. In an interview with the Cuban press, Nasser referred to the sacrifices that the Egyptians had to make to prevail in their revolution and told them, "like Egypt, Cuba would prevail." Expanding on this theme of affinity between the countries' struggles, Nasser added a note of solidarity and defiance: "We had similar difficulties to the ones the Cuban revolutionaries are having, but with a strong sense of unity we were able to repel the aggression of two great powers and carry on with our own revolution." [58]

These energizing words were to have a profound effect on Castro's speech to the United Nations. For the first time, a Latin-American leader connected the history, politics and actual problems of his country with those of nations in Africa and Asia and pledged that they had a future together. The mandate of the Cuban revolution was universal, and its appeal traveled far beyond the

---

56 Max Frankel, "Cuban in Harlem," *New York Times*, September 20, 1960, 1.

57 Max Frankel, "Nasser Asks Cuba to Join Neutrals," *New York Times*, September 26, 1960, 1.

58 "Como Egipto, Cuba prevalecerá: Nasser," *Revolución* (Havana), September 26, 1959, 1–12.

American continent. "The problems of Latin America are just like the problems of Asia and Africa," Castro told the General Assembly, and continued, offering his analysis of the power bloc structure:

> The world is divided among monopolies; the same ones we see in Latin America are to be seen in the Middle East. It is there in the Middle East where oil belongs to a number of companies that control powerful financial interests in France, the United States, Holland, England ... in Iran, Iraq, Saudi Arabia, Kuwait, Qatar, you name it, in each and every corner of the world.
>
> The problems that Cuba has had with the imperialist government of the United States are the same problems that Saudi Arabia, Iran or Iraq would have had if they had nationalized their oil. These problems are the same that Egypt had when it nationalized the Suez Canal. The same problems that Oceania had when it wanted to be independent, I mean, when Indonesia wanted to be independent; the same unexpected invasion that Egypt faced, the same unexpected invasion of Congo. Have the imperialists run out of excuses to invade? Never. They have always had some excuse at hand.[59]

For the first time, a Latin America leader constructed a history of the region using references from outside the defined frontiers of the Americas. Castro explained the Cuban revolution not only as a Latin American phenomenon but also as part of an emerging bloc of global proportions. His words carried the weight of the accumulated disenchantment with the United States and the hope that the newly emerging nations were on the verge of transforming the face of the international community.

Apart from the opportunity it gave him to meet with African-American leaders, Jawaharlal Nehru, and Gamal Abdel Nasser, his time in New York also allowed Castro to meet with Soviet leader Nikita Khrushchev. Hours before Khrushchev delivered his speech to the United Nations, he traveled to Harlem to meet the Cuban leader and told reporters that he found Castro a "heroic man."[60] The Cuban revolutionaries were making a remarkable impression on the Soviets, who for the first time since the beginning of the Cold War had received the support of a Latin American leader for an address to the United Nations.[61] The Soviets were flattered and responded in kind. Soviet representative Anastas Mikoyan later provided a sense of their emotional

---

59   Fidel Castro, speech to the United Nations, "Desarme: Apoyo a la URSS," *Revolución* (Havana), September 27, 1960, 7.

60   Harrison E. Salisbury, "Russian Goes to Harlem, Then Hugs Cuban at UN," *New York Times*, September 21, 1960, 1.

61   Max Frankel, 'Castro Plays Fan to Soviet Premier," *New York Times*, September 24, 1960, 3.

response to American Secretary of State Dean Rusk. "You must realize what Cuba means to us old Bolsheviks," Mikoyan told the Secretary of State, "We have been waiting all our lives for a country to go Communist without the Red Army. It has happened in Cuba, and it makes us feel like boys again!"[62] The Soviet theorists soon shifted their emphasis that the Communist party was the only vehicle to bring about revolutions in the Third World and began to accept that socialism could also emerge from the work of progressive "bourgeois nationalists" such as Fidel Castro.[63]

The Bay of Pigs Invasion: Between Nasser's Rhetoric and Soviet Support

After Castro returned from New York, more American companies were nationalized. The US retaliated by prohibiting all exports to Cuba except for unsubsidized foodstuffs and medical supplies on October 20, 1960.[64] These measures provoked a great deal of controversy within the United States, as the parallels to events in Egypt were particularly striking. According to Adlai E. Stevenson, soon to be appointed US ambassador to the United Nations, the economic embargo, short of weakening the Cuban revolution, would drive the Cubans towards the Soviet Union, and an "embargo will no more overthrow Castro than Mr. [John Foster] Dulles' economic sanctions against Egypt overthrew Nasser in 1956. Indeed, we may well have strengthened Castro's position with his people, as we did Nasser's."[65] Yet the decision was made. Cuba, described by Vice-President Nixon as an "intolerable cancer" on the Western Hemisphere, was placed under an economic embargo and the sugar quota fixed at zero.[66]

On New Years' Day 1961, the Cuban government announced its decision to restrict the number of personnel attached to the American embassy to a maximum of 11 and expel the remainder from Cuba. Eisenhower responded by severing relations with Cuba two days later. "There is a limit to what the United States in self-respect can endure. That limit has now been reached," an angry

---

62 John Lewis Gaddis, *We Now Know: Rethinking Cold War History* (New York: Oxford University Press, 1997), 181.

63 Gaddis, *We Now Know*, 182.

64 The embargo on Cuba would be comparable to the economic embargo on the People's Republic of China.

65 "Stevenson attacks Nixon on Cuban Plan," *New York Times*, October 26, 1960, 31.

66 "US Stops All Trade with Cuba: Dr. Castro Complains of Aggression, Fear of 'Large-Scale Invasion'," *The Times*, October 20, 1960, 12.

Eisenhower exclaimed.[67] The Eisenhower administration was prepared to act. A January 1960 meeting of the National Security Council revealed that the CIA and the State Department had been asking the president to approve a plan to assist political opposition to Castro's regime in Cuba since October 31, 1959, in an effort to make his downfall appear to be the consequence of popular discontent against Castro's policies and mistakes and not undue foreign influence.[68] Shortly thereafter, Cuban exiles began mounting sea-borne raids against Cuba's ports and planes dropped incendiary bombs to burn Cuba's sugar fields.[69] The success of these operations encouraged the CIA to seek President Eisenhower's authorization to target Cuba's sugar refineries. President Eisenhower, however, remained unconvinced by these tactics; he desired a more aggressive campaign against Castro himself. On March 17, Eisenhower approved a comprehensive plan against Cuba that included the international isolation of Castro's regime, increased funding for the opposition, and training of a paramilitary force outside Cuba.[70] The Eisenhower administration had already acquired some experience in removing nationalist leaders who had exhibited a tendency to wander too far outside the limits tolerable to Washington. Cuba was about to undergo the same experience that Iran and Guatemala had endured in 1953 and 1954, respectively. British Prime Minister Harold Macmillan had warned President Eisenhower that he must take actions against this "Caribbean Nasser" before it was too late. "Castro is really the very Devil," he and Eisenhower agreed

> He is your Nasser, and of course with Cuba sitting right at your doorstep the strategic implications are even more important than the economic ... I feel sure Castro has to be got rid of, but it is a tricky operation for you to contrive and I only hope you will succeed.[71]

A group of 300 guerrillas began CIA training in the United States and the Panama Canal Zone, after which they were moved to Guatemala. In June 1960, the CIA assembled the *Frente Revolucionario Democrático* (The Democratic National Front) as the political façade for this military campaign. By the end of the year the guerrillas were well trained, but the CIA decided that instead

---

67 "US Breaks with Cuba," *The Times*, January 4, 1961, 8.

68 Piero Gleijeses, "Ships in the Night: The CIA, the White House and the Bay of Pigs," *Journal of Latin American Studies*, 27.1 (1995), 3.

69 Gleijeses, "Ships in the Night", 3; see also R. Hart Phillips, "Planes Again Raid Cuban Cane Crop," *New York Times*, January 20, 1960, 3; "Cuba Says Bomber was from the US," *New York Times*, January 14, 1960, 3.

70 "Cuba Says Bomber was from the US," 3.

71 Gaddis, *We Now Know*, 182.

of having them infiltrate Cuba, they would be further trained to launch an amphibious invasion of the island at some point during 1961.

The final authorization for the invasion was left to the new US President, John F. Kennedy. Kennedy gave the operation the go-ahead.[72] Defectors from the Cuban Air Force began bombing Cuban airfields on the morning of April 15, 1961.[73] The planes, disguised as Cuban planes by the CIA, ran into mechanical problems shortly after the operation began and were of little use to the troops who had sailed from Nicaragua into a swampy area known as the Bay of Pigs.[74] Although the US government knew that Castro's regime was widely popular among the working class and the peasantry, they had left themselves no option but to believe their own propaganda that once the invasion began, the Cuban population would revolt against their government. Even the more pessimistic predictions proved fanciful. The invading forces, divided across four vessels each with an American adviser, landed in the Bay of Pigs; in less than 48 hours, they had been utterly defeated by an army that relied upon overwhelming support from the Cuban population. The American invasion, which the proxy forces hoped would come if their landing encountered difficulties, never materialized. The 1,180 survivors were taken prisoner and ransomed by the Cuban government for medical supplies and technical equipment valued at $62 million.

The invasion was a complete success, not for the United States but for Fidel Castro. Millions of Cubans rallied behind Castro in support of a revolution they regarded, above all else, as a nationalist revolution seeking the complete independence of their country. The Americans and the opposition within Cuba had been defeated by the legitimacy the population bestowed on Castro's regime. The revolution had been vindicated thanks to the millions of Cubans who decided to support it.

The Cubans sought to use this opportunity to reach some kind of *modus vivendi* with the American government. In August 1961 Guevara and Richard Goodwin, a close aide to President Kennedy, met to explore how the Cuban revolution and the United States could come to some kind of agreement. On behalf of the Cuban government, Guevara offered not to enter into any alliances with the Soviet Union in particular and the Eastern bloc in general— although Cuba would continue to have commercial, cultural, and diplomatic relations with all of them. In other words, they offered to transform Cuba into

---

72 Gaddis, *We Now Know*, 24–25. FRUS, "Foreign Relations of the United States, 1961-1963," in FRUS Vol. X, Cuba, January 1961- September 1962, (Washington, DC: United States Government Printing Office, 1997), 275.

73 "Cuba in Torment," *New York Times*, April 16, 1961, E 10.

74 "Anti-Castro Forces Land on Shores of Cuba," *The Times*, April 18, 1961, 12; also "President Bitter Over Cuba Failure," *The Times*, April 22, 1961, 8.

a kind of Finland in the Caribbean, with a neutral foreign policy and without an anti-American campaign on the continent. Kennedy refused to consider any such proposal. There was to be no negotiation with Castro in any form or under any terms. Instead of pursuing a negotiated settlement, Kennedy instead opted to authorize a new campaign against the Cubans. Called Operation Mongoose, it included further economic disruption and acts of sabotage on the island.[75]

The Bay of Pigs invasion and the events surrounding it are significant in many respects. As we have already noted, the Cuban people's response to the invasion demonstrated the broad legitimacy the revolution could already claim and further solidified Castro's regime. However, it also demonstrated the limits of Nasser's commitment to the Cuban revolution. The Egyptian response to the American-sponsored Bay of Pigs invasion fell short of any offers of meaningful assistance. Nasser authorized the National Union, Egypt's only legal political organization, to arrange a controlled demonstration in support of Cuba, and approximately 400 schoolboys were released from their classes to attend a rally, held in front of the American Embassy, at which they denounced the American invasion. The protesters, with their cries of "USA stop aggression against Cuba," were dispersed by the Egyptian authorities. From the American Embassy, the protesters marched across the Nile and attempted to invade an international agricultural fair being held at the time and at which the US had a large pavilion. Again, the police repulsed them before the situation got out of hand.[76]

Nasser had been following the news of the invasion while entertaining Yugoslavian leader Josip Broz Tito in Alexandria, and the two leaders, likely convinced that this, like Guatemala in 1954, was the end of another nationalist experiment in Latin America, signed a communiqué condemning the aggression in the most general terms possible. According to the joint communiqué released by the Egyptian and Yugoslavian governments, the invasion constituted "an attack against Cuba's independence and constitute[s] a denial of the principles of the United Nations and a breach of world peace."[77] Both presidents announced that they were "determined to take all available measures and extend every possible help to stop the foreign intervention."[78] The rhetoric,

---

75 "Anti-Castro Forces Land on Shores of Cuba," 12.

76 Jay Walz, "Nasser and Tito Vow Aid to Cuba," *New York Times*, April 20, 1960, 13.

77 "Joint Communiqué by the President of the Federal Republic of Yugoslavia, Josip Broz Tito and the President of the United Arab Republic, Gamal Abdel-Nasser, on April 19, 1961," President Gamal Abdel Nasser's Speeches and Press interviews, Cairo: Information Department, U.A.R., January–December, 1961, 102.

78 "Joint Communiqué by the President of the Federal Republic of Yugoslavia," 102.

however, was not supported by meaningful action, an express condemnation of the United States, or even a proposal to debate the question at the United Nations. Mere platitudes were of no use to the Cubans. The only country that had proven willing to arm the Cubans and bail out their economy was the Soviet Union. This was a defining moment for the Cubans. "We were no longer able to pretend that we could eat from two plates as Nasser was inviting us to do," concluded Jorge Serguera, Cuba's first Ambassador to Algeria. He concluded

> The Soviet Union proved to be a loyal friend of the Revolution. The Soviets showed their commitment to us. We had the Americans threatening and plotting against our revolution, and we had the Soviets offering us their friendship. Castro's decision to side with the USSR was clear to all of us.[79]

Indeed, Soviet economic and military aid was saving the Cuban revolution. Between 1959 and 1961, Cuban exports to the Socialist bloc were on the order of 74 percent of the country's total exports, where previously they had been less than 3 percent, and the share of its total imports coming from the Socialist block had jumped from 0.3 percent to nearly 70 percent. Most of this trade was with the Soviet Union itself,[80] accounting for nearly 50 percent of Cuban exports and 40 percent of imports. These levels of trade, although impressive, did not match pre-revolutionary Cuba's level of trade dependence on the United States.[81] Nevertheless, favorable terms of trade with the Soviet Union were used to finance a rapid process of economic diversification intended to eliminate the island's dependence on a single agricultural product, sugar, and finance its industrialization process.[82]

Cuba remained strongly identified with radical, anti-imperialist, and anticolonial causes, but it was evident that a worldwide military alliance of any kind between the Afro-Asian nations, Egypt and Cuba in particular, was not in prospect. After April 1961, Cuba made the strategic decision to ally itself within the Socialist bloc. The Cubans, according to Jorge Serguera, the first Cuban

---

79 Jorge Serguera (1932–2009) interview with the author, Havana, December 28, 2001.

80 Pérez, *Cuba: Between Reform and Revolution*, 355.

81 Pérez, *Cuba: Between Reform and Revolution*, 355.

82 The process of industrialization failed, as the Government reduced production of sugar, which resulted in declining revenues to import additional industrial equipment while simultaneously failing to provide the food required by the Cuban population. The US embargo and the migration of thousands of trained professionals also contributed to this failure. See Marifeli Pérez-Stable, *The Cuban Revolution: Origins, Course, and Legacy* (New York: Oxford University Press, 1999), 87–88.

Ambassador to Algeria, realized: "Neutrality was no longer an option after the Bay of Pigs:"

> We could not eat from two plates, as the Egyptians were doing. We had a mortal enemy, the United States of America, and a friend ready to help us, the Soviet Union. Together with the growing ideological identification with the principles of Socialism, there was not any doubt in our minds that our choice had to be the Soviet Union. What else could we do? We could not be neutral; it would have been immoral to be neutral.[83]

Nasser's "positive neutralism" was not an option for the Cubans. They were unable to play one superpower against the other for their own benefit. According to the rationale of the Cuban government, the revolution could not succeed if it failed to completely break with US dominance. That separation had to be total and unequivocal if the revolutionary programs were to succeed, and this assured the Cubans of perpetual American enmity. Again, it is important to recall that it was not primarily American hostility that drew the Cubans towards the Soviet Union, but rather that the Cubans themselves were actively seeking to disengage from the United States and asked the Soviets for assistance. Once the Soviets committed themselves to rescuing the Cuban economy and its military infrastructure, they became trapped in the Caribbean. Any withdrawal from Cuba would be a blow to the prestige of the Soviet Union.[84]

Isolated in the Americas, Welcomed into the Non-aligned Movement

As tensions between the superpowers over Cuba and other countries such as Germany and Vietnam increased, the leaders of nations that had proclaimed themselves nonaligned in the Cold War began to explore the possibility of calling a second "Bandung" conference of nations. The Egyptians, in close collaboration with the Yugoslav leader Josip Broz Tito, organized a preparatory meeting to establish the agenda and determine which states would be defined as nonaligned and then invited to participate in the meeting in Belgrade. Tito and Nasser controlled much of the conference's agenda, successfully sidetracking the idea of a conference of neutral nations proposed by Indian leader Jawaharlal Nehru.[85] Passive neutrality was not accepted as a working requirement for participation in the conference. In other words, the countries invited were expected to have a highly active foreign policy; yet it was also

---

83 Serguera, interview with the author. Havana, December 28, 2001.
84 Gaddis, *We Now Know*, 263.
85 "India's Fading Influence Among Neutrals," *The Times*, August 31, 1961, 6.

required that they not be militarily committed to either the Soviet or American bloc. The definition created at the preparatory meeting in Cairo stated: "a nonaligned state pursued a foreign policy of national independence based on peaceful coexistence, supported national liberation movements, and eschewed the multilateral military alliances and bilateral alliances with the great powers."[86]

Only 16 of the original 29 participants in the Bandung Conference were invited to attend.[87] Neither China nor North Vietnam, because of their ties to the Soviet Union, were invited. Moreover, Japan, Libya, and Jordan, because of their ties to the United States, were also excluded. The preparatory conference in Cairo concluded with a statement of support for the Cuban government and a demand that the United States transfer its base at Guantánamo Bay to Havana. Surprisingly, and perhaps in an effort to attract the less ideologically driven countries of Latin America, Mexico, Brazil, Bolivia and Ecuador were invited to attend the conference together with Cuba. Despite the invitation, all except Cuba chose not to participate.[88]

The first conference of nonaligned countries began on September 1, 1961, in Belgrade. Fidel Castro did not personally attend the Belgrade Conference and sent the Cuban president, Osvaldo Dorticós, in his place to head the Cuban delegation. Dorticós was unapologetic for the economic and social model adopted by Cuba's new stance in international affairs. As a full member of this new international entity, Cuba denounced the French occupation of Algeria and the "genocidal" Portuguese colonialism in Angola. Moreover, Dorticós rejected the nonconfrontational tone that Indian leader Jawaharlal Nehru had initially sought for the conference when he demanded the end of colonialism in Africa and called for the withdrawal of British troops from Kuwait and the Americans from Puerto Rico. Going further, Dorticós asked the conference to condemn United States action against Cuba in any proclamation made by the nonaligned countries professing the principles of self-determination. "How could we proclaim," Dorticós demanded, "to profess this principle without condemning the bombing of our cities and the invasion of our country by mercenary forces equipped and organized by the imperialist North American government?"[89]

---

86   Robert Mortimer, *The Third World Coalition in International Politics*, 2nd edn. (Boulder, CO: Westview Press, 1984), 12. See also "Seeking to Define Non-Alignment: Task Facing Cairo Delegates," *The Times*, June 7, 1961, 9.

87   The numbers were bolstered with invitations extended to other African, Latin American, and Middle Eastern countries.

88   Richard Eder, "Dorticos will go to Neutral Talk," *New York Times*, August 17, 1961, 9.

89   "Perfidia, Soborno y Guerra son Instrumentos del Imperialismo," *Revolución* (Havana), September 4, 1961, 6.

It is probable that the Cubans no longer harbored any illusions of a guarantee of military support from the nonaligned in the event of an attack by the United States; nevertheless, they were welcomed into the nonaligned movement, which meant that the diplomatic campaign launched by the United States to isolate the revolution had failed outside the Americas. On the continent, these efforts had centered on, but were not limited to, the expulsion of Cuba from the OAS. The previous year at an OAS meeting in Costa Rica, the United States had accused the Cubans of "walking hand-in-hand with the Sino-Soviet bloc,"[90] and the meeting ended with a condemnation of "Communist intrusion" on the continent, a walkout by the Cuban delegation in protest, and the issuance of a manifesto from Havana.[91] The manifesto, also known as the Havana Declaration, was a public denunciation of the regimes of the United States and Latin America. The Declaration elaborated, and denounced, a long list of wrongs:

> Latifundium, a source of poverty for the peasants and a backward and inhuman agricultural system; condemns starvation wages and the iniquitous exploitation of human labor by immoral and privileged interests; condemns illiteracy, the lack of teachers, of schools, of doctors and hospitals … condemns the discrimination against the Negro and the Indian; condemns the military and political oligarchies that keep our peoples in utter poverty, block their democratic development and the full exercise of their sovereignty.[92]

More provocatively, the Declaration cited the Soviet defense of the island as an "act of solidarity" and denounced the United Nations' failure to recognize Communist China.[93]

In January 1962, nearly four months after the Belgrade conference, at an OAS meeting in Punta del Este, Uruguay, the organization decided to suspend Cuba from the organization because its Marxist–Leninist ideology was "incompatible with the principles and objectives of the inter-American system."[94] Shortly after this meeting, on February 7, 1962, the United States imposed a full trade embargo on Cuba. The embargo prohibited US aid to Cuba or any country

---

90 "Cuba–US Clash at OAS Meeting," *The Times*, August 26, 1960, 8; "Rebuff for Cuba from O.A.S.: Communist Intrusion Placed on Agenda," *The Times*, August 9, 1960, 6.

91 "OAS Condemns Communist Intrusion," *The Times*, August 29, 1960, 8, and "Cuban Delegates Walk Out of OAS Conference," *The Times*, August 30, 1960, 8.

92 Fidel Castro, "Primera Declaración de la Habana," reproduced in Fidel Castro, *Obras Escogidas de Fidel Castro*, Tomo II, (Madrid: Editorial Fundamentos, 1976), 96.

93 Castro, "Primera Declaración de la Habana," 97.

94 Tad Szulc, "OAS Votes to Deny Cuba Any Inter-American Role; Prohibits Trade in Arms," *New York Times*, January 31, 1962, 1.

that furnished assistance to Cuba and prohibited ships from third countries engaged in such traffic from docking in the United States. It further prohibited US citizens and firms or their foreign subsidiaries from having any trade or financial relations with Cuba.[95] Castro responded to the expulsion from the OAS with a Second Havana Declaration. In this new manifesto, Castro again denounced the United States and stressed the worldwide revolutionary ethos that had emerged after the Second World War. "What is Cuba's history but that of Latin America?" Castro asked, "What is the history of Latin America but the history of Asia, Africa, and Oceania? And what is the history of all these peoples but the history of the cruellest exploitation of the world by imperialism?"[96] He concluded the Declaration by proclaiming: "The duty of every revolutionary is to make revolution."[97] Castro declared that Cubans would not "sit in the doorways of their homes to watch the corpse of imperialism pass by." Cuba, he vowed, would make revolution a reality.[98] By 1963, all Latin America countries except Mexico had severed diplomatic relations with Cuba. Cuba responded to these measures with renewed support for revolution on the continent and maintaining an active foreign policy within the Afro-Asian bloc.

After Belgrade, and because of continued American aggression, the Cubans again sounded-out the Egyptian leader on any kind of military alliance. The message from Egypt remained unchanged; Cairo would not commit any troops to Cuba. This became evident when the Cuban newspaper *Revolución* interviewed Nasser shortly after the Belgrade meeting. When Nasser was asked whether the Belgrade countries would consider aggression towards Cuba to be aggression towards the member states of the nonaligned movement, he lost no time in dampening Cuban expectations. This was not, according to Nasser, how the Conference was intended to operate:

> The Belgrade Conference was not a military alliance among the participant countries, but it laid down principles which have moral power. All the countries which participated in the Belgrade Conference will stand against any aggression launched against Cuba or against any other member-country. The Belgrade Conference calls upon all countries to solve their problems by peaceful means. We must take the moral power of the Belgrade Conference countries into consideration because it is a reflection of world public opinion and because it is the echo of the people's world conscience. No one can deny

---

95 "Cuban Embargo Statement and Text," *New York Times*, February 4, 1962, 22; and Domínguez, *To Make the World Safe*, 28.

96 Fidel Castro, "Segunda Declaración de la Habana," reproduced in Fidel Castro, *Obras Escogidas de Fidel Castro*, Tomo II, (Madrid: Editorial Fundamentos, 1976), 102.

97 Castro, "Segunda Declaración de la Habana," 131.

98 Castro, "Segunda Declaración de la Habana," 131.

the importance of this power. It is this particular power which stood beside us when an aggression was launched against Egypt. It supported all peoples in their struggle for liberty. It is in fact the reflection of the people's victory in their struggle against imperialism. It is the right of every country to choose the system which suits it best. The decisions of the Belgrade Conference stipulated this right and also stipulated non-intervention in the affairs of other countries, peaceful coexistence, putting an end to [the] cold war, and total disarmament.[99]

In short, Egypt would not commit forces to the defense of Cuba, not in April after the Bay of Pigs invasion and not now after the creation of the nonaligned movement in September 1961. The Cubans' dream of a united bloc of revolutionaries appeared nowhere in Nasser's plans.

Egypt remained the center of the anticolonialist and nationalist world for the Arabs and Africans north and south of the Sahara. The Cuban government, which had discovered Africa through its early contacts with Egypt, had arrived at the conclusion that they too, like Egypt, had a revolutionary role to play in Africa. In 1964, during the second nonalignment conference in Cairo, President Dorticós would acknowledge the new links between the Cuban government and the African continent. According to Dorticós, who again was the head of the Cuban delegation,

> It is very stirring for a Latin American, for a Cuban to speak in Africa; he knows that he can speak openly and sincerely and without reserve to the African peoples, just as it is possible to speak to all the peoples of the world who are involved in the intense and promising struggle for liberation and progress. This also explains the deep understanding which the distinguished representatives of the African peoples have shown in this meeting towards the cause of the Cuban people. It is the common denominator of all the African peoples today to struggle against centuries of oppression, subjection and discrimination, and we believe that the highly revolutionary mood of collective human effort of this meeting must affect the attitude of each one of us, must meet with our response and that it must be maintained and reflected in our resolutions.[100]

Cuba's commitment to ending colonialism and its desire to see the dawning of a new socialist era compelled it to act. Throughout the 1960s, the Cubans would fight for the success of that revolutionary ideal, beginning with the aid and support they gave to the Algerian revolutionaries. Subsequently, when the

---

99   President Gamal Abdel Nasser, "Speeches and Press—Interviews" (Cairo: Information Department, January–December 1962), 3.

100   Osvaldo Dorticós, *Cuba at the Second Conference of Non-Aligned Nations* (Havana: Foreign Ministry Information Department, 1964), 8.

Cuban government was providing support for other revolutionary struggles in Zanzibar in East Africa and Congo in Central Africa, Egypt remained a major hub through which arms and men would reach their final destinations. Nasser retained Cubans' respect and continued to be consulted on these operations, even after the Egyptian leader grew more cautious and began to regard such enterprises with less enthusiasm than he had in the 1950s.

Chapter 3
Algeria and Cuba: The Sister Revolutions

Gamal Abdel Nasser reignited nationalist demands in Panama in the 1950s. His leadership in the Afro-Asian group of nations was a source of inspiration in Cuba. It was soon clear that Egypt was not in a position to give Cuba any meaningful economic or military support, nor was the country interested in embracing Cuba's revolutionary mission in Africa. Algeria was to be a different case. Cubans regarded the Algerian revolution as a historical phenomenon identical to their own across the Atlantic. The Cuban government believed that they had a moral obligation to assist the Algerian revolution. Cuba's aid to Algeria not only opened the door to Cuba in the wider Afro-Asian bloc but also complicated Washington's efforts to isolate the Cuban regime and have some influence in the new Algerian government.

Cuba's Support for Algeria's War of Independence

Hopes for greater autonomy for the Arab majority in Algeria vanished shortly after the end of the Second World War. Under the new Statut de l'Algérie (the Algerian Code) adopted by the French parliament in 1947, Algeria remained under the legal fiction that it was another department of France, despite being under the authority of a governor-general appointed by Paris. The governor-general exercised his power with the help of a National Assembly composed of French Algerians, with a token representation of the local Arab population. The inability to negotiate a meaningful political accord with the French authorities began to radicalize a generation of Algerians that came to favor armed resistance to overthrow their colonial status.

Inspired by the defeat of the French forces by the Vietcong guerillas at Diem Bien Phu in Indochina early in 1954 and the French authorities' decision to grant self-government to the former colonies of Tunisia and Morocco, Algerians from different social sectors gathered supporters in Egypt and called for a general insurrection to begin on November 1, 1954. From Cairo, the different factions of the Algerian insurrectionary movement announced the formation of an umbrella organization in charge of the military and political campaign for the liberation of Algeria, the Front Libération Nationale (National Liberation

Front: FLN). The FLN organized guerrilla groups throughout Algeria and confronted both the French army and the paramilitary organizations created by French-Algerians.

Figure 3.1   President of Algerian Council Ahmed Ben Bella in Cuba in 1962

Source: © Getty Images

A year and a half earlier, another revolutionary movement had begun thousands of miles away in the Caribbean Island of Cuba. On July 26, 1953, in an attempt to begin a revolutionary process against the dictatorship of Fulgencio Batista, who had controlled politics in the country since 1933, a young upper-class lawyer-turned-revolutionary named Fidel Castro launched an attack on the *Cuartel Moncada*, the second-largest army installation in the country. Castro failed in this attempt to defeat Batista, but his military defeat catapulted him to the leadership of a broader movement that soon engulfed the entire country. Three years after the failure at the Moncada, Castro reorganized his forces in Mexico and launched another failed attempt against Batista in November 1956. Defeated and besieged, the insurgents regrouped their forces in the wilderness of the southeastern mountains, the *Sierra Maestra*, and from there expanded their forces until their final victory over the Cuban armed forces on January 1, 1959.

The future cadres of the post-Batista regime were school or university students when the Algerian revolution began in 1954. Many of them belonged to the upper echelons of Cuban society and had ample access to news from across the world. Armando Entralgo, a future Cuban ambassador to several African countries and later director of the *Centro de Estudios de África y del Medio Oriente* (Center for the Study of Africa and the Middle East: CEAMO) in Havana, Cuba, reflected,

> We grew up in a climate of revolutionary upheaval, not only in our country, but all over the world, at home we were fighting the dictatorship of Batista with his disgusting corruption and subservience to the United States, but as university students we were avid readers of what was going on around the world. We followed the confrontation of Egypt with the Europeans and Israel, we knew about the fight in Vietnam, the insurrection in Algeria, and of course about everything related to Latin America.[1]

Despite the fierce control over the press during the Batista dictatorship, the weekly *Bohemia* ran several articles favorable to the Algerian revolution during 1957, reinforcing the growing understanding among intellectuals and middle-class students that there was a connection between the two revolutionary movements.[2] As the revolutionary movement against Batista moved into the cities, more university students joined Fidel Castro's insurrectionary forces and brought with them their conviction that their own fight was connected with events in Africa, Asia, and the Middle East.

With the triumph of the revolution in January 1959, support for the Algerian guerrillas became the official policy of the new regime. The daily newspaper

---

1 Armando Entralgo, Director of the Center of Studies of Africa and the Middle East (CEAMO), former Cuban Ambassador to Ghana, interview by the author, December 30, 2001, Havana, Cuba.

2 Peter Trockmorton and Herb Creer, "¡Así es la guerra en Argelia! *Bohemia* (Havana), July 7, 1957, 8–10. Piero Gleijeses first noticed the existence of these articles in *Bohemia*. For a complete list of articles in *Bohemia* concerning Algeria, see Piero Gleijeses, *Conflicting Missions: Havana, Washington, and Africa, 1959–1976* (Chapel Hill, NC: University of North Carolina Press, 2002), fn 10, 406.

Revolución attacked French policies in Algeria while praising the guerrilla fighters. The tone of the newspaper's coverage can be gauged from an op-ed published in July 1961, which blasted the French Army's use of Napalm against the civilian population while applauding the Algerian rebels, who "after more than five years have demonstrated that neither the force of arms, nor the use of torture, nor the concentration camps are sufficient to put an end to the resistance against the colonial oppression."[3] Support for the Algerians was not confined to the local press. The leader of the Cuban revolution, Fidel Castro, used his first trip to New York to address the General Assembly of the United Nations in September 1960 to voice his support for the Algerian revolutionaries:

> In regards to the problem of Algeria, we are, I need hardly say, 100 per cent on the side of the right of the people of Algeria to independence. It is ridiculous—like so many ridiculous things in the world which have been artificially created by vested interests—to claim that Algeria is part of France. Similar claims have been made by other countries in an attempt to keep their colonies in other days. This so-called "integration" has failed throughout history. Let us turn the question upside down: suppose Algeria was the metropolitan country and it was to declare that part of Europe was an integral part of its territory? Such reasoning is far-fetched and devoid of all meaning. Algeria belongs to Africa as France belongs to Europe. This African people have been fighting a heroic battle against the metropolitan country for many years.
>
> Perhaps even as we are calmly talking here, the machine-guns and bombs of the Government of the French Army are attacking Algerian villages and hamlets. Men may well be dying, in a struggle in which it is perfectly clear where the right lies, a struggle that could be ending without disregarding the interests of that minority which is being used as an excuse for denying nine-tenths of the population of Algeria their right to independence. Yet the United Nations is doing nothing. We were in such a hurry to go into the Congo and are so unenthusiastic about going into Algeria! If the Algerian Government, which is a Government, for it represents millions of fighting Algerians, were to request the United Nations to send forces there also, should we go with the same enthusiasm? I hope that we should go with the same enthusiasm, but with very different purpose that is to say, for the purpose of defending the interests of the colony and not the colonizers.[4]

---

3 René Depreste, "La heroica Argelia," *Revolución* (Havana), July 21, 1961, 4.

4 United Nations General Assembly, Speech by Fidel Castro, Prime Minister of Cuba, Official Records of the General Assembly, Fifteen Session (Part 1) Plenary Meetings, New York, September 26, 1960, 132.

It did not take much time for the Cuban government to transform its endorsement of the Algerian revolution into something more concrete than political and diplomatic support for the FLN. In an unprecedented move, the Cuban authorities decided to contact the FLN in Tunis and offered the Algerians a sizable number of weapons at a time when the Cubans were themselves contending with constant military threats from Cuban exiles aided by the United States government. Jorge Massetti, an Argentinean journalist who had joined the Cuban revolution in the month preceding its triumph, was commissioned by Fidel Castro to negotiate with the Algerians and supervise the operation.[5]

On behalf of the Cuban government, Massetti agreed to send the Algerians 1,500 rifles, more than 30 machine guns, and 4 US-made 81 mm mortars with rounds, weapons that Cuba left aboard the Cuban vessel *Bahía de Nipe*. The *Bahía de Nipe* docked in the Moroccan port of Casablanca, and from there the arms were transported to Oujda, inside Morocco. The armaments were officially transferred to the FLN during the first two weeks of 1962.[6] The *Bahía de Nipe* returned to Cuba with dozens of Algerian war orphans; the Cuban authorities had offered to care for them until the end of the conflict.[7] Massetti remained in Algeria for a few months after the triumph of the Algerian revolution and went back to Cuba before again returning to Algeria for a completely different mission in November 1962.

The Cuban support for Algeria put at risk the initial support for the Cuban revolution of France's President, Charles DeGaulle. Militarily, it deprived the Cuban armed forces of weapons and personnel while distracting them from the urgent task of protecting their own revolution. Cuba's solidarity could not be regarded as anything other than an ideological identification with the Algerian struggle and the conviction that a new generation of nations oriented by similar political principles was emerging throughout Africa and Asia and now, after the Cuban revolution, in Latin America. As the Cuban Ambassador Jorge Serguera recalls,

---

5 Piero Gleijeses, *Conflicting Missions: Havana, Washington, and Africa, 1959–1976* (Chapel Hill, NC: University of North Carolina Press, 2002), 31. Also Jorge Castañeda, *Compañero: The Life and Death of Che Guevara* (New York: Alfred A. Knopf), 246–247 For an account of one of its protagonists, see Jorge Serguera Riverí, *Caminos del Che: datos inéditos de su vida* (México, DF: Plaza y Valdés), 54–55.

6 Gisela García Blanco, *La misión internacionalista de Cuba en Argelia (1963–1964)* (Havana: Dirección Política de las FAR, 1990), 16–17.

7 "Codo a Codo, Argelia y Cuba harán frente a sus destinos sin debilidad y con fe," *Revolución* (Havana), October 18, 1962: Segunda Edición, 6.

Our *comandante* was convinced, intimately convinced, that we had a moral duty, that we had to support those revolutionaries in the Arab World. He cherished their suffering and believed in their cause ... and they were loyal to the friendship we offered them.[8]

Algeria as Cuba's Bridge to the Afro-Asian World

The Algerians did not take long to respond to this early solidarity with their revolution from such a distant friend. The FLN leaders had excellent relations with Gamal Abdel Nasser, the leader of the emerging Afro-Asian bloc. The Algerians rapidly began to champion Cuba's cause in the Arab world, helping the Cuban revolution break away from its isolation, which was promoted by the United States in the Americas and the rest of the world. The Algerians were ready to place all geographic considerations aside and redraw the map of the world to consider Cuba another Afro-Asian country. If Cuba could enter the Afro-Asian bloc, its isolation in the Americas would be minimized and replaced with the welcome of a more populated and powerful power bloc. As an official Algerian newspaper of the time put it,

> The peoples of Asia and Africa have formed a coalition with Cuba. What happens in Cuba concerns them. They were deeply hurt by the events of Guatemala in 1954; after that there was Bandung, and in 1960, Fidel Castro has avenged the Third World. The great discovery of the 1960s is that The Third World is no longer "Afro-Asian." The living forces of Latin America have constantly expressed their support for our cause; they know from experience that the anti-colonialist fight and the anti-imperialist fight are one and the same combat.[9]

Two years later, and eight years after the beginning of their war of independence, the representatives of the Algerian revolution reached an agreement with the French authorities. According to the provisions of the Evian Accord, the Algerians held a referendum in which they could opt for total independence, full incorporation into France, or limited independence in a commonwealth with France. The referendum held on July 3, 1962 registered approximately 6 million votes in favor of and 16,000 votes against independence. After more than 130 years of French occupation, nearly eight years after their call for a general insurrection against the French authorities, and after the deaths of more than 1 million people and the uprooting of another 2 million, Algeria emerged

---

8 Serguera Interview with the Author, 6.

9 *El-Moudjahid*, September 8, 1960, no. 69, quoted in André Mandouze, *La revolution algerienne par les textes: documents du FLN* (Paris: Éditions D'Aujourd'hui, 1962), 63.

as an independent country.[10] The new nation had much to learn, but it was not ready to forget those who had supported it during its war of independence.

Algeria as an Obstacle to US Policy Towards Cuba

The leader of the new nation, the legendary revolutionary Ahmed Ben Bella, was invited to the United Nations to raise the flag of the newly independent Algeria, and to deliver his first address to the General Assembly in September 1962. Algiers announced that Ben Bella was planning to visit New York, followed by a visit to President John F. Kennedy in Washington, ending his trip to the Americas with a visit to Fidel Castro, the leader of the Cuban revolution, in Havana.

Despite initial protests regarding Ben Bella's visit to Havana, the Kennedy administration decided not to antagonize the Algerian leader but instead to use the meeting as an opportunity to "lay the groundwork for US influence on him." It was clear to the United States that Ben Bella was not a communist, but rather a "pragmatic" leader in need of further education as he "still clings to a lot of naive ideas and thinks in terms of a mélange of revolutionary clichés."[11]

During the meeting, which took place on October 15, 1962, President Kennedy lost no time in conveying to Ben Bella the United States policy towards the emerging nationalism across Africa and Asia. The President pointed out that "there seemed be [an] impression in Algeria that [the] world [was] divided into two blocs and that one led by [the] US favored nuclear tests, colonialism, and imperialism." Knowing that Ben Bella was going to Cuba in the next leg of his trip, Kennedy wanted to make it very clear that the United Stated had to abandon a preferred policy of isolationism in response to the growing threat that an expanding international communism represented to the world after 1945. While the United States wanted, according to the President, a "world of independent nations each with [governments] corresponding [to the] needs [of] its own people. Communists wanted uniformity tied together and directed by Moscow and Peking."[12]

---

10 Matthew Connelley, *A Diplomatic Revolution: Algeria's Fight for Independence and the Origins of the Post-Cold War Era*, (Oxford: Oxford University Press, 2002), 264–265.

11 FRUS, "Memorandum from Robert W. Komer of the National Security Council Staff to President Kennedy," in FRUS, 1961–1963, vol. XXI, *Africa* (Washington, DC: 1995), October 13, 1962, Document 71, 102   See also Peter Braestrup, "Colorful Ceremony Greets Ben Bella at White House; Kennedy Greets Algerian Leader," *The New York Times*, October 16, 1962, 1–3.

12 FRUS, "Telegram from the Department of State to the Embassy in Algeria," in FRUS, vol. XXI, 1961–1963, *Africa* (Washington, DC: United States Government

He then proceeded to explain to Ben Bella the complexities of politics in the Americas and the United States' role in confronting communism in the region. Kennedy argued that the United States had supported regimes that had fought against the expansion of communism. He cited the cases of the Dominican Republic, Venezuela, and Colombia, which were all "under liberal leadership and had fought for freedom and progress against regressive factions as well as against communists." He needed Ben Bella to understand that the American nations were "under attack" by Castro's Cuba, and that if they were undeterred, "the cause of independence in and sovereignty of nations might be defeated in Latin America."[13]

In a cordial but direct response, Ben Bella challenged the President. He reminded Kennedy of the similitudes between the Cuban and the Egyptian recent histories. The United States policy towards Nasser had forced him "little by little into [an] intolerable situation," where he had to accept armaments from the Soviet bloc. Ben Bella also argued that in Cuba "it [was] best [to] avoid nailing Castro to [the] communist camp [while] failing [to] give him any other choice." Unconvinced, Kennedy told Ben Bella that Castro was not a person he could trust. According to Kennedy, "Castro betrayed the Cuban revolution," by turning what many thought to be a national revolution into something very different to what he had promised. Castro, Kennedy argued, had "appended [Cuba] to [the] Soviet bloc."[14]

In a sense, both were wrong about Castro and the Cuban Revolution. Ben Bella was incorrect in assuming that Castro was a neutralist like Nasser, attempting to navigate the conflict between the United States and the Soviet Union. Castro had openly proclaimed his revolution to be socialist and embraced the Soviet camp the previous year to protect his country from another direct or indirect United States invasion. However, if, as Kennedy argued, Castro was not neutral, the US President was incorrect in assuming that he was a pawn of the Soviet Union. Castro was a revolutionary. He was fully committed to the historical mission of his revolution. His decision to embrace the Soviet Union was partly ideological but was mostly a tactical decision designed to save the Cuban revolution from continued military threat and the relentless economic embargo.

Kennedy appeared to have used Ben Bella to send a clear message to Castro. Despite his personal antipathy toward the Cuban leader, Kennedy warned Ben Bella that as long as there were no Soviet missiles in Cuba, he had no intention

---

Printing Office,1995). October 23, 1962, document 72, 105.

13 FRUS, "Telegram from the Department of State to the Embassy in Algeria," in FRUS, vol. XXI, 1961–1963, *Africa*, 105.

14 FRUS, "Telegram from the Department of State to the Embassy in Algeria," in FRUS, vol. XXI, 1961–1963, *Africa*, 106.

of transforming Havana "into another Budapest," in reference to the violent occupation of Hungary by the Soviet Union in 1956 after the country sought to break away from Moscow's political and economic influence. Ben Bella reminded Kennedy of Egypt's fight for its own independence in 1956, and hence of a parallel event, the Soviet invasion of Hungary. Nevertheless, Kennedy's final comment to Ben Bella on Cuba reiterated the US administration's position on armaments being transferred to Cuba by the Soviet Union:

> If those missiles included at any time types capable of striking at US territory, [the] situation would change to such [an] extent that [the] US would be forced [to] reconsider its position. The stronger the military build-up, the greater the danger. Cuba's best protection was its own people's support. [The] US does not want war against [a] small country.[15]

At this point, neither Kennedy nor Ben Bella had any notion of what was taking place in Cuba, but the CIA was analyzing the photographs taken the previous day by a U-2 reconnaissance plane evincing the presence of a much larger Soviet military build-up underway in Cuba at the same time that Kennedy was lecturing Ben Bella. Only one day after the meeting with Ben Bella, Kennedy would be informed of the presence of these bases in Cuba. News of the new military installation and the armaments it contained, however, would not be made public until October 22. Hence the Algerian Prime Minister was able to travel to Cuba before one of the worst crisis of the Cold War started.

"Acts of Valor and Gestures of Friendship:" Ahmed Ben Bella visits Havana

On Tuesday October 16, 1962, Ben Bella arrived in Havana for a two-day visit to Cuba. He was the first Arab head of state ever to visit a Latin American country. The Cuban government wanted this occasion to be an unforgettable one. Hence, businesses, schools, and universities were closed, and the entire city was slowed to a halt at midday to receive the Algerian leader. Havana had not witnessed such a rally since the celebration of the defeat of the Cuban exile invasion of April 1961. In contrast to his unremarkable previous visits to New York and Washington, the streets of Havana were packed with tens of thousands of Cubans who welcomed Ben Bella with an enthusiasm that took the Algerian leader aback. It was soon clear that Kennedy had failed to warn Ben Bella away from friendship with the Cubans. Shortly after his arrival, he told

---

15 FRUS, "Telegram from the Department of State to the Embassy in Algeria," in FRUS, vol. XXI, 1961–1963, *Africa*, 106–107.

the Cubans precisely what they wanted to hear in a time of heightened tensions with the United States: if Algeria had to take sides in this world, it would be with Cuba. In a message reproduced by the official newspaper *Revolución*, Ben Bella told Cubans that, "In times of happiness and sorrow, Algeria will always be on the side of Cuba."[16]

Ben Bella's visit was a major diplomatic success for Fidel Castro, and he would not easily forget this moment. Castro acknowledged the importance of Ben Bella's visit and thanked his guest for coming

> at a time in which the powerful Yankee empire is more determined than ever to exert its hatred and hostility toward our motherland, and pretends to impose upon us, by bribery and blackmail, a criminal economic and commercial blockade in the expectation of destroying the Cuban Revolution by starving it.

He also reassured Ben Bella's of his gratitude for his visit:

> To visit Cuba, when the Yankee imperialists have threatened to attack us at any moment, and drawn in blood our people's work is on your part, Mister Prime Minister, an act of valor and political courage that defines your character. It is also a gesture of friendship that we will never forget.[17]

Revolución noted that Ben Bella responded "with his phrases of revolutionary honesty," stating that, "in his motherland the events of the Bay of Pigs are remembered as a national festivity." Ben Bella, the official newspaper continued, "also underlined the similarities of the revolutionary process in both countries that have understood that socialism was the path towards liberty and happiness."[18]

A strong bond uniting the two leaders emerged as a result of Ben Bella's visit. His identification with the Cuban revolution was profound and sincere. Nowhere could one see the hand of the Soviet Union in the visit, nor were communist parties from any other country involved. Ben Bella understood the occasion as an historical encounter between two revolutions "in the path of the political and economic liberation" and between two peoples that "would never take different paths."[19]

Upon his departure from Cuba on October 18, the two leaders signed a joint communiqué stressing their commitment to "peoples that fight for their

---

16 "Saludo de Ben Bella al Pueblo de Cuba," *Revolución* (Havana), October 17, 1962, 1.

17 "Saludo de Ben Bella al Pueblo de Cuba," 6.

18 "Saludo de Ben Bella al Pueblo de Cuba," 6.

19 "Saludo de Ben Bella al Pueblo de Cuba," 6.

self-determination, independence and sovereignty." They condemned all forms of colonialism and neocolonialism and demanded the evacuation of foreign troops from other countries "including the Naval Base at Guantánamo." Castro congratulated Ben Bella for his "irrevocable determination to construct a new political, economic, social and cultural life through the path of socialism." For his part, Ben Bella pledged his support for the Cuban people's right to define its own path of development and defended the right, and the duty, of the Cuban government to defend its revolution. Finally, both countries elected to have diplomatic relations at the ambassadorial level.[20] Three months later, Castro would select his man in Algeria: the first ambassador to Algeria would be instrumental in solidifying the Cuban-Algerian relationship. Jorge Serguera Riverí, a former guerrilla fighter whom everyone knew by the nom de guerre of "*Papito*," was selected for the post and given Castro's unconditional support. He describes his appointment:

> It was in January of 1963 when Fidel asked me to come here to Havana and meet an official delegation from Algeria; I was called from my province of Matanzas, where I was the First Secretary General of the Party, to entertain the first official delegation of Algerians who had arrived to Cuba. When I arrived at Havana, Fidel told me right away that he wanted me to be the first ambassador of Cuba to Algeria, but that I would be more than a diplomat but also a facilitator, a bridge between him and Ben Bella. He told Ben Bella that I was there to help him with anything they needed.[21]

When Ben Bella returned to New York to fly back to Algeria, despite criticism of him in the United States media, the Kennedy administration downplayed the visit to Cuba and again demonstrated its patience with him. The Kennedy administration did not rushed to conclusions and typecast the young leader. *The New York Times* reported that according to some members of the Kennedy administration,

> [The] United States Government was reluctant to take Mr. Ben Bella to task at this delicate juncture when his new nation is just beginning to establish itself in international affairs ... The best hope, they said, was that "Mr. Ben Bella would acquire a more balanced understanding of affairs after a period of experience as the leader of an independent country."[22]

---

20 "Comunicado Conjunto Cubano-Argelino," *Revolución* (Havana), October 18, 1962, 4.

21 Serguera, interview with the author, see also Serguera, *Caminos*, 363–364.

22 "Ben Bella backs Cuba on US base; Joins Castro in Demand on Yielding of Guantanamo," *New York Times*, October 18, 1962, 14.

Yet, contrary to expectations in Washington, Cuban-Algerian relations would become stronger than anyone could have anticipated, due in part to the personal rapprochement between Ben Bella and Castro and the superpowers' confrontation—and alliance.

Algeria and Cuba's October Missile Crisis

The day before Ahmed Ben Bella's arrival in Washington, a U-2 reconnaissance aircraft from the American Strategic Air Command was flying over Cuba on a secret mission. Its objective was to identify the nature of new military build-up that had been taking place in Cuba since August under the auspices of the Soviet Union. That the Soviets were transferring armaments to Cuba had been known for months, but the Kennedy administration now wished to know whether the Soviet Union was installing armaments capable of reaching the United States.[23]

The United States had warned the Soviet Union of the dangers of furnishing those "impulsive Cubans" with weapons that could reach the United States.[24] In response to the accusations, Khrushchev had maintained that the armaments Castro was receiving from the Soviet Union were only of a defensive nature, and intended to provide Cuba with the weapons to defend itself in the event of an American attack.[25] Nevertheless, on October 16, the day Ben Bella arrived in Cuba, the President was informed that the Soviet bases on the island contained ballistic missiles that could reach the United States as far north as Seattle.

These findings provoked one of the most serious crisis of the Cold War. The United States regarded the installation of the missiles not only as a direct threat to its territorial security but also as a threat to its position in Europe. The Soviet Union could use the missiles in Cuba not only to attack the United States but also as a bargaining tool to challenge the US position in Europe or to secure a new agreement regarding the status of Berlin.[26] For its part, the Soviet Union regarded its weapons deliveries not only as an effective means of defending the Cuban government, as it officially announced, but also as a means of redrawing the map of the strategic distribution of nuclear arms. If the North Atlantic

---

23 Ernest R. May and Philip Zelikow, eds., *The Kennedy Tapes: Inside the White House During the Cuban Missile Crisis.* (Cambridge, MA: Harvard University Press, 1997), fn.10, 53.

24 Anatoly Dobrynin, *In Confidence: Moscow's Ambassador to America's Six Cold War Presidents (1962–1986)* (New York: Times Books, 1995), 68–70.

25 FRUS, "Memorandum of a Conversation, October 18, 1962," in FRUS, vol. XI, 1961–1963, *Cuban Missile Crisis and Aftermath* (Washington, DC: United States Government Printing Office), document 29, 110–114.

26 FRUS, vol. XI, 1961–1963, *Cuban Missile Crisis and Aftermath*, 162–163.

Treaty Organization (NATO) could place missiles near the border of the Soviet Union in Turkey, the Soviet Union believed it had the right place weapons 90 miles from the United States.[27]

President Kennedy demanded the immediate withdrawal of the Soviet weapons from Cuba in a television broadcast on October 22. In the meantime, Kennedy announced that

> [to] halt this offensive build-up, a strict quarantine on all offensive military equipment under shipment to Cuba is being initiated. All ships of any kind bound for Cuba from whatever nation or port will, if found to contain cargoes of offensive weapons, be turned back.[28]

The President also announced that the United States would hold the Soviet Union responsible for any missile launched from Cuba to any nation in the western hemisphere. He further warned the Soviet Union that any such incident would lead to a "full retaliatory response upon the Soviet Union."[29]Khrushchev immediately responded that those measures represented

> [a] serious threat to peace and security of peoples. [The] United States had openly taken [the] path of [a] gross violation of [the] Charter of [the] United Nations, [the] path of [a] violation of international norms of freedom of navigation on high seas, [and the] path of aggressive actions both against Cuba and against [the] Soviet Union.[30]

Khrushchev later fully rejected the American demands as an "ultimatum" that he deemed contrary to international law and the pillars of peaceful coexistence. Clearly he would not obey Kennedy's request.[31]

As the crisis was unfolding, Castro did not stand passively in the midst of this confrontation between superpowers. He had previously asked the Soviets for conventional armaments, but he had also accepted the offer to place nuclear arms on his island. Now, recognizing the possibility of a showdown between superpowers, he was convinced that an invasion of Cuba was imminent and that any conflict between the United States and the Soviet Union would involve the use of nuclear arms. Nevertheless, he was determined to prove to the Soviets that he was worthy of their continued political, economic, and military support.

---

27 FRUS, , vol. XI, 1961–1963, *Cuban Missile Crisis and Aftermath*, 170–171.

28 May and Zelikow, *The Kennedy Tapes*, 278.

29 May and Zelikow, *The Kennedy Tapes*, 279.

30 FRUS, vol. XI, 1961–1963, *Cuban Missile Crisis and Aftermath* , 170–171.

31 FRUS, vol. XI, 1961–1963, *Cuban Missile Crisis and Aftermath*, 186–187.

The entire island was prepared for the first chapter of a confrontation between the superpowers. The daily newspaper *Revolución* announced that the entire country needed to be prepared to confront what Castro regarded as a renewed invasion of the country. This time, however, unlike the amateurish attempt by Cuban exiles at the Bay of Pigs the previous year, the invasion would certainly be mounted by the American armed forces.[32] In a matter of days, more than 270,000 Cubans were mobilized and armed and had constructed ramparts and trenches across the island. The Cubans had the support of the Soviet soldiers who had been stationed in the country over the previous three months, whose determination to confront an imminent invasion of Cuba was shared by their commander, Serguei Bolanchenko: "We were ready to fight to our last man; we had nowhere else to go."[33]

The Cubans were expecting the worst. Castro himself saw little chance of a peaceful resolution: "A war appeared imminent; a first strike might take place at any time. I said to myself: If Cuba is in such unfortunate war, we will disappear from the map." Castro sought to ensure that Cuba was prepared to confront the United States with a nuclear response: "I inquired with the Soviet officer in charge of the armaments," Castro affirmed, "the missiles were ready, the air to air missiles were ready, everything was in place." The Cubans had determined their fate by accepting Soviet armaments, and their revolution had survived as long as it had thanks to the economic support of the Soviet Union. Even if October 1962 spelled the end of Cuba, Castro had no intention of disassociating from his ally.[34]

Outside of Cuba, negotiations between the superpowers continued. Both nations accepted the call of the Secretary General of the United Nations, U Thant, to avoid a confrontation at the quarantine line— an imaginary line in the Atlantic Ocean that signaled the beginning of the United States naval blockade of the island of Cuba. Perhaps taken aback by Castro's determination to take the crisis to its very end,[35] on October 26, Khrushchev wrote Kennedy a letter that continued to demand the end of the quarantine but also hinted that

---

32 Philip Brenner, "Cuba and the Missile Crisis" *Journal of Latin American Studies*, Winter (1994), 129.

33 Commander of Soviet Forces in Cuba, in *Cold War* [video recording], Jeremy Isaacs production for Turner Original Productions, Inc. Burbank, CA: Warner Home Video; Atlanta, GA : CNN Productions, 1998. v. 4.

34 Perhaps it was not. Cuba was still behind schedule in installing the bases. According to a historian of this crisis, Philip Brenner, the installation process was still in a very early phase despite Castro's belief that the process was almost complete. Of a total of 80 missiles, the Cubans were still waiting for 38 to arrive and for the complete installation of the 42 already in the country, of which only nine were fully operational by October 22. Brenner, "Cuba and the Missile Crisis," 131.

35 Brenner, "Cuba and the Missile Crisis," 132.

if assurances were given by the President and the Government of the United States that the USA itself would not participate in an attack on Cuba and would restrain others from actions of this sort, if you would recall your fleet, this would immediately change everything.[36]

He claimed not to be speaking for Castro but stated that once such a pledge was made, the government in Cuba would put an end to mobilization and "would appeal to the people to get down to peaceful labor."[37] He would formalize this offer the next day, but he added that the United States had to agree to dismantle NATO missiles in Turkey aimed at the Soviet Union.

Castro, who was certainly unaware of the accommodation being reached by the US and the USSR, was not prepared to remain passive while awaiting Soviet instructions. On the morning of October 27, he gave orders to open fire on any hostile aircraft flying over the island. That day, the Soviet officer in charge of the Strategic Air Missiles (SAM) disregarded Soviet instructions to avoid any provocation with the United States and, in obedience to Castro's orders, shot down an American U-2 flying over the island. That afternoon, the Cubans hit a low flying F8U-IP, a surveillance plane, which managed to return to its base. Despite the increase in tension generated by the downed plane, the superpowers were still moving closer to an agreement that completely excluded Cuba from the negotiation process.

On October 28, Khrushchev caved. In a radio address, he announced the following to President Kennedy:

The Soviet Government, in addition to earlier instructions on the discontinuation of further work on weapons construction sites, has given a new order to dismantle the arms which you described as offensive, and to crate and return them to the Soviet Union.[38]

The crisis between the superpowers was over.

Castro was infuriated:

We were irate, how did we learn about this? Through the radio, on the morning of the 28th they broadcasted that an agreement had been reached between the Soviet Union and the United States. That Kennedy was offering Khrushchev a guarantee! It really was a disgraceful agreement, it never crossed my mind they would do anything like this.[39]

---

36 FRUS, vol. XI, 1961–1963, *Cuban Missile Crisis and Aftermath* , 239.
37 FRUS, vol. XI, 1961–1963, *Cuban Missile Crisis and Aftermath*, 239.
38 FRUS, vol. XI, 1961–1963, *Cuban Missile Crisis and Aftermath*, 279.
39 Interview with Fidel Castro in Jeremy Isaacs' *Cold War*.

In fact, Khrushchev had not only agreed to dismantle the missiles but also subsequently agreed to the return to the Soviet Union of the non-offensive IL-28 bombers, which were already being transferred to the Cuban government.

The United States demanded that the United Nations serve as inspectors of the dismantling operation, but Castro completely rejected the presence of any monitoring authority in his country. Secretary General U Thant went to Cuba in an effort to convince Castro to accept the inspections, but he later reported that Castro had been in an "impossible and intractable mood"—"extremely bitter" toward the Soviets, the Americans, and even the Secretary General himself, "whom he seemed to regard as a lackey of the imperialists."[40]

Castro later agreed to inspections of the dismantling of the Soviet weapons in Cuba if the United States accepted five conditions: first, that the Guantánamo base, leased to the United States since 1901, be returned to Cuba; second, that the United States end its economic embargo; third, that the United States cease all subversive activities against Cuba; fourth, that the United States end the "pirate" attacks against Cuba from Puerto Rico and its mainland; and finally, that the US cease all violations of Cuban airspace.[41] The United States paid no heed to the Cuban government and continued to work directly with the Soviet Union over the Cuban crisis.

The superpowers had struck a deal behind Castro's back. Organized demonstrators against the Soviet Union flooded Havana, chanting, "Nikita, Nikita, Indian giver, you don't take back what you once deliver,"[42] while the official newspaper *Revolución* printed stories that depicted Cuban courage in the face of total war. The Soviets attempted to assuage the American reaction to the Cuban rejection of international monitors, blaming the rejection, in Khrushchev's words, on Cuba's immaturity as a nation: "Cuba is a young republic, the Cuban leaders being very able and devoted to their people are however young, expansive peoples—Spaniards in a word—to use it far from pejorative sense" (sic).[43] Castro refused to speak with Soviet Ambassador Alekseev, and when the Soviet envoy, Anastas Mikoyan, arrived in Havana to discuss *ex-post-facto* the Soviet position in the crisis, Castro refused to see him. Castro needed to show the Soviets that he would not be a pawn in their geostrategic conflict with the United States. Cuba had accepted the missiles to protect its revolution and because it believed in the cause of international socialism; therefore Cuba should have been treated as a peer, not as a pawn.

---

40 May and Zelikow, *The Kennedy Tapes*, 664.

41 "El Primer Ministro Fidel Castro, dió a la publicidad la siguiente declaración," *Revolución* (Havana), October 29, 1962, 1.

42 Brenner, "Cuba and the Missile Crisis," 134.

43 FRUS, vol. XI, 1961–1963, *Cuban Missile Crisis and Aftermath* , 519–521.

Castro felt betrayed by the Soviet Union and still a target of the United States. US-supported attacks continued during the months following the crisis, although they later subsided. On November 18, a terrorist squad bombed a Cuban factory. The Cubans now realized that the Soviets would not risk war with the United States over Cuban security. They had learned their lesson: if Cuba could no longer rely on the Soviet Union to defend it, then it would actively work for an alliance of Third World nations that would help defend the Cuban revolution and construct a revolutionary world. This approach was not without obstacles; Cuba remained blockaded by nearly all governments in the Americas, and its Soviet and Eastern European allies were no longer the trusted allies they were at one point. True revolutionaries still remained in other parts of the world, and Algeria was first on the list.[44]

In the middle of the Missile Crisis, Ben Bella had defended his trip to Cuba and declared "The Algerian and the Cuban revolutions had a set of goals that were common to both revolutions such as the end of colonialism, agrarian reform, the proscription of nuclear tests and the end of racial discrimination." He blamed the United States for its aggression against Cuba but refrained from closer involvement in the Cuban-US rivalry and presented his trip to the Island as his own attempt to "reduce the tension between the United States and Cuba."[45]

The Algerians were far from neutral on the conflict. The front page of *Revolución* reported the presence of former FLN combatants as members of the Internationalist Brigade established to aid the Cuban government in the event of an American invasion during the missile crisis.[46] These internationalists, acting with the approval of the Algerian government, declared to the press that they had fought against the French in Algeria. One member of the brigade (which, despite its members' enthusiasm, did not total more than half a dozen) openly stated, "If Cuba is invaded by the North American imperialism, I will fight alongside the Cubans, as I fought in Algeria."[47]

44 James Blight and Philip Brenner, *Sad and Luminous Days: Cuba's Struggle with the Superpowers after the Missile Crisis* (New York: Rowman & Littlefield Publishers, 2002), 77–88.

45 "Ratifica Ben Bella amistad entre Argelinos y Cubanos," *Revolución* (Havana), October 23, 1962, 3.

46 "Combatientes Argelinos a la brigada internacional," *Revolución* (Havana), November 1, 1962, 1–5.

47 "Combatientes Argelinos a la brigada internacional," 1–5.

Chapter 4
Algeria and Cuba: Partners in Revolution

The Cuban government saw the Algerian revolution a mirror image of its revolution, a door into the Afro-Asian world, and a partner in its campaign to ignite revolutionary processes in Africa and Latin America. Both Castro and Ben Bella were ready to take major risks in order to advance the cause of revolution.. Their partnership to ignite revolutionary processes in Africa and Latin America was a commitment to their revolutionary ideology as well as an act of defiance to both superpowers.

Cuba's Support for Algeria

After Ben Bella's visit to Cuba in October 1962, Cuba was fully committed to continuing its support for the Algerian revolution at all levels. One of the most striking parallels between the two revolutions was the dearth of medical personnel in both nations after their revolutions. In Cuba, more than 3,000 physicians out of a total of 6,000 and 700 dentists out of almost 2,000 departed the country, and the number of senior medical faculty at the University of Havana decreased from 200 to 17.[1] Cubans rushed to prepare a new generation of medical students, and after the first three years of revolution, the results were very promising. Castro pledged to help the Algerian revolutionaries with their medical shortages. In Havana, in front of a rally of medical students, Castro called for volunteers to go to Algeria and help the crumbling health care system. Castro explained to his own doctors, "In Algeria most of the doctors were French and many of them left the country after the revolution." The situation in Algeria was much worse than on the island. Castro continued, "Algeria, with four million people more than us, a great number of diseases left by colonialism; they have only half to a third of the doctors we have. They have a tragic situation in the health sector." He then asked for volunteers to go to Algeria: "Today, talking with our students, we told them that there was a need for fifty doctors to go to Algeria as volunteers, to go to Algeria to help

---

1 Louis Pérez, "*Cuba between Reform and Revolution*," 2nd edn. (New York: Oxford University Press, 1995), 343.

the Algerians." Castro counted on at least 50 volunteers to be sent almost immediately as part of a first medical delegation, but he promised that more would follow: "Just fifty! We are sure that many more are going to volunteer, as an expression of the spirit of solidarity of our people with our friends who are worse off than us, much worse off than we are."[2]

Castro's call for volunteers was answered by an enthusiastic group of internationalists. On May 23, 1963, a group of 55 doctors, nurses, and technicians left Cuba for Algiers on a mission whose duration was uncertain at the time. According to *Revolución*, "All doctors, professionals, and technicians have volunteered to serve for a period of not less than a year, while others will serve for a period of two to three years."[3] The delegation was presided over by the Cuban Minister of Health, Jose Machado Ventura, and consisted of surgeons, gastroenterologists, nurses, X-ray technicians, and optometrists. *Revolución* described a genuine sentiment of generosity on the volunteers' part and commended them for their sacrifice to the two revolutions. According to the official newspaper, members of the medical delegation expressed the "happiness that they felt in working together with a people who had fought so hard for their independence." Others, such as nurses Ana Maria Anglada, Onaida Aldereti, and Lucia Serrano, declared that they were ready to "help the Algerian people wherever the Algerian government wanted them to go."[4] Cuba's medical aid to Algeria would continue throughout the 1960s as new delegations were sent to provide services and help the Algerians develop a more efficient health care sector.

Despite the enthusiasm of the Cuban participants and the gratitude of the Algerian government, and although their revolutions were sisters and their revolutionaries brothers, there were clear cultural differences that were not made explicit by Castro but that the Cuban health personnel found difficult to understand. The unequal treatment of female doctors and nurses, for example, reflected the gender discrimination that the Cuban revolution had adamantly opposed, but was prevalent in Algeria.[5]

If the doctors in Algeria were increasingly aware of the cultural differences between the two revolutions, their leaders in Cuba were not. Despite the cultural and ideological barriers, the Cuban government was convinced that the Algerian revolution was walking the same revolutionary path as Cuba. Shortly after the arrival of the medical delegation, Ernesto "El Che" Guevara, Minister

---

2 "Atacó Fidel a los Cobardes," *Revolución* (Havana), October 18, 1962, 8. This chapter of Cuba's medical history was initially found in Gleijeses, *Conflicting Missions* on Cuba's medical contribution to Algeria, 35–38.

3 "Equipo Técnico de Cuba a Argel," *Revolución* (Havana), May 2, 1963, 1–4.

4 "Partió la Delegación Médica hacia Argelia, "*Revolución* (Havana), May 24, 1963, 4.

5 Gleijeses, *Conflicting Missions*, 38.

of Industries arrived in Algeria to participate in the festivities celebrating the independence of Algeria and to represent Cuba in an international seminar on economic planning. Guevara wanted to see the Algerian revolution first hand by traveling around the country.[6] At the end of his trip, Guevara was more convinced than ever that despite evident cultural differences, the Algerian revolution was Cuba's parallel revolution in the Arab world. "We were so convinced that we were running revolutionary processes that were so alike, we wanted so desperately to believe it that perhaps we did not pause to ponder the differences," concluded his travel companion Ambassador Jorge Serguera Riverí.[7] Guevara was so convinced of their common destiny that he declared to the international press in Algiers, "When I see something new in Algeria, it reminds me of Cuba: The same spirit, the same enthusiasm and perhaps the same lack of experience."[8]

The Algerian-Moroccan War of 1963: Cuba's First Military Campaign in the Arab World

Although the Algerians had the friendship of the Cuban government, they certainly could not count on the friendship of their immediate neighbors, Tunisia and Morocco. Ben Bella had been unequivocal in his support for a more active Algerian role in Africa north and south of the Sahara and in the Arab world. He was an ardent supporter of Pan-Arabism as espoused by Gamal Abdel Nasser, and he wanted to assist other African nations in breaking their colonial ties.[9] In May 1963, during the inaugural meeting of the Organization of the African Union (OAU) in Addis Ababa, Ben Bella called for continued struggle for the liberation of Africa. He stood before the African leaders and warned, "We must all agree to die a little or even completely for the liberation of the people still under colonial domination, so that African unity will not be an empty word."[10] Shortly after Algerian independence, Algiers was becoming the center for opposition groups and movements of national liberation from across the world, from Vietnam to South Africa.[11]

6   Serguera, interview with the author.

7   Serguera, interview with the author.

8   "Señala Che paralelo entre Cuba y Argelia," *Revolución* (Havana), July 24, 1963, 1.

9   David Ottaway, and Marina Ottaway, "*Algeria: The Politics of a Socialist Revolution*," (Berkeley, CA: University of California Press, 1970), 162.

10   Ahmed Ben Bella, Speech at OAU Conference, Adis Abeba (Ethiopia) May 23, 1963, quoted by Ottaway and Ottaway, *Algeria*, 163.

11   Ottaway and Ottaway, *Algeria*, 163.

Ben Bella's popularity had turned him into a menace to more conservative leaders in the region, who saw the Algerian as a threat to the internal stability of their regimes. Their animosity toward him, according to Ben Bella, was quite clear: "Our enemies had decided that the momentum of the Algerian revolution had to be broken before it grew too strong and carried everything in its wake."[12] In fact, Ben Bella's radical ideology clashed with that of a more moderate leader, Tunisian President Habib Bourguiba, and undoubtedly exacerbated the already tense Algerian relations with the conservative King of Morocco, Hassan II. A border dispute between the two countries escalated into a major conflict when the King authorized the invasion of the territory under dispute.

Shortly after the invasion, Algeria's Foreign Minister Abdelaziz Bouteflika informed the Cuban ambassador of the situation on the front. He told Ambassador Serguera that the Algerian army was unprepared for the impending invasion. As Ben Bella later recalled, "Our young army, fresh from a war of liberation, had no air cover (since we didn't have a single plane) nor armored transport, were attacked by the Moroccan forces in a terrain that left us in a disadvantage."[13] Jorge Serguera responded swiftly: "I told him [Bouterflika] straight to his face that I could call Fidel and explain the situation to him. After all, that was what I was there for, to help the Algerians in any way possible." Serguera promised Ben Bella he would discuss the possibility of obtaining Cuban troops and arms to defend the Algerian revolution.[14]

Informed through Serguera, Fidel Castro agreed to send help to the Algerians for a war in which he clearly saw the hand of the United States. Within a matter of days, the Cubans had dispatched a group of officials to Algeria to coordinate the arrival of arms and soldiers and to assure Ben Bella that Cuba would stand beside Algeria.[15] In Cuba, Fidel Castro's brother, the Armed Forces commander Raúl Castro, called for the formation of a group of volunteers who would leave Cuba to help a "sister country [that] was under attack from a reactionary, imperialist forces and that had asked for our help."[16] The Cuban army organized the *Grupo Especial de Instrucción* (Special Training Group or GEI) with the objective of training the Algerians in the use of the weapons Cuba was sending and, if necessary, fighting alongside the Algerian Army.[17] The volunteers were concentrated in three different training camps inside Cuba,

---

12 Ahmed Ben Bella, "Ainsi etait le 'Che'," *Le Monde Diplomatic* (Paris), October, 1997, 3.

13 Ahmed Ben Bella, ""Ainsi etait le 'Che'," 3.

14 Serguera, interview with the author. An account of these events is also in his memoirs: Serguera, *Caminos*, 370–371.

15 Gleijeses, *Conflicting Missions*, 43.

16 Gleijeses, *Conflicting Missions*, 43.

17 García Blanco, *La Misión Internacionalista de Cuba en Argelia*, 21.

and from there, they were transported to the ports of departure.[18] Most of the personnel left for Algeria on October 10, 1963 under the command of the seasoned revolutionary officer Efigenio Ameijeiras. Along with Ameijeiras, who was military commander of the GEI operations in Algeria, ambassador Serguera was appointed political liaison between the government of Algeria and the GEI.[19] Serguera was in charge of a total of 685 men, among them 26 officers, 19 sub-officers, and 640 soldiers, with special orders to help the Algerians. A word of caution came from Castro: Cubans were required to act with the utmost respect toward the Algerian revolutionaries. The military personnel were ordered never to act as experts above the Algerians and to observe the highest standards of behavior, including the absolute prohibition of alcohol and the total proscription of intimate relations of any type with Algerian women.[20]

On October 17, the Cuban vessels *González Lines* and *Camilo Cienfuegos* docked at the port of Oran loaded with 22 Soviet T-34 tanks, 100 well-armed trucks, and the rest of the Cuban personnel.[21] Their arrival in broad daylight destroyed the secrecy of the mission. French soldiers and the Spanish secret service noticed their arrival and witnessed the disembarking of the trucks and personnel.[22] Once in Oran, the Cuban soldiers made their way south to Bedeau, where they set up camp in an abandoned garrison that had once belonged to the Foreign Legion.

The Cubans were joined by a detachment of Egyptian troops sent by Gamal Abdel Nasser to fight in Algeria.[23] The Algerians put the Egyptians under the command of the Cuban troops, and together, they took control of Tinduf near the border with Morocco.[24] In Tinduf, the Cubans engaged the Moroccans with the objective of strengthening the position of the Algerian forces in future negotiations with Rabat. This engagement was Cuba's first on foreign soil and a baptism of fire in the fulfillment of the international dimension of their revolution.[25] The entire operation followed a plan that the Algerians and Cubans called "Operation Dignity." [26] Its objective was to take the offensive,

---

18   The three training camps were at La Chorrera, el Managuaco and La Cabana in Cuba. García Blanco, *La Misión Internacionalista*, 21.

19   García Blanco, *La Misión Internacionalista*, 21–22.

20   Gleijeses, *Conflicting Missions*, 44–45.

21   Serguera, *Caminos*, 372–373.

22   Serguera, *Caminos*, 372–373.

23   Ben Bella, "Ainsi etait le 'Che'," 3.

24   Serguera, *Caminos*, 375.

25   Serguera, *Caminos*, 374–375.

26   García Blanco, *La Misión Internacionalista*, 25.

capture as much Moroccan territory as possible, and, as the Cubans put it, "from this point, try to have negotiations with dignity."[27]

Cuban cooperation with Algeria was a clear signal to the world that the Cuban revolution was determined to stand by its friends and defend the revolutionary process across the world. One member of the Cuban detachment noted,

> The attitude of solidarity that the people of Cuba had for the cause of the Algerian people underlined the value of the internationalist solidarity in confronting the enemy and it showed the peoples of Africa that they could count on the support of the Cuban Revolution.[28]

The Cuban mission, however, was more than just a matter of fighting alongside the Algerians. Like the medical personnel sent months before, the soldiers were actively working to bridge significant cultural differences. The Cubans lost no time engaging in what they called "political work." The Cuban mission aspired to take the gospel of revolution to the Algerian people and to form a more solid revolutionary spirit among the Algerians. The Cubans made use of the few materials available to them at the time, especially

> speeches given by the Chief in Command, manuals of instruction, as well as several pieces of literature pertinent to the history of Algeria, the Algerian constitution, and themes related to the history of the African continent and the Islamic religion.[29]

In addition to formal political instruction, the Cubans used other sources for their political work. Pedro Rodriguez, a Cuban participant in the mission to Algeria, discussed the Cuban methodology:

> We organized a movie theater with a couple of movies we had, [and] later we received some from the embassy and a couple more came directly from Cuba ... we projected these movies in the towns nearby, we were accompanied by a translator, and we introduced the documentaries. In that way, we made our revolution known to the Algerians. We established links of identification with them by utilizing this form, and in another very powerful way, medicine. Doctors are an excellent political tool.[30]

---

27 García Blanco, *La Misión Internacionalista*, 28.
28 García Blanco, *La Misión Internacionalista*, 32.
29 García Blanco, *La Misión Internacionalista*, 36.
30 García Blanco, *La Misión Internacionalista*, 40.

More than 200 doctors and nurses had arrived in Algeria since May 1963, and by October, they were working alongside the military detachment in the war front.

The war was brief. Despite their preparation and training and the long trip, the Cuban forces never had to confront the Moroccan army in an open conflict. The presence of Cuban and Egyptian forces, their numbers helpfully exaggerated by the press, forced King Hassan II to accept the mediation offered by the Malian president Modibo Keita in Bamako.[31] Both parties accepted a reversion to the status quo, agreeing to return to the original pre-war borders. The Cubans left behind a better-trained and armed Algerian army:

> We began by transferring the weapons unit that we brought from Cuba to the Algerians. At the end, when we had to repatriate our soldiers, Fidel and Raúl Castro gave us orders to leave the trucks, cannons, and tanks with the Algerians. The Algerians were trying to buy arms from the Soviet Union, but in the meanwhile they needed the arms to prevent Hassan from launching new armed hostilities along the frontier.[32]

Paying Back in Kind: Algeria Assists the Revolution in South America

After the successful resolution of the Algerian-Moroccan crisis, and with the survival of the Ben Bella regime, the Cuban and Algerian governments were now ready to become more intensely involved in helping and promoting other revolutions in the Third World. Africa and Latin America were the targeted regions. Cuba, isolated from Latin America and closely monitored by the United States since the triumph of the Cuban revolution, found it difficult to provide assistance to other revolutionary movements in Latin America. Algeria, however, gave Cuba an entrance into Africa and the Middle East and served as a bridge between Cuban and Latin American revolutionary groups. In two cases, Algeria became an active participant in incipient revolutionary processes.

According to Ben Bella, Commander Ernesto Guevara first approached him with a request for help from Fidel, asking the Algerians for help in redirecting arms to Latin America. "My answer was, of course, a spontaneous yes," Ben Bella recalls.[33]

Their first joint venture would be the active encouragement of revolution in Argentina. The plan, according to the Cuban ambassador Jorge Serguera, was designed by El Che and counted on the direct knowledge and support of Ahmed Ben Bella. Its objective was to organize a revolutionary guerrilla cell,

---

31 Gleijeses, *Conflicting Missions*, 48.

32 Serguera, *Caminos*, 378.

33 Gleijeses, *Conflicting Missions*, 51; Ben Bella, "Ainsi etait le 'Che'," 6.

foco, in the Salta region of the northern Argentinean province of Córdoba and, from there, to extend the revolutionary process to the entire country.[34]

Jorge Massetti, the man in charge of the operation, was well known to the Algerians. Massetti was an Argentinean journalist who, in 1960, founded the Cuban news agency *Prensa Latina* and later became the first emissary of the Cuban revolution to the FLN. In 1961, Masetti had traveled to the region to deliver a shipment of arms from the Cuban government to the Algerian guerrillas. After being trained in Cuba and Algeria, Massetti and his men were scheduled to leave Algeria in the summer of 1963 and to gain entrance to Bolivia disguised as members of an Algerian economic mission. In Bolivia, Algeria's High Command had designated two men known only as Mohamed and Masmut to buy a farm near the Bolivian border with Argentina. According to the Cuban ambassador, Massetti and his men were supposed to regroup in Bolivia before entering Argentina and creating a *foco* in Salta.[35]

The guerrilla group landed in Bolivia and made several trips into Argentina to recruit participants for their revolutionary group. By September 1963, they had settled in Argentina, but despite all efforts, failed in their mission. It was soon too clear that they had been unable to adapt to the topographical challenges of the terrain and were no match for the better-armed and better-trained Argentinean army. The mission of Massetti and his men, "a handful of inexperienced youths, devoted but completely unfit for guerrilla warfare,"[36] collapsed in the first weeks of 1964. Massetti himself disappeared into the wilderness, never to be found again. In 1966, Ernesto Guevara would command a new revolutionary campaign in Bolivia, this time without the support of the Algerian government, though with identical results.

At the same time that it was providing assistance to the revolutionary project in Argentina, the Algerian government was giving a hand in helping to arm an incipient revolutionary movement in Venezuela. The revolutionary organization was directed by the *Partido Comunista Venezolano* (PCV), Venezuela's Communist Party, perhaps the only communist party that did not follow Moscow's directives. It rejected the idea of a peaceful coexistence between capitalism and socialism and embraced the revolutionary call of the Cuban revolution. In 1959, four years after the triumph of the Cuban revolution, the PCV created the *Frente de Liberación Nacional* (FLN), the National Liberation Front, as the political arm of the newly formed guerrilla movement.[37]

---

34 Serguera, *Caminos*, 56.

35 Castañeda, *Compañero*, 245–248, Serguera, *Caminos*, 56, Gleijeses, *Conflicting Missions*, 52 and Serguera, interview with the author.

36 Castañeda, *Compañero*, 248.

37 Brian Loveman and Thomas Davies, eds., *Che Guevara: Guerrilla Warfare*, 3rd edn. (Lincoln, NB: University of Nebraska Press, 1997), 221–224.

The FLN, through the Cuban embassy in Algeria, asked for an interview with the Algerian government. President Ben Bella met with Héctor Rodríguez, the FLN representative. He listened to Rodríguez's plans for the development of a revolutionary movement in Venezuela, and agreed to help.[38] Arms from Cuba were sent to Algeria and then rerouted to Venezuela along with a small donation of arms that the Algerians had in storage, a previous gift from the People's Republic of China. The weapons were transferred to Venezuela via Algeria using a European-registered wine export company as a front.[39]

Beginning in 1963 and continuing for two years, Cuban-trained men and Cuban arms routed through Algeria flowed into Venezuela. On November 28, 1963, the Venezuelan government publicly denounced Cuba as the country providing arms to the Venezuelan rebels after a three-ton weapon cache was discovered in the province of Falcón.[40]

Support for the Venezuela rebels continued. The last shipment of arms to Venezuela left Cuba on board the Cuban ship *The Uvero* which first headed to Guinea Bissau with arms that had been promised to the rebel forces in that country and then continued to Algeria.[41] The ship docked at the Algerian port of Skikda as planned but did not unload its containers. On June 19, 1965, the same day *The Uvero* docked, Ahmed Ben Bella was overthrown in a military coup d'état. At that moment, no one could predict what would happen to the revolutionary partnership of these two countries.[42]

The Campaign in Sub-Saharan Africa in the 1960s

The coup d'état was a setback for Cuba's revolutionary activities in South America, but it was a devastating blow to its campaign in Africa. Cuba's revolutionary campaign in Latin America was extremely difficult due to the close monitoring of its activities by the United States and the high degree of alert of every Latin American country. Any wrong move could trigger direct US intervention in Cuba. Havana therefore decided that it would be better to start in Sub-Saharan Africa, where the conditions for revolutionary upheaval were present (or so the Cubans thought) and where the United States was less omnipresent. "Then Africa became our first choice, as we wrongly thought

---

38 Serguera, *Caminos*, 146.
39 Serguera, *Caminos*, 244, 263.
40 Castañeda, *Compañero*, 245.
41 Gleijeses, *Conflicting Missions*, 99–100.
42 Gleijeses, *Conflicting Missions*, 52.

that the continent was ready for a revolutionary upheaval," reflected Armaldo Entralgo, Cuba's first ambassador to Ghana.[43]

A revolutionary Africa would not only fulfill the moral commitment of the Cuban revolutionaries to bring an end to colonialism in Africa, but also validate the Cuban position as an independent socialist country working on behalf of socialist revolutions with or without the help of the Soviet Union. By creating "two, three, many Vietnams," as Ernesto Guevara proclaimed to be the objective of Cuba's revolutionary call, the United States would be ultimately forced to intervene in Africa, leaving Latin America unprotected, and the revolution could come to that region. In the words of Serguera, "The African front was an attack on the other flank of the United States to cover our true objective: the fight in Latin America."[44]

In Algiers, the Cubans had been in contact with representatives of different national liberation movements in Africa. Over the course of several months, Cuban embassies were opened and staffed in Ghana, Mali, Guinea, and Tanzania. Nevertheless, most of the decisions related to these countries were made from Algiers by Ambassador Serguera. From Algiers, the ambassador traveled to Sub-Saharan Africa and reported back to Havana on the political situation in the region. Serguera recalls this period:

> I had to travel widely during my appointment as Ambassador to Algeria. I had to visit several countries in Sub-Saharan Africa, and I met with their leaders either in their capitals or in Algiers. Algiers at that time was the center of everything that was happening on that continent. It was more important than Cairo at that point![45]

During 1963 and 1964, Serguera and Ben Bella discussed the status of the revolutionary process in Africa and, according to Serguera, met frequently in the Cuban embassy in Algiers with all the accredited members of national liberation movements from different African regions. Serguera and Ben Bella discussed politics with them and had an opportunity to hear about their logistical and weaponry needs.[46] Serguera was not alone in his enterprise. In December 1964, six months before the coup against Ben Bella, he met Ernesto Guevara in Algiers. "El Che," Serguera recalls, "wanted to further explore the situation in Africa and study the different ways in which we could help them."[47] Guevara arrived in Algiers from New York, where he had addressed the United Nations

---

43 Entralgo, interview with the author.
44 Serguera, *Caminos*, 202–203.
45 Serguera, interview with the author.
46 Serguera, *Caminos*, 233.
47 Serguera, interview with the author.

General Assembly, repeating Cuban denunciations to the continuous attacks of the United States against the Island and renewing Cuban pledges of support for movements of National Liberation across the world.[48] Once in Algiers, Guevara met with Ben Bella, analyzed the situation in Sub-Saharan Africa, and met with representatives of various national liberation groups from the region.[49] Shortly afterwards, he and Serguera embarked on a tour encompassing Mali, Guinea, Ghana, Senegal, Congo Brazzaville, and Benin.

By the time Serguera and Guevara returned to Algiers from their tour of Sub-Saharan Africa, Guevara had decided to help the revolutionary forces of Congo against the conservative leader Moise Tshombe, who had been installed in 1964 with the help of the United States and Belgium armies. After they returned to the Cuban embassy in Algiers, "he told me exactly these words," ambassador Serguera remembers, "if there is a place in the world where we could kick the ass of the imperialists, it is Congo." Guevara was convinced that Cuba had a role to play in bringing the revolution to Congo, and that from there, the revolution would spread across Africa. Their optimism knew no boundaries, and in their revolutionary zeal, the Cubans overlooked a reality far more complicated than they could comprehend at the time. Their plan was to intervene in Africa on behalf of the revolution in order to "erase tribalism, regionalism, and the division between Anglophone and Francophone Africa."[50]

Ben Bella tried to warn Guevara that there was no possibility of a successful campaign in Congo: "I tried to point out that perhaps this was not the best way to help advance the revolutionary maturity that was developing on our continent." The Algerian leader argued with Guevara that outside forces might not be able to do what Africans had not done by themselves. He then told Guevara that "an armed revolution can and must find foreign support, but it first has to create the internal resources on which to base its struggle." Ben Bella did not have much success persuading the Cuban: "Che Guevara insisted that his own commitment must be total and it required his physical presence."[51]

Guevara also consulted with the Egyptian president, Gamal Adbel Nasser. He visited Egypt in February and again in March 1965. Again, the only witness to these meetings was Nasser's aide, Mohamed Heikal. According to Heikal, Guevara told Nasser of Cuban troops being transported to Congo to help the revolution there. Guevara explained his vision for the region to Nasser:

---

48 "Habló el Che ante la Asamblea General de las Naciones Unidas," *Revolución* (Havana), July 12, 1963, 2.

49 Castañeda, *Compañero*, 279.

50 Serguera, *Caminos*, 251.

51 Ben Bella, "Ainsi etait le 'Che'," 3.

I feel that we must do more for the revolution in the world and I thought I would come and do something in Africa. I have experience in revolutionary activities and organization and I think the situation is ripe in Africa.

Heikal recounts that Nasser, who was more versed in the affairs of Africa than Guevara, immediately replied,

You astonish me. What happened to all that you were doing in Cuba? Have you quarreled with Castro? I don't want to interfere, but if you want to become another Tarzan, a white man coming among black men, leading them and protecting them ... It can't be done.[52]

He warned Guevara that he had witnessed the same situation in Yemen: Nasser rushed to help the revolution there when the necessary materials and social conditions were not in place for a revolution. Again, according to Heikal, Nasser warned Guevara against this approach:

I experienced this in Yemen. When the Revolution started there, I jumped to its help, and although I received reports that the situation there was not right for revolution I said like you that the mere fact that it had started was a subjective element in itself and it should be helped. But then I discovered first, that it could not be helped from outside, second, that it would take a long time and much agony and while we can accelerate the historical process of the revolution we cannot jump over the natural and chemical process which creates the forces of Revolution.[53]

Ben Bella and Nasser, both more seasoned leaders than their Cuban allies with a profound knowledge of the complexities and the effects of tribalism and colonialism in Africa, were unable to convince the Cuban government, and much less the daredevil Guevara, of the impossibility of the task.

As predicted, Guevara's mission to Congo proved to be a complete failure, and by 1966, his military detachment had been defeated by inter-tribal interests and a lack of military preparation. Defeated in Congo, Guevara left for Bolivia to once again take on the revolutionary process in that country, only to die in its mountains on October 9, 1967.

---

52 Mohamed H. Heikal, *The Cairo Documents, the Inside Story of Nasser and his Relationship with World Leaders, Rebels and Statesmen* (Garden City, NY: Doubleday, 1973), 349.

53 Heikal, *The Cairo Documents*, 349.

Cuba, Algeria, and the Cold War: Neither Proxies nor Pawns

Cuba's relationship with Algeria cannot be explained from a traditional Cold War perspective in which superpowers averted open confrontation with each other, reverting instead to the manipulation of proxy states around the world in the pursuit of their strategic interests. Cuba did not fit this paradigm and did not act in Algeria on behalf of, and much less as a proxy for, the Soviet Union. Cuba's friendship and commitment to the Algerian revolution arose from the personal empathy between the top leaders of the Cuban revolution, especially Fidel Castro and Ernesto Guevara, and the Algerian leader Ahmed Ben Bella. They were convinced that a revolutionary process similar to the Cuban revolution was developing in Algeria, even before their triumph in 1962. The Cuban leaders were convinced that their destinies were united by a historical coincidence and that they were duty-bound to stand beside and aid these Arab revolutionaries whatever the situation, whether fighting against the French or forging ahead as an independent nation.

The Soviet Union was not present in this relationship, and in many instances, Cuba acted against the interests of the Soviet Union in its policy of seeking a peaceful coexistence with the United States. While the Soviets were attempting to consolidate their own economy and negotiating a more stable international system with the United States, the Cubans pressed hard to export their revolution and help their friends. After the Missile Crisis of 1962, the Cubans understood that they had to provide for their own defense. The best defense was to export their revolution and help their friends abroad. A good example of this strategy was Cuba's intervention on behalf of Algeria in its war against Morocco in October 1963. Cuba helped Algeria demonstrate its commitment to the success of the Algerian revolution without consulting or taking into account the interests of the Soviet Union or even the economic repercussions that intervening in the war would have on its own economy. Cuba's intervention in the conflict not only caused the country to lose its diplomatic relations with Morocco but also cost it a sugar contract with that kingdom at the height of the United States' economic embargo.[54] Jorge Serguera was unequivocal:

> We did not consult with the Soviet Union, least of all did we ask for permission of any sort whatsoever. Those were our arms, our soldiers, and our commitment to that revolution. The Soviets were not consulted, we were nobody's lackeys![55]

---

54 Domínguez, *To Make the World Safe for Revolution*, 175. Also Gleijeses, *Conflicting Missions*, 50.

55 Serguera, interview with the author.

Ahmed Ben Bella confirms ambassador Serguera's view. With regard to the armaments received from Cuba, Ben Bella recalls that the tanks "had been delivered to Cuba by the Soviet Union on the express condition that they were not to be made available to Third World countries, even communist countries such as Bulgaria, under any circumstances." Ben Bella was grateful for the Cubans who, "despite these restrictions from Moscow ... defied all the taboos and sent their tanks to the assistance of the endangered Algerian revolution in peril."[56]

Furthermore, the Cuban missile crisis left the Cuban leaders with deep resentment toward the Soviet Union. Even when the Cubans depended on Soviet economic support for their own survival and continued to receive aid throughout the 1960s,[57] they made sure that the Soviet Union knew that the Cuban revolution could not be treated the same as the Eastern European satellites. If Cuba's alignment with the Soviet Union had been a strategic decision to protect it from the United States, the country's commitment to revolutionary socialism was genuine.

The Afro-Asian Solidarity Conference held in Algiers in 1965 served as a forum for complaints voiced against the socialist bloc's treatment of the emerging Afro-Asian revolutions. This denunciation, aimed at the Soviet Union in particular, was delivered during the economic seminar at the conference on February 24. As Cuba's Minister of Industry and leader of the revolution, Ernesto Guevara, questioned the role of the more developed Socialist states toward the emerging revolutionary nations:

> A conclusion must be drawn from all this: the socialist countries must help pay for the development of countries now starting out on the road to liberation. We state it this way with no intention whatsoever of blackmailing or theatrics, nor are we looking for an easy way to get closer to the Afro-Asian peoples; it is our profound conviction. Socialism cannot exist without a change in consciousness resulting in a new fraternal attitude toward humanity, both at an individual level, within the societies where socialism is being built or has been built, and on a world scale, with regard to all peoples suffering from imperialist oppression.
>
> We believe the responsibility of aiding dependent countries must be approached in such a spirit. There should not be any more talk about developing mutually beneficial trade based on prices forced on the backward countries by the law of value and the international relations of unequal exchange that result from the law of value.

---

56 Ben Bella, "Ansi etait le 'Che',"3.
57 Pérez, *Cuba*, 355–356.

How can it be "mutually beneficial" to sell at world market prices the raw materials that cost the underdeveloped countries immeasurable sweat and suffering, and to buy at world market prices the machinery produced in today's big automated factories?

If we establish that kind of relation between the two groups of nations, we must agree that the socialist countries are, in a certain way, accomplices of imperial exploitation. It can be argued that the amount of exchange with the underdeveloped countries is an insignificant part of the foreign trade of the socialist countries. That is very true, but it does not eliminate the immoral character of the exchange.

The socialist countries have the moral duty to put an end to their tacit complicity with the exploiting countries in the West.[58]

No other Cuban leader was as blunt as Guevara in condemning the Soviet Union, but his speech accurately reflected the official opinion of the Cuban government. The economic forum was used as a platform to launch a foreign policy that was fiercely independent and committed to encouraging the expansion of anticolonial, anti-imperialist regimes regardless of the consequences to the superpower's peaceful coexistence. Ambassador Serguera recalled Guevara's pointed criticism of fellow socialist nations:

Che [Guevara] stated that there were socialist countries that needed technology, and that needed arms, and denounced the rich socialist countries selling that technology and arms as if they were gold. Was that a coherent attitude by the socialist states? Of course not, either we all were revolutionaries or we were not.[59]

Another witness to Guevara's speech, the Algerian leader Ahmed Ben Bella, was more cautious. Ben Bella was wary about the Cuban indictment of the Soviet Union. "We discussed his speech all night; he was fully aware of what he was going to say. He was an enormously charming man, but terribly dogmatic and stubborn in his ideological positions."[60]

Ben Bella's relationship with the Soviet Union was far from ideal. He resented the fact that the Soviet Union did not recognize their fight until the Evian Peace Agreements in 1962, eight years after their war for independence had begun.[61] Ben Bella had expelled the communists from his government immediately after he took power and, from the point of view of Ambassador Serguera, the

---

58   Carlos Tablada, *Che Guevara: Economics and Politics in the Transition to Socialism* (Sidney: Pathfinder, 1987), 162–163.

59   Serguera, interview with the author.

60   Castaneda, *Compañero*, 292.

61   Ottaway and Ottaway, *Algeria*, 157.

Algerian communists traveled to Moscow many times to ask the Soviets for help, but nothing resulted from those requests. It was only when Castro asked Ben Bella to sit and talk with the Algerian communists that the tension between them lessened. Thanks to Castro, the Cuban ambassador claims, "they started to find some common ground, and on some points, they found reason to have a closer relationship."[62]

Distant from both the United States and the Soviet Union geographically and ideologically, the Algerian government wanted to remain aloof from the conflict between the superpowers. Algerian neutrality in the Cold War derived from their identification with Nasser's positive neutralism and his Arab nationalism, an identification formed when Ben Bella lived in Cairo under Nasser's protection during the fight against the French occupation. Likewise, this positive neutralism was applied to the Sino-Soviet conflict. Algeria remained uncommitted to joining China in its revolutionary and anti-Soviet stance despite Beijing's recognition of the Algerian revolutionaries before 1962, a pledge of a US$50 million interest-free loan, and Premier Chou En–Lai's visit to Algeria shortly after its independence.

Cuba had taken sides with the Soviet Union in the Cold War, but this did not mean that it was willing to be treated as a pawn by Moscow. Algeria had remained faithful to the principles of neutralism that came from Cairo. Even though their political positions at the international level did not pose a problem for the advancement of their relationship, the cultural differences between Cuba and Algeria were more difficult to address. The Cubans embraced Marxism, proclaimed their state to be atheist, and promoted the role of women in a gender-equal society. The Algerians were far from these positions. Cubans were careful not to antagonize Algerian customs and beliefs to avoid damaging their relationship. Nevertheless, at the level of personal contact between Algerians and Cubans, the differences were evident, particularly during the period marked by medical brigades and military training. The Cuban ambassador claimed to have mentioned to the Algerian authorities that it was better to use French instead of Arabic for official practice while reserving Arabic for religious use.

> I proposed to the Algerian authorities that they must begin their literacy efforts in French, not Arabic. They needed a language in which science and technology could be transmitted, and Arabic clearly is not. Arabic was fine for their religious practices, but French is essential if you want to have some development, prepare scientists, and organize a modern educational system.[63]

---

62 Serguera, *Caminos*, 378.

63 Serguera, interview with the author.

Presented as a personal consideration without the endorsement of any Cuban authority, the suggestion did not go anywhere with the Algerians.

Washington's Struggle to Put an End to the Cuban-Algerian Partnership

The Kennedy administration was cautious about branding the Algerian revolution and its leaders as communist. The problem for the Kennedy administration was not Ben Bella's ideological orientation but rather the lack of one. Ben Bella was regarded as "ideologically immature, clinging to a mélange of revolutionary clichés." A year after his visit to Washington, the Kennedy administration was growing more impatient with Ben Bella's rising figure in the Afro-Asian bloc and his friendship with Fidel Castro.

Although the Kennedy administration had been willing to give Ben Bella time to realize that Cuba was not a good example to follow, the US was not seeing any change in Algeria's position since October 1962. During the presentation of credentials by the new Algerian Ambassador, Cherif Guellal, to the United States, President John F. Kennedy voiced his growing concerns. According to Kennedy, the Algerian government had aroused "sour American feelings" by dispensing a welcome to the Cuban delegate to the anniversary ceremonies of Algerian independence "beyond that accorded to anybody else."[64] He insisted that the Algerians had missed the point concerning Cuba. The President wanted to end the myth of the "sister revolutions" by insisting that "he appreciated Algerian identification with the successful Cuban guerrilla activities, but remarked that the action against Batista was not a serious war, with perhaps 100 killed. It was a political effort, while the Algerian was a bloody affair." The issue that Algeria needed to understand was that "Cuba was a pretty hard boiled Communist state, in a satellite relationship to the USSR being used to communize Latin America."[65]

The American press was more direct in its fears and mistrust of Ben Bella, especially after Ben Bella ordered the expulsion of some American journalists from Algeria days before the Algerian-Morocco conflict. *Newsweek* maintained that Algeria was just days away from becoming a Soviet satellite and that Ben Bella had a "definite timetable for establishing a Castro-type dictatorship." According to the news magazine, "Algeria's formal alignment with Cuban domestic and Russian foreign policies could come on the ninth anniversary of the revolution, Nov. 1." Ben Bella was reported as a great admirer of Castro, who compared the Algerian revolution to that of Cuba. The only hope,

---

64 FRUS, vol., XXI, 1961–1963, 124–126.
65 FRUS, vol., XXI, 1961–1963, 124–126.

according to the magazine, was that Ben Bella, "a lot less headstrong and a good deal shrewder than Fidel," would understand that by taking sides with the Soviet Union, he might lose US$350 million a year in aid from France, which not even the Soviet Union could provide. Nevertheless, Ben Bella's defection seemed so imminent that "State Department officials also believe Ben Bella has discarded his former loyalty to United Arab Republic (UAR) President Gamel Adbel Nasser, and now sees himself as a sort of African Castro, promoting and leading revolutions throughout Africa."

The explosion of the Algerian-Moroccan conflict brought further tension to the strained relations between the United States and Algeria. Both the Algerians and the Cubans were wrong in believing that the United States had supported King Hassan's invasion of Algeria. The State Department concluded that although Hassan might have had a good case, his claims to Algerian territory were part of other territorial conflicts with Spain and Mauritania. There was no doubt that the US should "turn him off this nationalistic kick before he gets everybody sore at him." Yet the problem was not an overambitious king but rather the implications that the conflict might have in terms of the Cold War. The United States was providing arms to King Hassan, who had accepted the US offer through the Mutual Aid Plan. On October 24, 1962, the State Department was informed that Egypt and Cuba were arming Algeria. The issue was how to prevent the conflict from escalating into an East-West conflict with the United States supporting a "pro-West Morocco at the expense of a pro-East Algeria."[66]

The Cuban and Egyptian interventions were seen more as an escalation into an East-West confrontation and less as a regional border dispute. The US knew it was difficult to protest Cuban and Egyptian aid while it was arming Morocco.

> There's not much we can do about Cuban or UAR [United Arab Republic] arms. Castro may be sending help without even asking Algerians. In any case, we're in a spot about protesting UAR (or even Cuban) response to BB's [Ben Bella's] arms appeal, when we and French are continuing regular arms shipments to Morocco (We have 31 jeep trailers landing now and 22 75-mm recoilless rifles, 143 jeep. 100,000 rounds carbine ammo and 7,000 rounds grenades and other artillery ammo due within the next two weeks). Ouch![67]

Despite earlier efforts at mediation encouraged by the United States, it was becoming obvious that the region would become the next point of East–West confrontation. The attempts at mediation failed, and as tension increased,

---

66   FRUS, "North African Region," FRUS, 1961–1963, vol. XXI, *Africa*, 33.

67   FRUS, "North African Region," FRUS, 1961–1963, vol. XXI, *Africa*, 26.

Washington was afraid of giving the "Soviets, Nasser and Cubans their chance to make a big pro-Algerian splash and make it hard for us not to back Moroccans."[68]

Fortunately for the United States, the conflict ended by the end of October 1963. Ben Bella never proclaimed any type of formal alignment with Cuba or with the Soviet Union. Cuba's influence in Algeria became less of an issue throughout 1964 as the United States attempted to accommodate Ben Bella's administration's growing and popularity in the region. According to an earlier assessment of the State Department,

> Ben Bella is a pain and will remain so, but he's more likely to be around for a while than Hassan. He seems to have done a good job so far of out-maneuvering his opposition. I think most specialists would agree that Hassan has even less life expectancy than BB [Ben Bella]. So we also want to be careful lest we end up backing the losing horse.[69]

This time, the Americans were wrong. Ben Bella's regime would not outlive Hassan's, and its end would be the end of an era of revolutionary partnership.

The End of the Cuban–Algerian Revolutionary Partnership

On June 18, 1965, the Cuban ambassador to Algeria, Jorge Serguera, had a private meeting with Ben Bella. They wanted to finalize some aspects of the next nonaligned movement conference that was about to happen in Algiers, and Serguera wanted to inform Ben Bella about Cuba's further revolutionary operations in Congo. Ben Bella told the Cuban ambassador how mistrustful he was becoming of Algerian Foreign Minister Abdel Aziz Bouteflika. He hinted to Serguera about his intentions of removing him from power. Serguera, who apparently knew from other sources that something might be developing against Ben Bella, tried to warn Ben Bella against Boumediene as well, but Ben Bella replied, according to Serguera, that Boumediene was an honest man, "*C'est un homme honnete.*" According to Serguera, "I could not say anything else; I left that question solely up to him. I left for Congo and pum! The following day colonel Boumediene toppled Ben Bella!! We had lost our friend in Algeria."[70]

The coup was a major blow to Cuban-Algerian relations. The Cuban government reacted with anger toward the plotters, but it could not take action to redress the events. Castro denounced those who participated in the coup, especially the Algerian Foreign Minister Abdel Aziz Bouteflika, as "the one

---

68 FRUS, "North African Region," FRUS, 1961–1963, vol. XXI, *Africa*, 24.
69 FRUS, "North African Region," FRUS, 1961–1963, vol. XXI, *Africa*, 34.
70 Serguera, interview with the author. Also, Serguera, *Caminos*, 388–389.

who undoubtedly masterminded the cuartelazo" and accused him of being a "right winger, known as such by the whole world and by the Algerian people; an enemy of socialism; in short, an enemy of the Algerian revolution."[71] Three days after the coup, Serguera was recalled by the Cuban government. In the meantime, in a clear message from the new government to the Cubans, the offices of the Cuban news agency *Prensa Latina* were stormed by the army, and several Cubans were harassed by the new authorities. Relations between Cuba and Algeria would never be the same. A year after the coup, there were no vestiges of a Cuban-Algerian policy for the liberation of Africa. Trade fell from US$3 million in 1965 to a mere US$200,000 a year later.[72]

Aside from the economic effects of the near cessation of trade on these two countries, the worst impact of the Algerian coup was political. Algeria ceased to be Cuba's partner in the liberation of Africa and Latin America. The new Algerian leadership wanted to focus its foreign policy exclusively in the Arab world, and abandon the revolutionary cause in Africa. Gradually, Algiers ceased to be the capital of the revolutionary movement in Africa, and the entire African liberation movement suffered a grave setback. Prominent revolutionary leaders on the continent, such as President Sekou Toure of Guinea and Kwame Nkrumah of Ghana, began to fear that the events in Algeria might incite members of their own armed forces to do to them what Boumediene had done to Ben Bella, and they concentrated more on their own local affairs than on the macro-dreams of the past that the Cubans had inspired.[73] Algeria also lost its prominence as a leader of the Afro-Asian movement. The Second Afro-Asian Solidarity conference, the so-called Bandung II, was scheduled to take place in Algiers on June 29, 1965, but was postponed until November 5. Algiers was selected to host the Second Afro-Asian conference in honor of its contribution to the liberation of Africa, but the new government was not enthusiastic about the idea. In addition, most participants denounced the new leadership and withdrew their participation in protest. Only the People's Republic of China and Indonesia, attempting to lure Algeria into their militant anti-Soviet camp, rushed to recognize the new government and supported the idea of Algeria as a host to the Afro-Asian conference.[74] As November approached, it was clear that Boumediene was not interested in "spending 150 million dinars [US$30 million] for a five-day invitation," as spending this much money was, in the

---

71 "Castro Rechaza el Golpe a Ben Bella," *Revolución* (Havana), June 27, 1965, 1.

72 Carlos Moore, *Castro, the Blacks, and Africa* (Los Angeles, CA: University of California Press, 1988), 217.

73 Ottaway and Ottaway, *Algeria*, 232.

74 Ottaway and Ottaway, *Algeria*, 173.

view of the new government, "not revolutionary".[75] The Second Afro-Asian conference was canceled as Algeria withdrew from the international spotlight.[76]

Regional politics were of more interest to the Algerian government. On a different occasion, Boumediene criticized Ben Bella's interests in Africa and his downplaying of Algeria's Arab identity. Boumediene recalled that Ben Bella used to tell his subordinates in government, "We must not act in Africa as Arabs because Arabism is hated there, but only as Moslem Africans leaving aside any idea of Arabism." Algeria's new regime was swift in denouncing this policy and declaring, "We are at once Arabs and Africans, and we must remain deeply attached to our Arabism in the sense of civilization and progress."[77] His professed Arabism was only welcomed by the Syrian government, which was at odds with Egypt and always pleased to see the fall of one of Nasser's trusted friends.[78]

Algeria's revolutionary commitment had ended. Nevertheless, those years of revolutionary alliance had been productive for the Cuban government. Algeria allowed Cuba to deepen its presence in Africa. Algiers had been the meeting place of many revolutionary groups and governments of Africa and the Arab World. Thanks in part to the revolutionary diplomacy of those years, the Cubans were well placed in the Afro-Asian bloc by 1965. The following year, the Cuban government agreed to host the new Bandung II. This time, it would take place in Havana and had a new name: the Tricontinental. As we will see in the next chapter, the Tricontinental Conference that took place in January 1966 was a major success for the Cuban revolution, which was finally recognized as being in the vanguard of the revolutionary world. Ben Bella was gone, along with the partnership between these two states. From this point forward, Cuba would have to support other groups and movements in hopes that they would take power and form revolutionary governments. As we will see in the next chapter, the forces of the Cold War and the power of the Soviet Union would freeze Cuba's adventures for a while until a new revival in Southern Africa in 1975. Other Latin American revolutionaries would meet their Arab counterparts in the 1970s but under different circumstances.

---

75   Ottaway and Ottaway, *Algeria*, 171–173, 202.

76   "Sin fijar nueva fecha: Aplazada la Afroasiática," *Granma* (Havana), November 2, 1965, 11.

77   Boumediene's interview with the Cairo newspaper *Al-Ahram*, 8–10 October, 1965 in Ottoway and Ottoway, *Algeria*, 241–242.

78   Ottoway and Ottoway, *Algeria*, 242.

Chapter 5
Cuba–Nicaragua and the Palestinian Movements 1968–1989

Figure 5.1 **Palestinian leader Yasser Arafat with Sandinista leader Daniel Ortega and members of Government's Assembly, Managua, July 21, 1980**

Source: © Austral Foto/ Renzo Gostoli.

The Nicaraguan, *Frente Sandinista para la Liberación Nacional* (FSLN), would write the next chapter between Latin American revolutionaries and the Arab world. An unexpected invitation to receive military training in Jordan and Lebanon in 1970 would forge a bond of solidarity between the FSLN, popularly known as the Sandinistas, and the Palestinian cause. With the military triumph of the Sandinistas in 1979, Nicaragua would be transformed into the strongest supporter of the Palestinian cause throughout Latin America. The Nicaragua of the 1980s would identify its own history with that of the Palestinian people, and Israel with the imperialism they claimed to be combating in Central America. Attentive to this articulation of history, Washington would recast the Sandinistas' support for Palestine as part and parcel of a global conspiracy orchestrated by Moscow and operationalized by Havana: an additional justification for its military campaign in Central America throughout the 1980s.

The Tricontinental: Havana Renews its Global Commitment to Revolution

The collapse of Ben Bella's government in June 1965 did not diminish Cuba's commitment to revolution in Africa, Asia and the Americas. In January 1966, Havana hosted the first Tricontinental Afro-Asian-Latin America Solidarity Conference and renewed its commitments to revolution across the world. The Tricontinental represented a unique opportunity for Cuba to further its role as a leader in the emerging world of newly independent nations. At the conference, Fidel Castro stressed the historical links between the Cuban revolution and the anticolonialist struggles of Africa and Asia. In discussing Egypt's role in the cause of anticolonialism, Castro emphasized the revolutionary elements of Egypt's recent history. After all, it was Egypt that brought into itself the tripartite invasion of France, Israel and Great Britain in 1956, setting an example that would be followed by other nations across Africa and Asia. Yet with the 1959 revolution in Cuba, "the dogmas of geographical fatality were shattered", bringing the Americas into the Afro-Asian community of newly liberated nations.[1]

The Tricontinental also served as an opportunity for Cuba to continue its ideological rejection of the Soviet Union's efforts to accommodate itself into a "peaceful-coexistence" with the United States. All revolutionaries, Castro argued, had the "right as well as the duty to help the peoples that are fighting for their own national liberation." Those who were seeking a compromise with the West had ceased to be true Marxist-Leninists. In this call for total revolution, Cuba reiterated its determination to work with those movements fighting Western imperialism, whether communist or not, as it had during its years of solidarity with Algeria.

A year later, Guevara wrote a letter to the states and movements of national liberation that had participated in the Tricontinental. The letter represented the official path set by the Cuban government and called upon the Tricontinental delegates to continue their guerrilla efforts. In his letter Guevara argued:

What role shall we, the exploited people of the world, play? The peoples of three continents are watching and learning a lesson for themselves in Vietnam. Since the imperialists are using the threat of war to blackmail humanity, the

---

1 "La batalla es total y a fondo. Los tres continentes deben ser uno solo," *Granma*, January 6, 1966., 4.

correct response is not to fear war. Attack hard and without letting up at every point of confrontation—that must be the general tactic of the peoples. But in those places where this miserable peace that we endure has not been broken, what shall our task be? To liberate ourselves at any price ... The fundamental field of imperialist exploitation comprises the three underdeveloped continents: America, Asia, and Africa. Every country has also its own characteristics, but each continent, as a whole, also presents a certain unity.

In this statement, Guevara hints at the difficulties of spreading the revolution to the Arab world because of Israel's presence as a counterpart to progressive forces in the region. According to Guevara,

The Middle East ... has its own contradictions and is actively in ferment; it is impossible to foretell how far this cold war between Israel, backed by the imperialists, and the progressive countries of that zone will go. This is just another one of the volcanoes threatening eruption in the world today.[2]

No longer a model for revolution, the Arab world was allowing the Vietnamese guerrillas in South Vietnam to take center stage as they fought first against the French and then the United States. Guevara pleaded for the existence of many Vietnams as the key to defeating the United States.

How close and bright would the future appear if two, three, many Vietnams flowered on the face of the globe, with their quota of death and their immense tragedies, with their daily heroism, with their repeated blows against imperialism, forcing it to disperse its forces under the lash of the growing hatred of the peoples of the world! And if we were all capable of uniting in order to give our blows greater solidity and certainty, so that the aid of all kinds to the peoples in struggle was even more effective—how great the future would be, and how near![3]

After the Tricontinental, the Cuban government created the Organization of Latin American Solidarity (OLAS), an agency charged with helping revolutionary movements in Latin America. The agency was instituted to boost the guerrilla movement in Latin America and would eventually support movements of liberation throughout the world.

For their part, the Soviet Union had no alternative but unenthusiastically to support the Tricontinental. The Soviets hoped to have some control of events in Havana and prevent the Cubans from siding with the People's Republic of

---

2 Ernesto Guevara, "Mensaje a los pueblos del mundo del comandante Ernesto Guevara a través de la tricontinental," *Granma* (Havana), April 17, 1967, 4.

3 Guevera, "Mensaje a los pueblos," 6.

China, which was by then in direct confrontation with Moscow.[4] It became clear, however, that Havana was seeking a position of leadership in the revolutionary world and, in so doing, displacing the Soviet Union with its revolutionary discourse and actions. By openly supporting North Vietnam, demanding better terms of trade among the Socialist nations or no trade at all if it was based on capitalist terms and calling for revolution throughout the world.

Despite Cuba's commitment to spreading revolution in Latin America, followers of the Cuban strategy were suffering major defeats at the hands of local armed forces. In Guatemala, the Rebel Armed Forces (*Fuerzas Armadas Rebeldes*, or FAR) and the November 13 Revolutionary Movement (*Movimiento Revoluciónario 13 de Noviembre*, or MR-13) failed to ignite a revolution. In spite of its overt actions, such as the killing of American Ambassador John Gordon Mein and several high-ranking members of the military, the guerrilla movement could not withstand counterattacks from the Guatemalan Army. The guerrillas were also contending with internal divisions; the death of guerrilla leaders Marco Antonio Yon Sosa and Luis Turcios Lima also created difficulties.[5]

The Venezuelan Communist Party rejected Soviet leadership and embraced the Cuban revolutionary strategy, but two years into the Cuban Revolution, guerrilla groups that had appeared throughout the Andes, such as the Armed Forces of National Liberation (*Fuerzas Armadas de Liberación Nacional*, or FALN) were losing strength. Internal divisions, defections, and the military might of Venezuela's armed forces led to the demise of the guerrilla movement in Venezuela. The amnesties offered by the national government decimated the ranks of the guerrilla movement so severely that it had almost disappeared by 1967 .[6]

In neighboring Colombia, a country with a revolutionary movement older than that of Cuba, several guerrilla groups, including the Revolutionary Armed Forces (*Fuerzas Armadas Revolucionarias de Colombia*, or FARC), the National Liberation Army (*Ejército de Liberación Nacional*, or ELN), and the Popular Liberation Army (*Ejército Popular de Liberación*, or EPL), were for the most part either confined to unpopulated areas or forced to run from the army rather than to confront it.[7]

---

4 James G. Blight and Philip Brenner, *Sad and Luminous Days: Cuba's Struggle with the Superpowers after the Missile Crisis* (Lanham, MD: Rowman & Littlefield Publishers, 2002), 109.

5 "A Guerrilla Dies," *New York Times*, October 06, 1966, 46

6 "Venezuela Reports Attack On Last Guerrilla Force," *New York Times*, November 13, 1966, 23

7 "Guerrillas in Colombia Reported Hunt by Government Drive and Internal Feuds," *New York Times*, January 24, 1971, 13; "Latin Guerrillas Said To Be Losing;

Bolivia was home to the most striking failure of a revolutionary movement in Latin America. More memorable than the defeat itself was the disappearance of Ernesto "Che" Guevara who was killed in Bolivia, on 9 October 1967.[8]

The Cuban–Soviet Clash

From Guatemala to Bolivia, the Cuban revolutionary model failed to ignite revolutions across Latin America in the late 1960s. Cuba took on an almost religious commitment to promoting revolution after its perceived abandonment by the Soviet Union during the missile crisis of 1962. However, military defeats on the continent made Castro more vulnerable to Soviet economic and political pressures.

In 1967, Soviet Foreign Minister Aleksey Kosygin advised the Cubans to end their support for revolutions in the Third World. In June 1967, shortly after meeting with President Johnson in the United States, Kosygin went to Havana to deliver his message to Castro. Historically, Moscow had been opposed to the achievement of power through revolutions brought up by movements of national liberation, instead of a communist party. Its efforts to build a working relationship with the United States had started to materialize, and Moscow did not want Cuba to interfere in this new rapprochement. Castro's revolutionary activities in Latin America infuriated the Americans and threatened the new relationship between the superpowers. Moscow had openly criticized Guevara's campaign in Bolivia and ordered the Bolivian Communist Party not to collaborate in his military campaign, and they had publicly congratulated the Venezuelan Communist party for rejecting Cuba's assistance.[9]

Kosygin's mission to Havana, however, was unsuccessful. In June 1967, the Cubans were hoping for good news from their campaigns in Bolivia and the rest of Latin America. They believed that if revolution triumphed in Bolivia, Cuba's position as a leader of the Third World would be indisputable. Castro was resolute and rejected the Soviets' insistence that he ended his support for the guerrilla movements. He accused the Soviet Union of abandoning its Arab allies in the recent Arab-Israeli War and of making broad concessions to the West in pursuit of a *modus vivendi* with the United States. One example of Castro's rejection of the Soviets came in August 1967 at the closing session of the OLAS. He used this opportunity to denounce the Socialist bloc for trading

---

Severe Setbacks Reported in Incidents in 3 Nations," *New York Times,* September 11,1967, 13

8 Juan de Onis, "Setback to Castro: Many Latins would see Guevara's Loss as Signs 'Revolution' had Failed," *New York Times,* October 11, 1967, 18.

9 Blight and Brenner, *Sad and Luminous Days,* 122–123.

with Latin American countries that were aligned with Washington. According to Castro, "If internationalism exists, if solidarity is a word worth pronouncing, the least we can expect from any state in the socialist bloc is that no financial or technical aid is rendered to any of these governments."[10] He warned the Soviet Union that he was not going to be blackmailed:

> No matter how difficult the circumstances, no matter how big the problem we face, nobody will be able to put our dignity and our revolutionary consciousness against the wall! If that had been the case, the directorate of our party would have surrendered a long time ago, confronted by the gravest and mortal peril that imperialism is to us, because of our political stance.[11]

Castro wanted the Soviets to know that he was not their puppet. To stress his independence from Moscow, Castro even refused to break diplomatic relations with Israel, a policy that Moscow had advocated in the aftermath of the June 1967 Six-Day War. Castro rejected the break with Israel and reminded everyone in attendance that supporters of the revolution had not cut off ties with Albania when every country in the socialist camp had done so. He noted that revolutionaries had only reluctantly broken with the Federal Republic of Germany after recognizing the Democratic Republic of Germany. Pure ideology, rather than a Soviet directive or good commercial prospects, would determine Cuba's foreign policy, Castro emphasized. "Otherwise, we could have found millions of reasons to reconcile ourselves with the imperialists."[12]

News of the military catastrophe in Bolivia only hardened Castro's resolution.[13] On January 26 1968, Fidel Castro addressed a secret meeting of the Central Committee of the Communist Party of Cuba and denounced the Soviet Union for abandoning Cuba during the 1962 Cuban Missile Crisis. Castro criticized Nikita Khrushchev, the Soviet leader at that time, for acting like an imperialist in compromising with the United States, and neglecting the security of Cuba. Castro also denounced Soviet leaders for their lack of commitment to the revolution in the Third World. Referring to the Soviet abandonment of both Cuba in 1962 and Egypt in 1967 during the Six-Day War against Israel, Castro questioned the value of Soviet assistance:

> It is indeed incredible that a country 90 miles away from the United States, and ready to fight that enemy, should have to hear the views of their senior [Soviet]

---

10 "Fidel en la clausura de OLAS," *Granma* (Havana), August 11, 1967, 5.

11 "Fidel en la clausura de OLAS," 5.

12 "Fidel en la clausura de OLAS," 5.

13 "Castro, in Interview, Confirms Soviet-Cuban Rift," *New York Times*, December 21, 1967, 17.

specialists telling it that it would only be able to resist for 72 hours. If this is not an insinuation of surrender, if this is not a suggestion of impotence, if this is proletarian internationalism, if this is the correct method, if this is their way of guiding and encouraging the revolutionary movements, then it is no wonder that the Arabs in the UAR [United Arab Republic] got stomped in a matter of hours![14]

Two days later, on January 28 1968, the Cuban government announced that a group of conspirators had been discovered in the Communist Party and would be prosecuted. The "microfaction" of 37 members was headed by the leader of the former Popular Socialist Party (PSP),[15] Aníbal Escalante, and had received help from a number of unspecified officials within the Soviet Embassy. They had provided the Soviets with information about Cuba and had encouraged Moscow to apply sanctions to their own government.[16]

The USSR had little patience for the constant criticism coming from Cuba, particularly Havana's misgivings over Soviet behavior during the 1962 Missile Crisis. In an open signal of displeasure with the Cuban revolutionary campaign, the Soviet Union began to establish diplomatic and commercial relations with the Latin American governments that Cuba had pledged to topple or had denounced as reactionary.[17] The Cubans reacted with indignation to these diplomatic moves, but the Kremlin wasted no time in demonstrating its economic power over Cuba. Oil dispatches to Cuba started to diminish, and in January 1968, the Cuban government began rationing gasoline for the first time since 1959.[18] Soviet technical assistance and military supplies to Cuba were also put on hold in 1968.[19]

The message to Castro was clear: Cuba continued to depend on Soviet economic support and could not afford to lose its favourable trade terms with

---

14 Fidel Castro, Meeting of the Central Committee of the Communist Party of Cuba, January 26, 1968, as transcribed in Blight and Brenner, *Sad and Luminous Days*, 71.

15 The former Communist Party of Cuba before the revolution of 1959.

16 Blight and Brenner, *Sad and Luminous Days*, 33.

17 Sam Pope Brewers, "Colombia and Soviet Resuming Relations; Colombia and Soviet to Resume Diplomatic Ties Broken in 1948," *New York Times*, January 20, 1968, 1; and Juan de Onis, "Russians with Sample Cases," *New York Times*, September 8, 1968, E5.

18 "Rationing of 'gas' is begun in Cuba," *New York Times*, January 4, 1968, 11.

19 Jorge Domínguez, *To Make a World Safe for Revolution: Cuba's Foreign Policy* (Cambridge, MA: Harvard University Press, 1989), 72–77. An almost open confrontation between the Cuban government and the Soviet Union ensued with the prosecution in Cuba of pro-Soviet members of the government. See Juan de Onis, "Castro says 'Nyet' to the Russians," *New York Times*, February 4, 1968, E4, and "Pro-Soviet Cubans are Found Guilty," *New York Times*, February 3, 1968, 3.

the Soviet Union. On August 23 1968, Castro went on national television to discuss the recent Soviet invasion of Czechoslovakia. Voicing his approval for the invasion, Castro finally appeared to be signaling his intention to reach a working relationship with the Soviet Union.[20] In a televised speech to the nation and in what was most likely the most difficult speech of his tenure, Castro argued that the invasion, though regrettable, was justifiable:

> First, I wish to quickly make the important statement that we considered Czechoslovakia to be heading toward a counterrevolutionary situation, toward capitalism and into the arms of imperialism. This is the operative concept in our position regarding the action taken by a group of socialist countries. That is, we consider that it was unavoidable to prevent this from happening—at any cost, in one way or another.
>
> ... What is not appropriate here is to say that the sovereignty of the Czechoslovak state was not violated. That would be fiction and a lie. The violation was flagrant, and on this we are going to talk about the effect on sovereignty and on legal and political principles. From a legal viewpoint, it cannot be justified. This is quite clear. In our judgment, the decision regarding Czechoslovakia can be explained only from the political viewpoint and not from a legal viewpoint. Frankly, it has absolutely no legality.
>
> ... The essential point to be accepted or not accepted is whether the socialist camp could allow a political situation to develop that would lead to the breaking away of a socialist country, to its falling into the arms of imperialism. And our point of view is that the socialist camp has the right to prevent this in one way or another ... We acknowledge the bitter necessity of sending those forces into Czechoslovakia; we do not condemn the socialist countries that made that decision. [21]

The *Frente Sandinista de Liberación Nacional* (FSLN): 1961 to 1967

Fidel Castro's decision to align Cuba closer to the Soviet Union had profound effects on small revolutionary groups in the Americas. This was particularly evident in Nicaragua. The history of Nicaragua's Sandinistas was one of

---

20 "Castro Expresses Support of Invasion; Denounced Dubcek," *New York Times*, August 24, 1968, 14; and *Obras Escogidas de Fidel Castro, Tomo II* (Madrid: Editorial Fundamentos, 1976), 182–231.

21 "There was a march towards a counterrevolutionary situation in Czechoslovakia, they were marching towards capitalism and towards the imperialists arms. It was necessary to stop this one way or another, in any form or shape," *Granma* (Havana), August 24, 1968, 1–5.

incessant defeat until its final victory over the dictatorship of Anastasio Somoza Debayle on July 19 1979.

Carlos Fonseca Amador, the founder of the *Frente Sandinista de Liberación Nacional* (FSLN), was a committed member of Nicaragua's Socialist Party (PSN). The PSN commissioned him to attend the Sixth World Congress of Students and Youth for Peace and Friendship in Moscow in 1957. Fonseca admired the material and social progress achieved by the Soviet Union and Eastern Germany, and he supported the Soviet stance on international affairs, particularly Moscow's path to peaceful coexistence with the West. For Fonseca, there was no question of deviation from Moscow's leadership. The Cuban revolution in 1959 shocked Fonseca and the members of his generation who aspired to social change. The Cuban revolutionaries proved that a nationalist movement could succeed without the guidance and control of what many had begun to perceive as fossilized communist parties.[22]

Revolutionaries outside Cuba had been welcomed in Havana since 1959. Fonseca joined the "Rigoberto López Pérez" brigade, a guerrilla group manned and trained by the new Cuban government. On the continent, the Honduran armed forces and the Nicaraguan National Guard swiftly surprised and defeated the guerrillas at El Chaparral near the Nicaraguan border. To the PSN, this came as confirmation that armed struggle was not feasible in Nicaragua and that the only way to achieve victory was by following Moscow's prescription for change through the electoral system. Fonseca, who miraculously escaped the El Chaparral defeat after being wounded and incarcerated, ended up in Havana. Defeat reinforced his commitment to form a broader movement of national liberation that was independent of the Socialist Party. With inspiration from Augusto Cesar Sandino, a nationalist leader who led a successful guerrilla resistance movement to the US Marines' occupation of his country from 1927 to 1933, Fonseca organized a guerrilla group. Sandino had also fought against a political and economic system controlled by a handful of families. Fonseca's movement followed the Cuban guerrilla model. His militia was organized in the jungle and in the countryside; over time the movement gathered enough strength to descend on Nicaragua's cities in a nationwide insurrection against the dictatorship of the Somoza family, in power since 1936.

The FSLN, a new Cuban-oriented guerrilla group, moved to Rios Coco y Bocay in northern Nicaragua. Throughout 1962, the FSLN sent combatants through Honduras. In 1963 a poorly armed force of 63 men with scant knowledge of the terrain and no contacts with the non-Spanish-speaking local

---

22 Carlos Amador Fonseca, *Un Nicaragüense en Moscú* (Managua: Centro de Publicaciones de la Secretaría Nacional de Propaganda y Educación Política del F.S.L.N., 1980), 78.

population braced themselves for a serious defeat. They were unprepared for hunger and illness, the jungle, and Somoza's feared National Guard.

Pancasán

The FSLN prepared itself for a second guerrilla offensive in Pancasán in northern Nicaragua later that year.[23] Pancasán had no roads and was a journey of several days from the northern town of Matagalpa. The terrain surrounding Pancasán appeared to be more hospitable than that surrounding Rios Coco y Bocay. Moreover, the Spanish-speaking peasant population in Pancasán was thought to be more easily converted to the revolutionary cause. However, the FSLN's fate in Pancasán would be no different to that in the Rios Coco y Bocay operation of 1963. The guerrilla operation began in May 1967, but defectors soon informed the National Guard of the guerrilla hideouts, and by late August, Pancasán had become a second military catastrophe. In less than four months, the FSLN was defeated by more than 400 members of the better armed National Guard. The survivors decided to call off the fighting and departed for Honduras.[24]

Despite their military defeats, the leaders of the Frente Sandinista decided to continue their fight. The defeat was terrible by any measure, but Pancasán was a point of no return. Looking back on the events, Humberto Ortega, a member of the Frente Sandinista and a future Minister of Defense of Nicaragua, reflected on the defeats and on the FSLN's decision to press further:

> Ours was a long-term fight, there was no way we could go backwards; the defeat was immense, but we decided that we were not going to capitulate and we were not going to ally ourselves with any traditional organization. It was all or nothing. In spite of Somoza's continued repression, we decided to go on. But let me tell you, we were probably no more than a hundred militants.[25]

---

23 Matilde Zimmermann, *Sandinista: Carlos Fonseca and the Nicaraguan Revolution* (Durham, NC: Duke University Press, 2000), 96.

24 Zimmerman, *Sandinista*, 98.; In a similar way "Rosendo" (an alias) explains that "due to those casualties of destiny our guerrilla movement does not have much international support because Pancasán happened roughly at the same time that El Che embarked to Bolivia. We could not have the same projection [as] a guerrilla movement commanded by Comandante Ernesto Che Guevara, yet at least after Pancasán other movements began to know about us." Centro de Historia Militar, Ejército de Nicaragua, Carpeta MR. R-001-C-015 No. 000402,3.

25 Interview with General Humberto Ortega, former commander of Nicaragua's armed forces, August 14, 2002, Managua, Nicaragua.

In a desperate effort to prove to friends and foes that they were still alive, the FSLN organized a series of urban operations in October 1967. These urban actions further intensified the regime's repression of the few militants who remained. Within a year, the FSLN's major leaders had either been eliminated, were in jail, or were on the run from Somoza's wrath. "At the close of 1967 we were in a dire situation, after the debacle of Pancasán, and the urban setbacks, we began a slow but intense process that we called the 'accumulation of forces in silence'."[26]

Cuba's Restrained Support for Revolutionary Movements After 1968

By the early 1970s, Castro was interested in re-establishing diplomatic and commercial relations with Latin American countries that had been severed when Cuba was expelled from the Inter-American System in the early 1960s. Salvador Allende's triumph in Chile's 1970 election opened up the possibility for a transition to socialism through the electoral system, soon Cuba would have a friend in South America. Following Chile's lead, Peru, Barbados, Guyana, Jamaica, and Trinidad and Tobago began to break the economic and diplomatic embargo of Cuba followed later on by countries such as Colombia and Venezuela.[27]

A shift in Cuba's policy toward revolutionary movements in the region began to be more evident. Latin American revolutionaries could count on Cuba's support, but it was only to be given to those revolutionary movements capable of presenting a viable military option.[28] For a small and defeated movement like the Sandinistas, Cuban support was absolutely crucial. Without support from Cuba, the Sandinistas would not find support elsewhere. An early history of the FSLN notes the despair felt during those years:

We made our foreign contacts abroad, mostly in Cuba, because everybody was arriving there. In Cuba, we established relations with the most developed movement of National Liberation in Central America: the Revolutionary Armed Forces of Guatemala. The Salvadorian guerrilla movement was only just being born from the Communist Party, and the Costa Rican PRA ... well, we basically taught them how to arm and disarm a gun ... In Latin America, only

---

26 Interview with General Humberto Ortega.

27 "Visitor Castro Finds a Friend Or Two," *New York Times*, November 14, 1971, 5. "A Step Toward Cuba," *New York Times*, January 29, 1973, 28; "Venezuela to the Forge," *New York Times*, January 1, 1975, 16.

28 Piero Gleijeses, *Conflicting Missions: Havana, Washington, and Africa 1959–1976* (Chapel Hill, NC: University of North Carolina Press, 2002), 220–222.

our Cuban comrades were behind us ... We only began to receive the solidarity of other revolutionary organizations in 1978. Before that we had nothing. We made everything from scratch; we only had the Cubans, and the Palestinians who gave us a hand in 1970. They trained some of our comrades, but after that nothing. Nothing.[29]

After 1968, the Sandinistas could no longer rely on Cuba as their major, or only supplier, of armaments and training. Reflecting on the opportunities available to them, Ortega concluded:

Cuba was very generous with us. The problem was that by 1970 the defeat at Pancasán was written all over our foreheads, and we could not offer anything to the cause of revolution in Latin America. Plus, the Cubans were in this very complicated moment of their relationship with the Soviet Union. Cuba was closed for us. We needed somewhere else to go for the training of our cadres, weapons supply, and financial assistance. Oscar Turcios and I had trained in North Korea before. That was a very valuable experience, but perhaps because it was too far, or for other reasons I really do not recall, North Korea was not an option. Then we received news from our representatives in Europe that something might come up in the Middle East.[30]

FSLN Training in Jordan and Lebanon

In the early afternoon of September 6 1970, a series of plane hijackings shocked the world. More than 400 passengers on four different planes were taken hostage by the Popular Front for the Liberation of Palestine (PFLP) as they flew to New York from Amsterdam, Frankfurt, and Zurich. Three of the airplanes were diverted to the Middle East—one to Egypt and the other two to Jordan—where they would later be blown up. The passengers were used in negotiations for the release of Palestinians held prisoner in Europe and Israel.[31]

All did not go well for all the hijackers. The commandos in charge of El-Al flight 219, which took off from Amsterdam, were foiled by the airline crew. The plane landed safely at London Heathrow, where two severely injured hijackers were taken by the authorities. One of the hijackers was identified as 24-year-

---

29 Historia del F.S.L.N. (Rosendo) 1968–1970 (Ernesto) Carpeta MR. E-001, C015, No. 000401 Centro de Historia Militar, Ejército de Nicaragua, 16.

30 Interview with General Humberto Ortega.

31 "4 Jets Hijacked; One, a 747, Is Blown Up; Arab Group Says It Took Planes; El-Al Foils Move," New York Times, September 7, 1970, 1.

old Palestinian commando Leila Khaled.[32] Her companion, who died en route to the hospital, was 27-year-old Nicaraguan-American, Patricio Arguello.[33] Although little was known at the time about Arguello, he participated in these terrorist acts on behalf of the FSLN along with another Nicaraguan, Juan Jose Quezada.[34]

By 1970, neither the Soviet Union, with its urgent need to mend fences with the West, nor Cuba, besieged by economic and military setbacks, was of much help to the FSLN. The Sandinistas turned to their commands in Western Europe. The Sandinistas in Europe included Oscar Rene Vargas and his brother, Gustavo Vargas.[35] The brothers lived in Switzerland, where it is known that Oscar Rene was studying sociology at the University of Geneva.[36] These individuals in Switzerland, as well as other Sandinistas throughout the continent, were in constant contact with political parties from Europe's old and new left. They were also connected to members of various radical organizations, such as Germany's Baader-Meinhof, the Italian Red Brigades, and several national liberation movements from the Third World.

> Like regular students, we met these people at University meetings and in café discussions where we analysed the situation in Vietnam, in Africa. We talked to them about our fight in Central America. It was common to get in contact with these people everywhere,

recalls Rene Vivas, another Sandinista studying in Germany.[37]

In Switzerland, the Vargas brothers, in the company of other members of FSLN, established their first contact with the Popular Democratic Front for the Liberation of Palestine (PDFLP) and the Popular Front for the Liberation of

---

32 Leila Khaled, *My People Shall Live: The Autobiography of a Revolutionary*, ed. George Hajjar (London: Hodder and Stoughton, 1973), 179–206; also, Bernard Weinraub, "Woman Hijacker feels 'Engaged to the Revolution'," *New York Times*, September 9, 1970, 19.

33 "Slain Airliner Hijacker a U.S. Citizen," *New York Times*, September 15, 1970, 16.

34 Departamento de Propaganda y Educación Política del F.S.L.N., *Un pueblo alumbra su historia* (Managua: Centro de Publicaciones 'Silvio Mayorga', 1981), 29, 34.

35 "[Flores] was very much trusted by the Front's commander Carlos Fonseca because he was the brother of one of our men who died at Pancasán." Interview with Rene Vivas, member of the group of Sandinistas that traveled to the Middle East, August 16, 2002, Managua, Nicaragua.

36 They all lived a comfortable life because they came from families in Nicaragua that could support their studies in Europe, "We call them 'los pashas' the pashas because for us the other Sandinistas in Europe, they were rich." Interview with Leticia Herrera, a Sandinista trained in Lebanon, August 23, 2002, Managua, Nicaragua.

37 Interview with Rene Vivas.

Palestine (PFLP). The FSLN made contact with the Palestinian organizations through their connections with the Fourth International and the Trotskyist movement.[38] The Palestinians had established camps in Jordan, where they invited European sympathizers to train in an effort to bring more publicity and solidarity to their cause. Once the Nicaraguans and Palestinians connected, the Sandinistas were invited to the training camps of the PDFLP and then to those of the PFLP, where most of the training for the hijackings actually occurred.[39]

A first group of Sandinistas traveled to Jordan, most likely in the early spring of 1970. The group included FSLN members Augusto Montealegre, Patricio Arguello, Gloria Gabuardi, and Juan Jose Quezada, who apparently had travelled from Cuba.[40]

After the training, which likely ended in the late spring or early summer of 1970, Gabuardi and Montealegre managed to return to Europe and later traveled to Nicaragua. Although little is known about Arguello and Quezada's whereabouts after their participation in the training camps, they did travel to Europe sometime before the end of the training in late May or early June and remained in Europe until the plane hijackings of September 6. The Sandinistas later claimed that Juan Jose Quezada participated in the hijacking of the British jet bound for London on September 9 to rescue Leila Khaled.[41] It is also possible that he participated in the TWA hijacking that occurred three days earlier on September 6.[42] From Jordan, he managed to escape with the other Palestinians and in Beirut met up with another group of Nicaraguans who had arrived in Lebanon for training in October 1970.[43]

This second group of Nicaraguans who were trained by the Palestinians had been scattered throughout the world in such places as England, Western Germany, the Soviet Union, and Cuba. Those living in the Soviet Union

---

38 There is no record of the precise way in which the contact were established or the first contact persons on each side. This is a reconstruction as told to the author by Rene Vivas, Leticia Herrera, and Humberto Ortega in interviews, and correspondence with anonymous, 2001–2002.

39 Interview with Rene Vivas.

40 Interviews with Rene Vivas and Leticia Herrera, and Melania Vega de Uriza, *Conozcamos nuestros héroes y mártires de la lucha anti-imperialista*, vol. 1 (Managua: Instituto de Historia de Nicaragua y Centroamérica, 1982), 74–75. Oscar Arauz Palacios might have belonged to this first group as he too was living in Cuba after the hijacking of a plane in Costa Rica with Quezada. Yet Rivas, Herrera, and Valdivia's article coincides with having him in the second group.

41 Bernard Weintraub, "B.O.A.C. Jet Joins Others in Jordan," *New York Times*, September 10, 1970, 1.

42 See also Quezada, *Un Puelo alumbra su historia*, 29; and de Uriza, *Conozcamos nuestros héroes*, 74–75.

43 Jose Valdivia, "Con el Al-Fatha," *Nuevo Amanecer Cultural*, February 27, 1983, 1, 3.

were studying at the Patrice Lumumba University in Moscow. The group was composed of Leticia Herrera and her husband Rene Tejada, Jose Valdivia, Evenor Calero, and Denis Enrique Romero Zamoran. In marked contrast to the Sandinistas living in Switzerland, those based in the Soviet Union came from very poor social backgrounds and had been beneficiaries of fellowships allocated by the Soviet Union to students from the Third World. Leticia Herrera described how her background molded her politics:

> I came from a very poor family; my father was a shoemaker and he belonged to the shoemakers union during the dictatorship of "*los Somozas*." In the 1960s, my whole family left Nicaragua for Costa Rica because the repression was getting so strong that our lives were in peril. I had retained a strong connection with my country, and I had a profound desire to join the Frente. In 1968 I won a scholarship to study at the Patrice Lumumba University in Moscow. I was going to study chemistry there. In Moscow I met several Nicaraguans who were involved in some way or another in the FSLN, and we formed a very cohesive group.[44]

Apart from the fact that their scholarships were given by the Soviet government to study in Moscow, the Nicaraguans there had no other relationship with Soviet authorities. In fact, as Herrera explains, they were viewed with suspicion by the Soviets because they did not belong to the Communist Party:

> They [the Soviets] were suspicious of people from Movements of National Liberation; we just felt comfortable when we went to the Cuban embassy to socialize and get some news from Latin America, but we had reason to believe that the Soviets had a clear idea of who was who, and they most likely did not like us going to the embassy.[45]

It is very likely that the Soviet Union had nothing to do with the initiation of contacts between the Palestinians and the Nicaraguans. What is not clear is the extent of the Cuban government's knowledge. Because some of the Nicaraguans left for Europe from Cuba en route to the Middle East, the Cubans might have had knowledge of their plans. Even if the Cubans knew something, they were not directly in control of the Sandinistas' participation in the PFLP training program. Leticia Herrera explained that Oscar Turcios, a member of the National Directorate who had been accused of being a Maoist and expelled from the Lumumba University in the 1960s, arrived in Moscow to inform the group about their secret mission in the Middle East.

---

44 Interview with Leticia Herrera.
45 Interview with Leticia Herrera.

Apart from those studying in the Soviet Union, there was another group of Sandinistas in Germany. This group was composed of Enrique Schmitt, who was studying economics in Cologne, Rene Rivas, who was studying chemistry at the University of Heidelberg, and Eduardo Contreras, who was living in Berlin. They were joined by Jacobo Marcos Frech, a psychiatrist whose grandparents emigrated from Bethlehem to Nicaragua in 1913 and who was living in London at the time. Rene Vivas commented on the experience:

> We all [the so-called Germans] met in Cologne, and we met with Jacobo. We all knew each other since we were *chavales* [kids] back in Managua. The idea sounded interesting; it was a way for us to get some training and be ready to return to Nicaragua at some point in the future. It also was a great way to know more about the history and organisation of the Palestinian movement.[46]

The group based in the Soviet Union travelled to France, where they met up with the group coming from Germany, Jacobo Marcos, who was coming from England, and Pedro Arauz Palacios, who was coming from Cuba.[47] Leticia Herrera and Rene Vivas recalled, "We met together for the first time in a park in Paris in July of 1970."[48] In Paris, the group created its own organization. According to Herrera, Pedro Arauz was appointed as the leader of the operation with Eduardo Contreras second in command: "Since Contreras spoke the most English, he basically was in charge of everything."[49] At some point during the summer, the group traveled together from France to Switzerland, where they met up with their Swiss contacts. From Geneva, they travelled to Palermo, Italy, where they boarded a cargo ship: "We docked in Alexandria after a month going from one place to another. In Egypt we went to Cairo, and then to see the pyramids, and shortly after we boarded again en route to Lebanon."[50] They learned of the failure of Leila Khaled and Patricio Arguello's operation on their way to the training camps in the Middle East. According to Herrera:

> That only confirmed our resolution to go with the Palestinians and receive the training with them. After Patricio's death, there was no way we could have

---

46 Interview with Rene Vivas.

47 Again, it is possible that Arauz had come earlier. The National Guard wrote in his criminal record in October that "the individual is being trained in Amman, Jordan, by the Palestinian guerrillas." He may have been receiving training by the time of the annotation, or have already left Jordan. Centro de Historia Militar, Ejército de Nicaragua, Arauz-Palacios: MR E-001; C-014, No. 000377.

48 Interviews with Leticia Herrera and Rene Vivas.

49 Interviews with Leticia Herrera and Rene Vivas.

50 Interviews with Leticia Herrera and Rene Vivas.

backtracked. This training became our moral obligation with the *Frente* and with his memory.[51]

This second group of Sandinistas, composed of those coming from Germany and the Soviet Union, arrived in Beirut in the fall of 1970. They received military and political training from the PFLP in the Baalbeck area close to the Syrian-Lebanese border. The training they received appeared not to have been very relevant or significant to military operations. Leticia Herrera laments the whole episode: "Such a long trip to obtain training that at the end was so elementary. Plus, we ended paying a high price: the death of one of our own dear ones."[52] The death of Arguello came as a shock to the group; it instilled a sense of community among the members of the group based on the memory of their dead comrade but did not necessarily enhance their relationship with the Palestinians. Herrera described her mixed reactions to the whole experience, which were reminiscent of the encounters between Cubans and Algerians in the early 1960s:

> I felt morally obliged to go after I knew that Arguello had been killed, but in regards to our experience there, the language and the idiosyncratic differences were just too great a barrier to having meaningful dialog with each other. At the end, it was just a great opportunity to know other lands.[53]

Language, according to Rene Vivas, might have been the toughest barrier: "We only had English as our medium of understanding, and we both spoke it badly."[54] Another participant, however, wrote about the importance of the experience in terms of broadening his understanding of the situation in the Middle East. Jose Valdivia offered a different perspective on the weeks spent in the PFLP camps and the history of the events unfolding in front of him. Writing about his experience, Valdivia stated:

> It was in Lebanon where we, for the first time, saw in a direct way and with our own eyes the disproportionate and difficult to fathom tragedy of the Palestinian people. Expelled from their own land by the Zionist usurper, Palestinians were forced to settle in neighboring Arab countries whose governments were more interested in preserving their unequal and unjust privileges and always regarded their presence with indifference, fear, and mistrust.

---

51 Interviews with Leticia Herrera and Rene Vivas.
52 Interview with Leticia Herrera.
53 Interview with Leticia Herrera.
54 Interview with Rene Vivas.

In Lebanon, Jordan, Egypt, Syria, and other countries, Palestinians were cramped in camps that lacked even minimal infrastructure, in an inexplicable and shameless contrast to the oil-rich Arab world swimming in opulence and dollars.

Despite these difficult circumstances, the Palestinian people were able to achieve a vanguard role in the Arab world with its fight, a bloody fight full of sacrifices against the Zionist invaders. They were and they have always been a vanguard people in the fight against usurpation and Zionist enslavement.

In October of 1970 from the Palestinians' camps in Beirut, we saw long lines of trucks with young Palestinian combatants en route to Jordan. The Monarchy of this country in alliance with the backward tribes of the desert and Israel had cowardly attacked the refugee camps and the Palestinian military forces. It was a fratricidal war, provoked by the unchecked fear that the Palestinian presence, with its more advanced mentality and with its more progressive political positions, was a threat to the anachronistic social order of Jordan with its backwardness, its lack of culture and tradition of surrendering to foreigners. The war against the Palestinians in Jordan was evidently a criminal manipulation of the backward sectors of this country by the Zionists. The Arab world had to pay a high price for these kind of mistakes. It was not difficult to understand there that divided peoples are easily dominated. What an old imperial tactic!![55]

After the training in Lebanon, the Sandinistas returned to Europe, where the group dispersed. The "Germans" returned to Germany, whereas the others began their homeward journey via Europe and Mexico. In Guerrero, Mexico, they met two Sandinista leaders—Henry Ruiz and Tomas Borge—and received instructions on future FSLN actions against Somoza. In approximately February or March, Denis Enrique Romero Zamoran, Evenor Calero, Jose Valdivia, Pedro Arauz, Juan Jose Quezada, Jacobo Marcos, Leticia Herrera and her husband, Rene Tejada, traveled to Honduras.[56] From Honduras, they entered Nicaragua on May 7 1971.[57] In 1973, Enrique Schmitt and Rene Vivas returned to Nicaragua from Germany. Vivas and Henry Ruiz would later form the guerrilla column known as the "Chema Castilla", which would remain in operation almost until the end of the revolution in 1979.[58]

Most of those trained in the Middle East went on to become high-ranking leaders within the FSLN and were killed by the National Guard before the triumph of the revolution in 1979. Denis Enrique Romero died in June of 1971 in the town of Esteli; three months later, the Guard killed Evenor Calero in the

---

55 José Valdivia, "Con el Al-Fatah," *Nuevo Amanecer Cultural*, February 27, 1983, 1–3.

56 Leticia Herrera agrees with Jose Valdivia.

57 Interview with Leticia Herrera.

58 Interview with Rene Vivas.

city of León. Juan Jose Quezada led the organization of a peasant movement in the regions of Bijao, Cerro Grande, and Waslala. He was attacked by a peasant and would later die in the hands of the National Guard on September 18, 1973 while recuperating from his wounds in the town of Nandiame.[59] Rene Tejada, who became a military trainer for the FSLN, died on January 10, 1975 while attacking a National Guard garrison, the Cuartel Wasala, in the town of Dipina.[60] Eduardo Contreras became responsible for the internal command of the FSLN in 1973 and participated in several military operations during 1974. While in exile in Cuba, he became responsible for the establishment of relations between the FSLN and Panama, Mexico, Venezuela, and Peru. By the mid-1970s, these countries had begun to take the FSLN seriously as an organization, believing that it had a chance of winning power in Nicaragua. Contreras was gunned down by Somoza's National Guard on November 7, 1976.[61] Pedro Arauz, known by his alias "Federico", became a member of the National Directorate of the FSLN and leader of the FSLN's urban commandos. He died on October 17, 1977 on the "Masaya-Tipitapa" highway.[62] Finally, Enrique Schmitt, who survived the triumph of the revolution, became Minister of Communications but died in 1983 while fighting counterrevolutionary forces.

Despite their divided opinions about the military utility of the training, the Sandinistas reported that their experience in the Middle East reinvigorated their commitment to their revolution in Nicaragua and opened their eyes to the complexities of a new region. Although they did not realize it at the time, the Palestinians would reap the political dividends of this relationship when Nicaragua stood out as the most solid advocate of the Palestinian cause in the 1980s. Soviet pressure on Cuba only made the Sandinistas more resourceful and proactive in their connections with the organizations they made contact with in Western Europe. In this regard, the Sandinistas managed to fly under the Soviet radar, as they organized their people and took advantage of the training offered by the Palestinians in a gesture of international solidarity.

Cuba Breaks with Israel

Cuba had maintained diplomatic relations with Israel since the days of Fulgencio Batista. Cuba-Israel relations remained healthy in the lead-up to the Cuban revolution in 1959, although Cuba's rhetoric towards the Middle East was critical of Israel. In Cuba, Jews who desired to leave the country after the

---

59 de Uriza, *Conozcamos nuestros héroes*, 74–75.

60 de Uriza, *Conozcamos nuestros héroes*, 64–65, and interview with Leticia Herrera.

61 de Uriza, *Conozcamos nuestros héroes*, 56–57.

62 de Uriza, *Conozcamos nuestros héroes*, 70–71.

revolution were not subjected to the same public scorn that was reserved for other citizens. Instead of being branded as *gusanos* (worms), if they opted to leave for Israel, they were assigned the benign judicial status of "repatriated". Jews who remained in Cuba were afforded the same rights as the rest of the population. Synagogues continued to operate, and the government provided special requirements during Passover. Moreover, in an act of respect towards Israel, the Cuban government declared a three-day national mourning period after learning of the death of President Yitzhac Ben-Zvi in April 1963.[63]

Despite its positive relations with Israel, Cuba invited a Palestinian delegation to the Tricontinental Conference held in Havana in January 1966. Ibrahim Abu Sitta headed the Palestinian delegation, which was composed of a generation of Palestinian leaders about to be replaced by the new movement emerging in 1967.

Whereas the Tricontinental Conference passed a motion condemning Israel, the Arab countries circulated an early draft of a motion condemning Zionism as "an imperialist movement by nature," but this motion was rejected in the plenary meeting.[64] The final declaration of the Tricontinental protested "the presence of imperialism in South Africa and of Zionist Colonialism in Palestine". It also called for "the restoration of the legitimate rights of the Arab peoples and their right of return to their usurped land".[65]

At the closing of the OLAS conference in August 1967, three months after Israel's defeat of the Egyptian, Jordanian, and Syrian armies in the Six-Day War, Castro was more direct in his reproach of Israel, but he still refused to break diplomatic relations with Tel Aviv, focusing instead on the Soviet Union and what he perceived as a lack of support from the Soviet Union for Egypt during the Six-Day War. In an effort to make a distinction between Moscow and Havana, Castro did not break diplomatic relations with Israel, even though such a severance was being promoted by the Kremlin and the rest of the Socialist bloc, except Romania. At the OLAS conference, Castro argued that:

A state at the service of imperialist aggression, like Israel, takes over a large part of the territory of other nations, it establishes itself on the very shores of the Suez Canal and now even claims the right to participate in the operation of the canal. The case is such that all it has yet to demand is that a pipeline be installed

---

63 Shapira Yoram and Edy Kauman, "Cuba's Israel Policy: The Shift to the Soviet Line," *Cuban Studies*, 8 (1978), 22. The authors, based on a Latin American *Jewish Congress Information Bulletin* (Buenos Aires), 86 (September 12, 1973), speculate that this was the reason why Fidel's visit to Algeria was canceled back in 1963. Specials thanks to Ambassador Ibrahim Souss for his insights on Palestinian foreign relations.

64 Yoram and Kaufman, "Cuba's Israel Policy," 24.

65 "La Tricontinental," *Granma* (Havana), January 6, 1966, 4.

from the Aswan Dam to irrigate the Sinai. And they are there and no one knows until when. And the more time passes, the longer they will stay. This is the order imperialism wants to establish. These are the laws imperialism wants to impose on the world.[66]

Six years later, Cuba still refused to break relations with Israel. Fidel Castro's speech at the Non Alignment Movement meeting in Algiers in September 1973 certainly represented a direct confrontation of Israel but fell short of a breaking off of relations with Tel Aviv:

Whom should we blame for having armed, supported, and sustained the aggressor Israeli state in its war against the Arab countries and in its occupation of the land where the Palestinians have all the right to live in peace? The United States' imperialism.[67]

In sharp contrast to his message at the meeting in Havana, this time Castro fully supported the Soviet Union. Challenging those countries that were critical of the USSR, Castro responded: "Others lament that the first socialist state in the history of human kind has become a military and economic power. We, the underdeveloped countries, the exploited countries, we don't lament this. Cuba is overjoyed with this."[68]

The new leader of Libya, Moammar Al Qaddafi, left the conference room as Castro was giving his speech. He later opposed Castro's closeness with the Soviet Union and decision to maintain diplomatic relations with Israel. Cuba's credentials in the Arab world were being challenged. Qaddafi said, "We have no objection to the Cuban system, but we object to its presence among the nonalined (sic) group because this presence is similar to the presence of any other communist country such as Czechoslovakia or Hungary." He then added, "If we were to allow a state which is a U.S. satellite to attend the conference it would say about the United States what Castro said about the Soviet Union."[69]

---

66 Fidel Castro, "Discurso Pronunciado por el Comandante Fidel Castro Ruz, Primer Secretario del Comité Central del Partido Comunista de Cuba y Primer Ministro del Gobierno Revolucionario, en la Clausura de la Primera Conferencia de la Organización Latinoamericana de Solidaridad (OLAS)," August 10, 1967, available at http://www.cuba.cu/gobierno/discursos/1967/esp/f100867e.html

67 Fidel Castro, "Discurso Pronunciado por Fidel Castro Ruz, Presidente de la República de Cuba, en la IV conferencia de Paises No Alineados." Argel, Republica Argelina Democratica y Popular, September 7, 1973. Available at http://www.cuba.cu/gobierno/discursos/1973/esp/f070973e.html

68 Castro, "Discurso Pronunciado por Fidel Castro Ruz."

69 Cairo MENA 1973-09-07 "Al-Qadhdhafi Answers Castro," as published in *Daily Report. Middle East and Africa. Supplement. Materials on Fourth Nonaligned Conference in Algiers*

Challenged by Qaddafi and pressured by the environment at the conference, Castro finally decided to break relations with Israel and invited Arafat to visit Cuba.[70]

The FSLN and the Palestinian Movement

The emergence of an independent Palestinian movement dates back to the Six-Day War in June 1967. The war constituted a major defeat for the Arab states, and left Israel in control of the West Bank, the Gaza Strip, and the Golan Heights. It also created a new wave of displaced Palestinians, who primarily migrated to Jordan. Moreover, the June War proved to the Arab world that Arab armies, despite their numerical superiority, were no match for the Israeli army. Although the war was a defeat for Arab armies in general, it was particularly devastating for the generation that had emerged from the first Arab-Israeli War with a pledge to destroy Israel.

As much as the war in 1967 was a setback for the Palestinian people, it gave them freedom from many years of domination by other Arab nations. Now on their own, the Palestinians' objective was to confront the Israeli army in the newly occupied territories of the West Bank and Gaza Strip. Writing about the significance of the defeat, the historian Fouad Ajami has concluded that "for more than a decade, it had been an article of faith that the hope of doing something for the Palestinians rested on Nasser and his army: That was Egypt's burden and role."[71] After 1967, it was up to the Palestinians to raise the standard for their own struggle and thus challenge other Arab states to assist them in their movement for national liberation. In the words of George Salameh, one Palestinian fighter stationed in Gaza and later the PLO's Ambassador to Latin America, "We did not allow any more pictures of Nasser in our camps. Who was Gamal Abdel Nasser after all? *Un perdedor!* A loser! 1967 showed us that Nasser was nothing. We had to fight our own fight."[72]

Part II, FBIS-MEA-73-186-S on September 9, 1973. Supplement number 35 Under the heading Materials on Fourth Nonaligned Conference in Algiers II, *FBIS*, 79.

70 Algiers Voice of Palestine——1973-09-08 "Revolutionary Leader Arafat meets head s of State in Algiers," as published in *Daily Report. Middle East and Africa. Supplement. Materials on Fourth Nonaligned Conference in Algiers Part III*, FBIS-MEA-73-191-S on October 2, 1973. Supplement number 36 Under the heading Materials on Fourth Nonaligned Conference in Algiers Part III, *FBIS*, 31; 'Israel Receives Confirmation of Cuban Diplomatic Break,' *New York Times*, September 11, 1973.

71 Fouad Ajami, *The Arab Predicament: Arab Political Thought and Practice Since 1967* (Cambridge: Cambridge University Press, 1981), 105.

72 Interview with George Salameh, PLO ambassador to Nicaragua, August 15, 2002, Managua, Nicaragua.

By August 1967, Yasser Arafat and his organization, Al-Fatah, had begun operating in the West Bank and Gaza. Free from Egyptian and Jordanian control and learning from the experiences of the Chinese and Vietnamese, Al-Fatah began to create a "revolutionary authority" in the occupied territories. Other Palestinian movements, such as the Arab Nationalist Movement (ANM), explained the defeat by the Israelis as the consequence of the inability of the Arab regimes to mobilize millions of armed citizens as had occurred in Vietnam. Furthermore, the ANM and others criticized the Socialist bloc for its inability—or perhaps unwillingness—to help its Arab allies because of either its entanglement with China or its erroneous desire to secure peaceful coexistence with the West.[73] Despite Arafat's enthusiasm, the ANM was cautious with regard to its confrontation of Israel, particularly before people in the occupied territories were armed and trained and had established a good source of weapons.

The caution of the Palestinian ANM did not deter Arafat. His goal was to create in the West Bank the conditions for a spontaneous popular insurrection similar to the one that had occurred between 1936 and 1939. This insurrection, Arafat hoped, would establish the conditions necessary for creating secure bases that would evolve into semi-liberated zones from which the Israelis could be challenged. The first ANM operations began in the West Bank and in the Golan Heights, where the ANM created an alliance with a small organization called the Palestinian Liberation Front (PLF), which had already been involved in collecting abandoned arms in the Golan Heights and constructing safe houses in the West Bank and Jordan. The two organizations merged, and the newly formed organization began operations with an attack on the Ben Gurion International Airport at Lydda on December 11 1967. The Popular Front for the Liberation of Palestine (PFLP) was born.

By January 1968, the Palestinians were taking the initiative in their own war of liberation. They dragged along an older generation of Palestinians, who had entrusted their hopes for liberation in the Arab regimes and who, since 1964, had run the Palestinian Liberation Organization (PLO). Three months later, Al-Fatah, together with PLO forces, confronted the Israeli army in the village of Karama. Although it was a military defeat for the Palestinians, Karama served as a turning point for Arafat's political career. He was catapulted into a position of undisputed leadership within the Palestinian movement; meanwhile, the PFLP, which did not participate in Karama, lost much of its appeal among the Palestinian population.

Just as Al-Fatah was increasingly being recognized as the leading Palestinian group, the PFLP began an internationalist campaign against Israel and its

---

73 Yezid Sayigh, *Armed Struggle and the Search for State: The Palestinian National Movement, 1949–1993* (Oxford: Clarendon Press, 1993), 159.

allies. Beginning in 1968, as a response to Al-Fatah's growing power, the PFLP began to plan and carry out a terrorist campaign beyond the Middle East. The rationale for this campaign was to provide the Palestinian resistance with greater visibility throughout the world and to enhance the image of the PFLP among the Palestinian people.[74] "It was in this revolutionary campaign that we met the Nicaraguans", recalls Bassam Abu Shariff, a former PFLP spokesman. "At the time, there was a crisis in the revolutionary movement. They were frustrated in Europe. As an alternative to being strained in Europe, we offered them the possibility to express their internationalism through our campaigns."[75]

In the Middle East, particularly in Jordan and Lebanon, the PFLP, together with the Popular Democratic Front for the Liberation of Palestine (PDFLP)—an organization that had emerged shortly after 1968—hoped to transform Amman into a second Hanoi and Jordan into North Vietnam, or a source of men and weapons for the struggle in the occupied territories. The radical PDFLP claimed to have the backing of several hundred militia members but more likely had a maximum of 150 supporters. The PDFLP lambasted the Soviet Union for its lack of commitment to revolution and praised China, Vietnam, and Cuba for their support. The organization attracted radical Arabs, Trotskyites, and many other European groups that had flocked to their own camps with those who had gone to the PFLP.[76]

A conflict soon erupted between the PDFLP and the PFLP for the leadership of the Palestinian Left. The radicalism of the FDFLP forced the PFLP further to the left, as the latter organization did not want to lose ground to the former, which was the smaller group.[77] The FDFLP sought to achieve a revolution of the masses and rejected terrorist acts committed by a few high-profile individuals against civilians. The Popular Front rejected this position and continued its campaign of terrorist activity throughout Europe in 1969. Not only was the Popular Front terrorist campaign rejected by the PDFLP, but it was also soundly denounced by Arafat, who, in early 1969, declared "We categorically oppose and reject such attacks on aircraft, for they come at a time when we are making political gains."[78] "This campaign was an irresponsible utilization by the PFLP of their relationship with other non-Palestinian peoples", George Salameh concurred. "The fact that the PFLP got the Sandinistas involved in this desperate action degraded the Sandinista cause and our own fight" concluded

74 Sayigh, *Armed Struggle*, 213.

75 Interview with Bassam Abu Sharif, former PFLP spokesman, July 22, 2001, Ramallah, West Bank.

76 Dana Adams, 'Palestinians Ties Growing Abroad,' *New York Times*, April 5, 1970, 17; and Sayigh, *Armed Struggle*, 231.

77 Sayigh, *Armed Struggle*, 232.

78 Sayigh, *Armed Struggle*, 215.

Salameh. He [Patricio Arguello] was the first Nicaraguan martyr of our fight. They used the Nicaraguans irresponsibly!"[79]

By March 1969, Arafat had been elected chairman of the PLO, and the organization had become recognized as the primary representative of the Palestinian cause. It was clear that Arafat did not want the PLO's mission to become entangled with the actions of an organization that, despite an impressive rate of successful military acts, was losing its grassroots support and had begun to be plagued by internal dissent and fatal divisions. Only after Arafat's visit to Moscow in February 1970 did the Kremlin began to show some sympathy towards the PLO. Although Arafat did not meet with high-ranking Soviet authorities, but with members of the Afro-Asian solidarity office, he began to receive favorable reviews in the Soviet press.[80] Still, a somewhat favorable opinion of Arafat did not necessarily mean support for the Popular Front, whose international terrorism was opposed by Kremlin leaders.[81] The Soviets deemed George Habash's PFLP responsible for the creation of an international crisis and the ensuing conflict in Jordan. The Soviets also rejected the PDFLP for their embrace of Maoism and their utilization of the Leninist diagnosis, which the Soviets considered to be evidence that the organization was suffering from "the childish disease of leftism".[82]

By the time the second group of Nicaraguans was undergoing training, the situation in the Middle East had grown even more tense. On 26 July 1970, Nasser accepted a ceasefire with Israel along the Suez Canal. Jordan followed suit four days later. The PFLP scorned Nasser for his actions, and he responded by expelling the PFLP from Egypt and cutting off its funding.[83] The next phase of the confrontation was with King Hussein, a figure regarded by all movements as both weak and expendable. The PDFLP and the Popular Front

---

79 Interview with George Salameh.

80 John K. Cooley, *Green March, Black September* (London: Frank Cass, 1973), 157.

81 Bernard Gwertzman, "Arafat Ends Soviet Visit Without Sign of Success," *New York Times*, February 21, 1970, 2.

82 E Dmitriev and Vladimir Petrovich Ladeĭkin, *Put'k miru na Blizhnem Vostoke* (Moscow: Mexhdunarodnye Otnosheniia, 1974), 63, as quoted by Roland Dannreuther, *The Soviet Union and the PLO* (New York, St. Martin's Press, 1998), 45. Also Komsomol'skaya *Pravda*, April 12, 1970, quoted by Sayigh, *Armed Struggle*, 250, also criticized the PFLP hijackings and described the PFLP as "an extremist group led by the reactionary Lebanese (sic) politician Habash, which bears the responsibility for hijacking."

83 Nasser counted on the support of the Soviet Union. *The New York Times* reports that *Pravda* clearly rejected the position of China and the Palestinian groups that rejected the cease fire. See Bernard Gwertzman, "Moscow Assails Nasser's Critics," *New York Times*, July 31, 1970, 1.

were convinced that they would prevail over Hussein in a swift and decisive fashion. They were both wrong.

The King repelled the attacks by the Palestinian guerrillas and by the end of 1970 had forced them out of Jordan. Only one Sandinista, Juan Jose Quezada, was in Jordan at that time, and thus the group did not take part in the confrontation. Quezada was stranded in Jordan after the conflict erupted, but he managed to make his way into Lebanon, where he joined the rest of the Nicaraguan group.[84] On 13 October 1970, around the time that the second group of Nicaraguans arrived in Lebanon, King Hussein and Arafat signed an agreement in Amman. By signing the agreement, Arafat and the PLO recognized the sovereignty of Jordan and pledged to respect the independence of the Kingdom by removing forces from the towns and villages and promising not to bear arms outside their training camps. The harshness of the Jordanian response to Palestinian defiance forced the PLO to accept most of the conditions demanded by the King of Jordan. The PFLP, however, declared that it would not abide by the agreement and continued what it branded as guerrilla warfare to seize power in Jordan.[85] The Jordanian police and army responded swiftly and harshly to the PFLP and PDFLP's continuing military actions, which plunged the organizations into profound military and political crisis.[86] Defeated and divided, the groups lacked the power they once enjoyed within the Palestinian movement and were mostly defunct by the time the Sandinistas gained power in Nicaragua nine years later.[87] "We had great relations with Daniel Ortega [the President of Nicaragua from 1979 to 1990] because we fought together in 1970", recalled Abu Ali Mustafa, the political leader of the PFLP. Mustafa glossed over the fact that while the Sandinistas tried to maintain relations with all Palestinian factions, they treated Arafat as the true president of a future Palestinian state. The PFLP did not want the historical record to be rewritten; they had established the first Sandinista-Palestinian relationship. Mustafa continued,

> We trained their people in 1970, and one of them died in our operations, but this was our fight. The Nicaraguans knew this, and Ortega once welcomed Habash [the historical leader of the PFLP] to Nicaragua. As to why Abu Amar [Yasser Arafat] says that the relationship has been with them … well the answer is easy. Abu Amar thinks he has been the father of all revolutions, including Khomeini's.[88]

---

84 Valdivia, "Con el Al-Fatah."

85 Sayigh, *Armed Struggle*, 277.

86 Sayigh, *Armed Struggle*, 280.

87 Eric Pace, "Purge Demanded Among Fedayeen," *New York Times*, November 4, 1970, 13.

88 Interview with Mustafa Abu Ali, former leader of PFLP, July 22, 2001, Ramallah, West Bank.

In conclusion, the Soviet Union appears not to have had a role in arranging the training in Cuba or encouraging the training in the Middle East. The long-standing and uninterrupted relationship between Al-Fatah and the Sandinistas, which Arafat would later claim had existed, does not appear to be supported by the historical record either. It should be noted again that Arafat had emphatically rejected and condemned the hijacking campaign carried out by the PFLP. The organization's decision to proceed with the plane hijackings was clearly an ideological one. Moreover, the hijackings occurred at a time when the PFLP urgently needed to demonstrate to others, particularly Arafat, that they maintained broad support within the Palestinian community.[89] Finally, the evidence suggests that the links between the Sandinistas and the PFLP ended after 1970, when a completely new chapter began with the PLO under Yasser Arafat's control.

The FSLN Government and the Palestinian Movement

With the triumph of the Sandinistas against Somoza's dictatorship in July 1979, the Arab world would reemerge as a model for Latin America's revolutionaries. The new narrative of Nicaragua's history would present the PLO and the Nicaraguan movement for national liberation as allies in a common struggle against American imperialism and two of its proxies: Israel and the Somoza regime. According to this narrative, the allies had been united ever since their joint military training in the 1970s. Nicaragua would serve as the most enthusiastic supporter in Latin America of the Palestinian fight against Zionism; likewise, the Palestinians would open doors in the Middle East for the new Nicaraguan government.

There is no evidence of encounters between the Sandinistas and Palestinians after 1970. According to Jacinto Suarez, a Sandinista who was partially in charge of international relations for the FSLN during the 1970s and a former Nicaraguan ambassador to the USSR, "Once the last group returned at the end of 1970, there were no other [Sandinista] groups there. The terrain conditions [in Lebanon] and the training they could provide us were not what we needed

---

89 As Barry Rubin rightly concludes: "This trio—the pro-Syrian PFLP-GC, the Pan-Arab PFLP, and the Marxist [P]DFLP—and their leaders remained Arafat's and Fatah's main rivals. Over the next 20 years they would alternately restrain or fight Arafat, marching in and out of the Fatah dominated PLO and astonishing the world with acts of terrorism … over the years, their fortunes rose and fell and passed through endless rivalries and alliances with Arafat, Arab states, and one another." See Barry Rubin, *Revolution Until Victory? The Politics and History of the PLO* (Cambridge, MA: Harvard University Press, 1994), 31.

for our own type of fight.''[90] After 1970, the aid and training that the Sandinistas received was beginning to flow from other sources. The Sandinistas had become the leading guerrilla group in Central America despite their internal divisions and Somoza's continued attempts to confront their increasing power. By late 1977 and 1978, the Sandinistas had begun to garner support from progressive leaders in Latin America who threw their support behind the Sandinistas and against the 40-year-old dictatorship of the Somoza family. Direct support came from Jose Figueres and Rodrigo Carazo, two consecutive presidents of neighboring Costa Rica; General Omar Torrijos, the nationalist leader of Panama; and Carlos A. Perez, the President of Venezuela. General Humberto Ortega, the future commander of the Nicaraguan armed forces, explained some of the support received by the Sandinistas: "Fidel [Castro] gave us arms, CAP [Carlos Andres Perez of Venezuela] gave us money, and Torrijos also gave military and logistical support. We channelled the arms through Costa Rica in due time."[91]

Despite the enthusiasm of these regional leaders for the Nicaraguan revolution, no support was more important than Cuba's. "By 1978 we were a guerrilla group worthy of Cuba's support", remembers General Humberto Ortega:

> We met Fidel Castro after we had made a respected guerrilla group of ourselves. He [Castro] met us—the members of the [FSLN] directorate—in his own office, and he began to have a direct involvement in our cause. He had reasons to believe in us.[92]

Indeed, Castro was perhaps invigorated by his recent successful campaign in Angola. He was also likely surprised by the advances that the Sandinistas alone had achieved on all fronts. Therefore, Castro reignited Cuba's commitment to full involvement in the cause of armed struggle in Latin America 11 years after the defeat of Guevara's guerrillas in the Bolivian Andes. With total conviction that victory was possible for the FSLN, Cuba became the Sandinistas' main provider of weapons, training, and other essential support.[93] In addition, Havana became the centre of the FSLN's international activities.

---

90 Interview with Jacinto Suarez, ambassador to the USSR and FSLN international representative in 1978, August 12, 2002, Managua, Nicaragua.

91 Interview with General Humberto Ortega. The memoirs of how the FSLN acquired its relationship with these presidents can be found in Sergio Ramírez, *Adios muchachos: una memoria de la revolución Sandinista* (Mexico: Aguilar, 1999), 121–135.

92 Interview with Humberto Ortega.

93 Jorge Castañeda, *Utopia Unarmed: The Latin American Left After the Cold War* (New York: Knopf, 1993), 59, n. 9.

"It was in Havana that we reestablished contact with the various Palestinian groups", recalls Jacinto Suarez. Because the Cubans had allowed the Palestinian groups to open offices in Havana, the Sandinistas were able to connect with all of them. The Sandinistas signed two communiqués: the first with the PLO in February of 1978[94] and a second with the PDFLP later that year.[95] The February 1978 communiqué with the PLO marked the beginning of a new relationship between the FSLN and the Palestinians. The Sandinistas recognized the PLO as the "only legitimate representative" of the Palestinian people and pledged Nicaragua's support for the creation of a Palestinian state in the "territories that constitute the Palestinian homeland".[96] The training of 1970 reemerged as a solid foundation for Palestinian-Nicaraguan solidarity. "The internationalism of both peoples had been sealed with the generous blood of Sandinista combatants who fell for the just cause of the Palestinian people in the year of 1970",[97] stated the PLO-Sandinista communiqué, heralding the foundational encounter between the two movements.

The communiqué signed in Havana left no doubt about the future political position of the Sandinistas. The parties expressed their "extreme concern at the use of imperialism by the racist state of israel (sic) as a provider of technical and military aid as well as economic support and weaponry to the Somoza family."[98] Israel's support for the Somoza family was well known. The first Somoza ruler of Nicaragua, Anastasio Somoza García, had been a diplomatic supporter of the state of Israel, and ever since, Nicaragua had been a client of the powerful Israeli arms industry. Somoza had supported the cause of partition during the creation of the Jewish state in Palestine in 1947.[99] Furthermore, Israel had defied the arms embargo imposed on the Somoza regime by the US months before its final collapse.[100]

In August 1979, one month after the triumph of the revolution against the Somoza dictatorship, Yasser Arafat sent a diplomatic delegation to Nicaragua that was received with the highest honours by the Sandinista-controlled junta of National Reconstruction. The PLO now branded the FSLN as a "sister in

---

94 Comunicado Conjunto OLP-FSLN, *Gaceta Sandinista*, 3.2 (1978), 23.

95 Comunicado Conjunto FDLP-FSLN, Habana-Cuba, *Gaceta Sandinista*, 3.3/4 (1978).

96 Comunicado Conjunto OLP-FSLN.

97 Comunicado Conjunto OLP-FSLN.

98 Comunicado Conjunto OLP-FSLN.

99 After a strong lobby and perhaps a substantial kickback. Ignacio Klich, "Latin America, the United States and the Birth of Israel: the case of Somoza's Nicaragua," *Journal of Latin American Studies*, 20.2 (1988), 389–432.

100 "Alleged Israeli Arms Shipments to Nicaragua," Memorandum from Secretary of State to Embassy in Tel Aviv, June 1979.

the fight against imperialism".[101] The delegates congratulated the Sandinistas for the triumph: "We are thrilled to see the triumph of the Nicaraguan people. When we congratulate the people, we congratulate ourselves because victory belongs to all the peoples that fight for their liberation."[102]Arafat's visit to Nicaragua to celebrate the first year of the Sandinista revolution was a major event for the new government. The Nicaraguans gave Arafat a hero's welcome reminiscent of Ben Bella's visit to Havana in 1962. Upon his arrival, Arafat called both the Palestinian and the Sandinista revolution "two halves of one whole". The Palestinians inscribed Nicaragua's revolution into the history of the Middle East. Likewise, the Nicaraguans considered the Palestinians to be part of the revolutionary process of Latin America. According to Arafat, both revolutions were part of the same fight against "imperialism" and "Zionism".[103]

In addition to identifying politically and ideologically with the PLO, the Sandinistas looked to the PLO for assistance. The PLO had valuable contacts with Middle Eastern governments that might potentially provide an economic lifeline for Nicaragua. Soon after the opening of diplomatic relations, Henry Ruiz, an official representative of Nicaragua, and Ahmed Sulaiman (Abu-Ala), the director of the economic department of the PLO, signed an agreement of understanding between the two entities. The PLO pledged to serve as an agent of Nicaragua's financial and commercial interests in the "Arab region". Moreover, given the dire economic situation in which the Nicaraguan government found itself, the PLO pledged to make all efforts to try to find external financial assistance for Nicaragua, starting immediately.[104] The Nicaraguan government was advised to open an account in the Beirut Commercial Bank; this Bank would become the locus of Nicaraguan finances in the Middle East. In addition, the PLO pledged to train Nicaraguans in the financial and agroindustrial sectors and agreed to send technical personnel to help modernize the Nicaraguan banking, agricultural, and pharmaceutical industries.[105] The Sandinistas pledged, in

---

101 "Delegados de la OLP en Jornada de Acercamiento con nuestro Pueblo," *Barricada*, August 24, 1979, 1.

102 "Delegados de la OLP en Jornada de Acercamiento con nuestro Pueblo,".,6.

103 Yasser Arafat, "Ahlán wa Marhabá bi Yasser Arafat: Bienvenido Yasser Arafat," *Barricada*, July 22, 1980, 1, 5.

104 "Acta de Conversaciones entre la Delegación de la Organización para la Liberación de Palestina, de la Dirección Nacional del Frente Sandinista de Liberación Nacional, miembros de la Junta de Gobierno de Reconstrucción Nacional y los Organismos Estatales de Nicaragua," *Archivo Ministerio de Relaciones Exteriores de Nicaragua*, August 16, 1980.

105 "Acuerdo de Colaboración Técnica," *Archivo Ministerio de Relaciones Exteriores de Nicaragua*, August 15, 1980.

return, to award an unspecified number of scholarships to Palestinians wishing to study in Nicaragua.[106]

The PLO would also serve as a broker for Nicaragua with the Libyan and Iranian governments, with which the Palestinians had excellent relations. According to Othman Abu Garbia, Yasser Arafat's deputy for ideological and political affairs and an associate of Abu Jihad who brokered the contacts with Iran:

> We did not train them [the Sandinistas] militarily or give them any meaningful weaponry support. They did not need it. They needed these economic contacts, and Abu Jihad helped them to establish contact with the Libyans and, later on, with the visit of Ernesto Cardenal [Nicaragua's Minister of Culture], with the Ayatollah Khomeini.[107]

The Israeli army's invasion of Lebanon in June 1982, destined to eliminate the Palestinian presence in that country, further intensified the identification of the Sandinistas with the Palestinian cause. By this time, Nicaragua had been transformed into Israel's new opponent in Latin America and the strongest supporter of the Palestinian cause. The Nicaraguans viewed their commitment to the Palestinian cause as part of their own destiny, as part of their own "fight against imperialism". Accordingly, the official newspaper in Managua connected the internal fight for total control of Nicaragua that the Sandinistas were still waging and the events in Lebanon: "Our solidarity is also our destiny." The Palestinians "are in Beirut in the war front, we are at the strategic rear guard represented by a victorious Revolution…"[108]

In addition to breaking all diplomatic relations with Israel, Nicaragua was engaging in a "combative march against Hitler's sons," according to the official governmental newspaper, *Barricada*. This newspaper, which gave ample coverage to the marches against Israel after the invasion of Lebanon, stressed the links between the Palestinians and the Sandinistas against their common Israeli enemy. "While the Zionists inundate the land of Lebanon with blood and

---

106 According to the Palestinian Ambassador George Salameh, "probably around sixty students came to Nicaragua, very few ended their studies, by 1987 there were eight students, six graduated: one in medicine, other in journalism, and two in medicine."

107 Interview with Othman Abu Garbia, 26 July 2001. The Libyan government agreed to lend Nicaragua, US$100 million on 30 March 1981. There were other accords by which Libya guaranteed to sell Nicaragua its requirements of oil, and help it with its agricultural sector. Agreement between the Republic of Nicaragua and the Jamahiriya Arabe Libia Popular Socialista. Archivo Ministerio de Relaciones Exteriores de Nicaragua.

108 "Las calles son del pueblo: nuestra solidaridad es también nuestra defensa." *Barricada*, June 26, 1982, 3.

encircle Beirut," an "endless" march against Israel was departing "in Managua, from the very same place where Israeli arms were used by Somoza's guard to massacre more than one hundred patriots."[109] In July of that year, Father Miguel D'Escoto, Nicaragua's Minister of Foreign Affairs, and Father Ernesto Cardenal, Nicaragua's Minister of Culture, went to Beirut to "personally inform brother Yasir Arafat of the total solidarity of the Nicaraguan people and the revolution, the heroic life or death struggle, the struggle of free fatherland or death, that they are waging in the city of Beirut." [110] D'Escoto and Cardenal failed to bypass the Israeli encirclement of Beirut and thus were unable to meet with Arafat in person, but their presence in Lebanon signaled to Israel and the United States the Nicaraguan solidarity and commitment to the Palestinian cause.

The further radicalization of the Nicaraguan revolution increased the growing hostility of the United States towards the government in Managua. This was the beginning of a long and protracted military conflict between US armed groups and the Sandinistas, both inside and outside Nicaragua.[111] By the end of 1982, Ariel Sharon, Israel's Minister of Defense, had visited both Honduras and Costa Rica, a visit which infuriated Nicaragua. The Sandinistas saw the visit as a provocation to Managua and the beginning of a rearmament campaign in Central America against the Sandinistas. Nicaragua's Foreign Ministry referred to the visit as a part of the attempt by the United States to use "imperialism to make Honduras the Israel of Central America".[112] Nicaragua blamed the United States for making "plans to destroy the Sandinista people's revolution". This destruction would be carried out by Reagan's transformation of Honduras into a "small Central-American Israel".[113]

---

109 "Marcha Combativa contra Hijos de Hitler," *Barricada*, June 26, 1982, 1; "Nicaragua rompe toda relación con Israel," *El Nuevo Diario*, August 6, 1982, 1.

110 Managua Radio Sandino Network, July 15, 1982, "Culture Minister Cardenal on Mideast Visit," as published in *Daily Report. Latin America*, FBIS-LAM-82-138, July 19, 1982.

111 Hal Brands, *Latin America's Cold War* (Cambridge, MA; Harvard University Press, 2010), 189.

112 Managua Domestic Service December 11, 1982, "Communique on Sharon Visit to Honduras," as published in *Daily Report. Latin America*, FBIS-LAM-82-239 on December 13, 1982, under the headings Nicaragua, Central America, 20.

113 Managua, *Barricada*, January 25, 1983. "Editorial Sees Reagan 'Israelizing' Honduras," as published in *Daily Report. Latin America*, FBIS-LAM-83-022 February 1, 1983 under the headings Nicaragua, Central America.

The Reagan Administration and the Sandinista–Palestinian Relationship

The Nicaraguans and the Palestinians were not the only parties stressing historical connections and their common struggle against imperialism via the proxies of the Somoza family and Israel. The United States under President Ronald Reagan was making similar connections to justify its campaign in Central America against Nicaragua. Soon United States branded the Sandinistas a threat to American interests in the region, and to Nicaragua's neighbours in Central America. Ronald Reagan, who took office in 1981, particularly saw the Sandinistas as a regime controlled by the Soviet Union and Cuba; and, saw the Sandinistas' links to the Palestinians as evidence of a global terrorist network that needed to be countered in Central America before it reached the United States.[114]

Cuba viewed the Sandinista victory as a major triumph. Starting with Nicaragua, and rapidly expanding throughout the isthmus of Central America, revolution was, finally, on the rise in the 1980s in Latin America. The prospects for revolution seemed promising after so many years of defeat. The Soviet Union, which had been a fierce critic of guerrilla movements, was now supporting Nicaragua and Cuba militarily, economically, and diplomatically.[115]

Washington became alarmed by what it regarded as another example of global Soviet expansion. The Reagan administration saw the Nicaraguan-Palestinian connection as evidence of a new expansionist wave of Soviet communism in the Third World that now was spreading from Angola to Afghanistan and from Ethiopia to Nicaragua.[116] Nicaragua, in particular, became an obsession of Ronald Reagan's administration. Even during his electoral campaign, Reagan denounced the Sandinistas as a Soviet and Cuban springboard for Marxist Leninism in Central America. Once in power, Reagan's prescription seemed as clear as the diagnosis: the Soviet Union's advance in Latin America must be stopped and the Cuban-Sandinista alliance defeated before it spread throughout Central America.[117] Robert McFarlane, who was by 1981 an adviser to Secretary

---

114 United States State Department, "The Managua Connection: The Sandinistas and Middle Eastern Radicals," *Public Diplomacy Office Review* (467315), 5 (Washington, DC: United States State Department, August, 1985).

115 Brands, *Latin America's Cold War*, 195–198.

116 United States State Department, Bureau of Intelligence and Research. "Developing Soviet-Nicaraguan Relations," (Washington, DC: United States State Department, 1981) 1981, 1–9; Frank Church, "America's New Foreign Policy," *New York Times*, August 23, 1981, SM8.

117 Carlos Fuentes "Dominoes—Again?," *New York Times*, September 19, 1980, A27.

of State Alexander Haig, explained to a Joint Hearing of Congress how the world was seen from the White House:

> We had just witnessed a five-year period where the Soviet Union tried out a stratagem of sponsoring guerrilla movements that would topple moderate regimes, and install their own totalitarian successor, and they had a phenomenal success—from 1975 to 1980, in Angola, Ethiopia, South Yemen, Cambodia, Afghanistan, Mozambique, Nicaragua, and so on.[118]

The administration felt that the expansion of communism urgently had to be rolled back. This sense of urgency was thought to be essential to demonstrate the administration's commitment to preventing the expansion of communism to other countries, including the Philippines, Pakistan, and Saudi Arabia. According to McFarlane:

> If you are sitting in the Kremlin watching this and you had evidence that the United States could not even cope with this phenomenon where it was more important to them—not in Vietnam; right at home—and if you are a Kremlin leader, the precedent of failing where it ought to be easiest to win might well encourage the Soviet Union to continue this stratagem and to pour more money into it, as opposed to other kinds of European orientation or Japanese or Chinese.[119]

The United States' campaign against Nicaragua was intense and multifaceted. It included the arming of a counterrevolutionary force to fight the Sandinistas; the strangling of Nicaragua's economy; military operations in the region; and a relentless public campaign against the Sandinistas. The Office of Public Diplomacy for Latin America and the Caribbean, directed by Otto Juan Reich, was in charge of this campaign. Reich's mission was to "clarify the issues, clearly state our policies and generate domestic and international support for our program [in Central America]".[120]

Part of the public diplomacy campaign was designed to depict Nicaragua as a surrogate of communist powers with dangerous links to a network of

---

118 House Select Committee to Investigate Covert Arms Transactions with Iran and Senate Select Committee on Secret Military Assistance to Iran and the Nicaraguan Opposition. *Testimony of Robert McFarlane, Joint Hearings on the Iran-Contra Investigation*, 100th Congress, 1st session, 1988, vol. 100-2, May 13 (Washington, DC: United States Government Printing Office, 1987), 190.

119 *Ibid.*

120 William P. Clark, "Tasking for Central America Public Diplomacy," Memorandum for the Special Planning Group, The White House, July 12, 1980, 2.

terrorist states and organizations inspired and coordinated by Moscow and Havana. Therefore, the events of September 1970 were presented as part of a continuous relationship between the Sandinistas and Yasser Arafat's PLO predating 1970. Accordingly, friends of Israel, and the enemies of the PLO and the Sandinistas, could find a common denominator to unite them in support of the controversial policies emanating from the White House.[121] Failure to support the administration was seen not only as indifference to the expansion of communism but also as tacit acceptance of the expansion of a terrorist network in Central America and the Middle East. According to one of the Public Office's publications:

> The PLO [Palestinian Liberation Organization] made its international debut in 1966 in Havana, Cuba, at the First Conference of the Organization of Solidarity of the Peoples of Asia, Africa, and Latin America (also known as the Tri-Continental Conference). At this conference, Fidel Castro brought together 500 delegates from radical leftist groups around the world to devise a strategy for what they called the global revolutionary movement.
>
> Results of that conference soon became apparent. In the months following the conference, guerrilla training camps appeared in various countries, with major clusters in Cuba, the Soviet Union, Lebanon, and Libya. Members of the PLO were among the first to be trained in the Cuban and Soviet camps, thanks to the close ties developed at the Tri-Continental Conference.[122]

A plan of action began to emerge as the Office continued to piece together its history of revolutionary movements. Guerrilla training camps began to be installed in various countries such as Cuba, the Soviet Union, Lebanon and Libya. Although no specific date was provided, the State Department affirmed that the PLO members were among "the first to be trained in the Cuban and Soviet camps, thanks to the close ties developed at the Tri-Continental Conference."[123] After utilizing Cuba and the Soviet Union for their training, the Palestinians began to train people in their own camps in Lebanon and Libya.

---

121 Congressman Courter summarizes the list: "Not only is the Soviet Union, not only is Cuba, but countries such as Czechoslovakia, North Korea, organizations such as the PLO, Muamar Kadaffi's Libya are likewise helping the Sandinistas in Central America." House Select Committee to Investigate Covert Arms Transactions, *Testimony of Robert McFarlane*, 192.

122 United States State Department, "The Managua Connection: The Sandinistas and Middle Eastern Radicals" *Public Diplomacy Office Review* (467315), 5. Washington. D.C. August 1985.

123 United States State Department, *Sandinistas and Middle Eastern Radicals*, 1.

After setting up the first training camps in Lebanon,[124] The Department argued, the Sandinistas arranged for the training of "at least 50 to 70 of its members".[125] Once the training had begun, the Sandinistas participated in the PFLP hijackings and fought alongside the Palestinians in the attempt to dethrone King Hussein of Jordan in September 1970.[126] Set in those terms, the threats to the US and the Western Hemisphere could not be more clear, and present. The need for action urgent and necessary.

The State Department proclaimed with certainty that by 1978, the relationship between the PLO and the FSLN had intensified. Moreover, officials claimed that "[as] the Sandinista guerrilla actions increased in intensity, so did the rate and amount of PLO aid".[127] After the Sandinista's successful revolution in July 1979, the links to the PLO grew stronger, as Nicaragua became the recipient of PLO-brokered Libyan and Iranian economic and military aid. These connections offered further evidence, the White House argued, that Nicaragua had been incorporated into this "axis of terrorist nations"[128] and would undoubtedly prove to be a springboard for further PLO activities in Central America.[129] As President Reagan reminded the American people in a radio address, "Over 7,000 Cubans, Soviets, East Germans, Bulgarians, Libyans,

---

124 Eileen Scully, "The PLO's Growing Latin American Base," *The Heritage Foundation Backgrounder*, August 2, 1983, 4. Scully claims that "joint PLO-Cuban training of Sandinistas begun in Lebanon, Algeria, and Libya" and that the training began with Pedro Arauz and Thomas Borge, then Minister of Interior.

125 Scully, "The PLO's Growing Latin American Base," 1. Neil C. Livingstone and David Halevy, *Inside the PLO: Covert Units, Secret Funds, and the War against Israel and the United States* (New York: William Morrow and Company, 1990), concurs with the State Department claiming that Fidel Castro himself put Palestinians and Sandinistas in contact. "By using PLO as a proxy, Cuba could further disguise its extensive collaboration with the FSLN," and affirmed that "more than two hundred Sandinistas received training in PLO/PFLP camps in first Jordan and later Lebanon," 157. Jillian Becker, *The PLO: The Rise and Fall of the Palestine Liberation Organization* (New York: St. Martin's Press, 1984) argues that it was after a meeting between Fidel Castro and Yasser Arafat in Algiers in May 1972 that the PLO started to cooperate in the training of Latin American guerrillas, 166–167.

126 United States State Department, *The Sandinista and Middle Eastern Terrorist*, 2.

127 United States State Department, "The Managua Connection," 4.

128 United States State Department, "The Managua Connection," 6, 7; United States State Department, *Sandinistas and the Middle Eastern Radicals*, 9, 10.

129 United States Department of State and Department of Defense, "The Sandinista Military Build-up," May 1985, Department of State Publications 9432 (Washington, DC: Bureau of Public Affairs, 1985), 34; United States Department of State and Department of Defense, "Background Paper: Central America," May 27 (Washington DC: Bureau of Public Affairs, 1983), 6; United States Department of State and Department of Defense, "Nicaragua Military Build-up and Support for

PLO, and other bloc and terror groups are turning Managua into a breeding ground for subversion. A delegation of Nicaraguans is now in Iran."[130]

The administration justified the public campaign against Nicaragua on these grounds. The campaign was also intended to legitimize the secret connection between the Reagan Administration and the government of Israel, which first provided Honduras with Kfir warplanes. Later, this secret relationship orchestrated the channeling of arms confiscated from the PLO by the Israeli army in the 1983 operation "Tipped Kettle" to the Nicaraguan counterrevolutionary militia. Finally, Israel was used to circumvent the Congressional prohibition against arming a counterrevolutionary militia, which ultimately became known as the Iran-Contra Affair.[131]

The Failures of the 1980s

The Sandinista revolution of 1979 gave new impetus to the revolutionary ethos of Latin America. Answering the pluralistic call of the Nicaraguan revolution, the Sandinistas formed a government that included all ideological sectors and class interests. Some of these groups were soon displaced from power, as the revolution moved decidedly to the left. Nicaragua soon embarked on a program of agrarian reform and a campaign against illiteracy with the support of Cuba. Nicaragua was also prepared to work with Cuba and, and now the Soviet Union, in the expansion of socialism across Central America.[132] Soon after the Somoza regime's collapse, the Sandinistas encountered major roadblocks that they could not overcome. Ultimately, these obstacles derailed the revolution and turned it into an endless spiral of civil conflict. The Reagan administration, of

---

Central American Subversion," July 18 (Washington DC: Bureau of Public Affairs, 1984), 22–23. 2–23.

130 Ronald Reagan, "Radio Address to the Nation on Tax Reform and the Situation in Nicaragua," December 14, 1985. Available at http://www.reagan.utexas.edu/archives/speeches/1985/121485a.htm. On the need to redouble aid to the counterrevolutionaries Vice-President Bush had said before that the Nicaraguan government was "helped by massive new supplies of weapons from their allies in the Soviet Union, East Germany, Bulgaria, North Korea, Vietnam, Cuba, The PLO, Libya, Iran and other radical states." See the communiqué released by the Office of the Press Secretary, The Vice President's Office, Washington, DC, "Excerpts from Remarks by Vice President George Bush; Austin Council on Foreign Affairs," Austin, Texas, Thursday, February 28, 1985, 1.

131 United States District Court for the District of Columbia, *United States of America vs. Oliver L. North*, Criminal No. 88-0080-02 GAG, 1988, 1–15.

132 Brands, *Latin America's Cold War*, 196.

course, viewed the revolution as an expansion of international communism and pledged to destroy it.

The covert and overt war against the Sandinistas forced Managua to devote the majority of its meagre public resources to the defense of the revolution. The entire country mobilized to fight the war against the counterrevolutionary forces, known by their Spanish name, the *Contras*. In fighting the *Contras*, the Nicaraguan government became increasingly less tolerant of local and international opposition. The government militarized Nicaraguan society, thus exacerbating the economic crisis. [133] Over the years, tired of war, the Sandinistas watched their popular support decline as opponents emerged over the course of ten years and finally took power through elections held in early 1990. Returned to power after a decade of being shunned, the old elite shifted their country back into a close alliance with the United States and maintained a distance from the Palestinian movement. By 1992, Nicaragua had reestablished diplomatic relations with Israel.[134]

Other guerrilla groups in Central and South America also failed to hold on to power; indeed, most of them had disappeared, at least militarily, by the early 1990s. Leftists in El Salvador organized a guerrilla movement having spent years trying to implement widely supported social reforms and being ignored by the Salvadorian elite. Their military organization, *Frente Farabundo Martí para la Liberación Nacional* (FMLN), waged a war and, at times, appeared close to winning. Ultimately, the war between the FMLN, the army, and the Salvadorian elite ended in a bloody stalemate. Only with the help of the United Nations in 1992 did the parties reach a peace agreement that put an end to the civil war. The agreement did result in the partial opening up of the political system and the amelioration of some of the problems that had forced the left to take up arms in the first place.[135]

As radicals dismantled their training camps and abandoned their arms throughout Central and South America, the whole "edifice of socialism" collapsed around the world. By the 1980s, the vital resources that had arrived from the Soviet Union to sustain the Cuban economy, at the rate of US$8–10 million per day, began to dry up. Soviet aid to the Sandinistas also declined.[136] To free resources from the military for use in the civilian sector, Gorbachev

---

133 Brands, *Latin America's Cold War*, 215.

134 Managua Radio Nicaragua Network 1992-10-06 "Relations Reestablished with Israel," as published in *Daily Report. Latin America*, FBIS-LAT 92-197 on October 9, 1992 under the headings Nicaragua, Central America, 10.

135 Brands, *Latin America's Cold War*, 216.

136 Brands, *Latin America's Cold War*, 216, 217. "Gorbachev's "gift" to Bush in Nicaragua." Available at http://www.nytimes.com/1989/05/18/opinion/gorbachev-s-gift-to-bush-in-nicaragua.html?

actively pursued positive diplomatic relations and a broad range of nuclear and conventional weapons negotiations with the United States. Gorbachev thought that the Polish, East Germans, Czechoslovakians, Rumanians, Hungarians, and Bulgarians, all set free from the constraints imposed upon them, would freely choose to remain in an alliance with the Soviet Union. Towards the end of the 1980s, however, the Eastern Europeans, despite guarantees of independence from Moscow, toppled their governments and rejected any further alliance with the Soviet Union. By the early 1990s, the Union of Soviet Socialist Republics was also disintegrating, as emergent nationalist forces demanded the right to secede from Moscow. In December 1991, the most important state of the socialist bloc imploded in a bloodless revolution.

In Cuba, Castro rejected the Soviet's political and market reforms and called for "rectification", or a return to the ideals and principles of the revolution before the realignment of 1968.[137] Cubans were asked to brace themselves for difficult times. Over the next five to seven years, trade with Eastern Europe collapsed altogether, and trade with the Soviet Union went into a downward spiral. Imports of Soviet products could only be obtained if paid for in hard currency at market prices. The development of Cuban socialism came to a halt as the country's economy cracked under the pressure imposed by a lack of oil, resources, food, and consumer goods. Cubans were again called upon to embrace major personal sacrifices in what the government called the *período especial*, or "special period", a grim warlike time when food rations became stricter and blackouts more widespread. Even the health system—once the hallmark of the Cuban revolution—could no longer provide patients with necessary medications. Public transportation stopped, and industries and factories were forced to reduce their work schedules or close altogether for lack of parts and raw materials.[138] In Latin America, the Cuban dream of a radical world united in its commitment to revolution was a matter of the past and, with the defeat of the Sandinistas, so was the uncompromised support of Nicaragua to the Palestinian cause.

By the late 1990s, a new generation of leftist leaders began to emerge across the region. The Arab World would be again a point of identification in their defiance of what by the early twenty-first century seemed a solid unipolar world dominated by the United States.

---

137 Joseph Treaster, "Castro Scorning Gorbachev Model," *New York Times,* January 11, 1989. Avilable at http://www.nytimes.com/1989/01/11/world/castro-scorning-gorbachev-model.html?

138 Jo Thomas, "The Last Days of Castro's Cuba." Available at http://www.nytimes.com/1993/03/14/magazine/the-last-days-of-castro-s-cuba.html?

Chapter 6
"My Heart Beats with Millions of Arab Hearts": Venezuela and the Arab World

Latin American revolutionaries were in retreat by the end of the twentieth century. The collapse of the Sandinista government in the 1989 elections, and the peace agreements between governments and guerrilla groups in El Salvador and Guatemala, confirmed the end of revolutionary movements across Central America. Cuba survived as a socialist regime, but its economy was in shambles as a result of mistakes of its own making, the continuing economic embargo imposed by the United States, and the collapse throughout the 1980s of its main trading partners in the socialist bloc.

The world around them was also changing. The Cold War, the economic, political and strategic conflict between the United States and the Soviet Union had come to an end at the closing of the 1980s. In this *new world order*," as the President of the United States called these times, both superpowers voted in the Security Council of the United Nations in favor of a military response to the invasion of Kuwait by the Iraqi leader Saddam Hussein in August of 1990. In a matter of months the former Soviet ally was forced to leave Kuwait by the United States-led military coalition. The end of the Cold War, and the events in the Gulf, opened the door to a first encounter in what many saw as the start of a wider peace process between Arab countries and Israel, and between Israel and the Palestinians. A first encounter, sponsored by both superpowers, took place in Spain, in October 1991. The Madrid peace conference led to further talks that ended in 1993 with a promising peace accord signed in Oslo two years later between Palestinians and Israelis.

Two years before the end of the twentieth century, when encounters between Latin American revolutionaries and the Arab world seemed confined to the footnotes of the history of the Cold War, Hugo Chávez captured the presidency of Venezuela. In the next 14 years, Chávez would emerge from Caracas as one of the most vocal critics of a new world order dominated by market-driven liberal democracies led by the United States. The Venezuelan President would again revive the idea of an Arab world historically connected to Latin America, fighting hand in hand for political and social freedom and against imperialism.

Figure 6.1   Hugo Chávez with the Iraqi president Saddam Hussein, the first visit of a Head of State to Iraq since 1991, Baghdad, August 11, 2000

Source: © AFP-INA

The History of OPEC and Venezuelan Nationalism

Oil Nationalism from a Venezuelan Perspective

A different Venezuelan had first introduced the Middle East to his country 40 years earlier: Juan Pablo Pérez Alfonzo. A former Minister of Mines and Hydrocarbons in Venezuela, an intellectual and committed nationalist, Pérez Alfonzo awakened and educated a generation of Latin Americans to the nationalist struggles of the Middle East and their relationship with Latin America's own political and economic history. He followed closely the political development in Iran and Egypt and their struggles to have full ownership of their own natural resources. Pérez Alfonzo warned his readers in Latin America to think beyond the world presented to them by the foreign media. In particular he wanted Venezuelans to understand the dynamics of what was going on in Iran. "Mossadegh was not the improvised Prime Minister that the press, controlled by the international forces of capitalism, tried in vain to caricaturise after his brave nationalisation of [Iran's] oil industry," he cautioned his readers.[1] On the contrary, Iran was an example of the region's continuous struggle for ownership and control of the country's natural resources against the interests of large multinational oil companies and the empires behind them.

Pérez Alfonzo reminded his audience across Latin America that Iran had been occupied by both the Soviet Union and Great Britain during the Second World War. After the withdrawal of both powers from the country, Mohammed Mossadegh was one of the few political leaders who stood firm against both the Soviet oil interests in the north of his country and against the British concessions in the south. After long negotiations and threats from Moscow, the Soviets finally left Iran in 1946 without extracting further concessions, but negotiations with the British Anglo Iranian oil proved more complicated. After the war, in response to the rising nationalist sentiment in Iran, the Anglo Iranian Oil Company presented a supplementary agreement to the general framework of royalties that it "surreptitiously argued" was based on the 50/50 system in place in Venezuela since 1950. Mossadegh, at that time the head of the Oil Commission in the Iranian Parliament, led the opposition to the offer, arguing that it did not "protect the interests of Persia".[2] The eventual failure of this initial negotiation convinced Mossadegh that "nationalisation was the only way out for the country, given that negotiators were using all their skills to keep their colonialist exploitation," concluded Pérez Alfonzo.[3]

---

1 Juan Pablo Pérez Alfonzo, "El Camino de Mossadegh," *Política: ideas para una nueva América*, 61.6 (1967), 16.

2 Pérez Alfonzo, "El Camino de Mossadegh," 20.

3 Pérez Alfonzo, "El Camino de Mossadegh," 20.

A fierce nationalist, Pérez Alfonzo was also critical of the local elites and their alliances with foreign capital to the detriment of the broader interests of the nation. In the case of Iran in particular those elites created the social and political instability that gave the upper hand to foreign interests. "Only those who have suffered similar abuses and humiliations could understand the events that followed," Pérez Alfonzo warned his Latin American readers. In the midst of major confrontations in Iran, Prime Minister Ali Razmanara was assassinated in March 1951, and the Shah was forced to appoint Husein Ala' as Prime Minister.

Pérez Alfonzo had met Ala' years earlier. While living in the United States as the Iranian Ambassador, Ala' had been approached by a delegation sent by Pérez Alfonzo, then Minister of Development, to organize the first official visit of the Venezuela government to Iran. The visit never took place because a coup d'état in Venezuela in 1948 sent Pérez Alfonzo into exile and led to the cancellation of all plans for meetings with other oil producing countries. In any case, Hussein Ala's term in office was brief because the Shah could not postpone demands for the reappointment of Mossadegh as Prime Minister, which occurred on April 30 1951.[4]

In Parliament, Mossadegh won approval for the Nationalisation of Oil Law on May 2, 1951. In the months that followed, Pérez Alfonzo recounts, Iran successfully responded to the challenges of the United Kingdom at the United Nations Security Council and the International Court of Justice.[5] Nevertheless, a dire turn of events was looming as the United Kingdom approached the United States with an offer to reduce its participation in oil extraction in Iran in favor of American companies. With this offer, Pérez Alfonzo argued, American capitalists joined the British counterparts in their control of Iranian oil. The offer, "awakened the ambition of American capitalists", he concluded. He warned his readers in the Americas that these capitalists had at their service "not only their economic power but also their powerful paramilitary forces always working hand-in-hand with powerful economic interests for the conquest and control of other people".[6] By 1953, the Central Intelligence Agency (CIA), in cooperation with its British counterpart, launched a campaign against Mossadegh that would oust him from power on August 19 of that year.

The expulsion of Mossadegh from power reminded Pérez Alfonzo of Venezuela's own history. In 1948, Venezuelan President Romulo Gallegos was ousted in a military coup d'état at a time that the country was trying to bring "some justice in the economic relations [between Venezuela and] ... international capitalism". Pérez Alfonzo reminded his audience that a liberal

---

4 Pérez Alfonzo, "El Camino de Mossadegh," 23.
5 Pérez Alfonzo, "El Camino de Mossadegh," 27–28.
6 Pérez Alfonzo, "El Camino de Mossadegh," 29.

democrat such as President Gallegos was sacrificed to serve the same interests that toppled Mossadegh in Iran in 1953.[7] The events in Iran, as painful as they were for him, strengthened Pérez Alfonzo's determination to become a driving force behind the creation of what would later be known as the Organization of the Petroleum Exporting Countries (OPEC). Had there been responsible governments across the Arab World and Latin America that were conscious of what was a stake in Iran in 1953, the situation might have been completely different as early as the 1950s, he further argued.[8]

The need to create an organization to defend oil producers' interests did not arise solely because of the events in Iran – the idea had been present since the end of the Second World War. "It was precisely in 1947, when Venezuela was taking a more active role in handling its oil wealth managed by foreign companies," that the US was making a transition from being an exporter to a net importer of oil. Cheap oil that was now arriving from the Middle East was used as a threat to Venezuela's future ability to engage large and wealthy companies in meaningful negotiations with the government. However, "it was also at that time that Venezuela became conscious of the community of interests that would forge a common front of solidarity against opposing interests". A meeting in Caracas during the National Petroleum Congress (*Convención Nacional de Petróleo*) in September 1951 would serve as the stage for an encounter that would be critical to the history of both regions. The Saudi representative, Abdullah Tariki, attended this Congress and established the first direct contacts between the largest oil-producing countries and Venezuela. Unfortunately, the Venezuelan dictator at the time, Marcos Pérez Jiménez, had no intention of challenging the interests of the large transnational oil companies and did not follow up on the advances made by the Saudis.[9]

The nationalisation of the Suez Canal Company by Gamal Abdel Nasser was a major encouragement to those nations seeking to own and administer their natural resources. According to Pérez Alfonzo, with its success, Egypt "encouraged" nations that sought "progress and economic liberty". Based on Nasser's success, the Arab League called for the first Arab Oil Congress to take place in Cairo in April 1959 and the Arab countries invited both Venezuela and Iran. With Marcos Pérez Jiménez gone, the new government of Venezuela appeared ready to work with Iran and his Arab counterparts. The Venezuelan delegation actively participated in the initial drafting of a document that embodied the common nationalist principles driving all oil-producing nations

---

7 Pérez Alfonzo, "El Camino de Mossadegh," 30.

8 Juan Pablo Pérez Alfonzo, "Organización de Países Exportadores de Petróleo (OPEP)," *Política*, 45.6 (1966), 8.

9 Pérez Alfonzo, "Organización de Países Exportadores de Petróleo," 7.

present at the meeting.[10] The downward spiral in the prices of oil caused by overproduction gave the countries meeting in Cairo more urgency to create OPEC in Baghdad on September 14 1960. Pérez Alfonzo was convinced that Venezuela and the rest of the OPEC members would use the new institution as an instrument to confront "with a strong force those who had been unjustly taking advantage of their weakness".[11]

Oil Booms and Busts

The strategy paid off. Thirteen years after the creation of OPEC, oil industries were nationalized across the board and governments were establishing market prices by a system of quotas that controlled the supply of oil to markets across the world. The price of oil soared from US$3 to US$10 per barrel. By 1980, the price of oil gained another US$30 and reached US$40 per barrel.[12] Oil was giving Arabs and Latin Americans what revolutions could not: real independence from foreigners interests and the potential for full development. The influx of the extra revenue allowed governments across the Atlantic to dream big: "In the Middle East, it was the era of the 'Great Civilisation'; in Latin America, the epoch of "La Gran Venezuela."[13]

"Sowing the oil" proved to be more difficult than expected. By 1974, the newly elected President Carlos Andrés Pérez had US$10 billion to transform his country of 12 million people into "La Gran Venezuela".[14] Pérez intended to achieve 20 years of industrialisation in five, and to accomplish this goal he would invest resources in the soon to be nationalized oil, steel, and hydroelectric sectors.[15] Under the control of the executive and without significant supervision from the other branches of government, the state apparatus expanded at a rate never before observed in the history of Venezuela. This expansion came with little accountability, transparency, and efficiency.[16]

Soon public expenditures grew out of control, and revenue mismanagement brought high levels of corruption and increasingly unsatisfied demands from citizens who got used to a powerful omnipresent state. With the collapse of the Shah's regime in Iran in 1979, oil prices increased again from US$12.70 in 1978 to US$28.67 in 1980 providing some relief to the coffers of the Venezuelan

---

10 Pérez Alfonzo, "Organización de Países Exportadores de Petróleo," 10.

11 Pérez Alfonzo, "Organización de Países Exportadores de Petróleo," 11.

12 Terry Lynn Karl, *The Paradox of Plenty: Oil Booms and Petro-states*, vol. 6 (Berkeley, CA: University of California Press, 1997), 3.

13 Karl, *The Paradox of Plenty*, 3.

14 Karl, *The Paradox of Plenty*, 71.

15 Karl, *The Paradox of Plenty*, 125.

16 Karl, *The Paradox of Plenty*, 136.

government. Nevertheless, mismanagement of public revenue continued unabated. After another brief increase resulting from the Iran-Iraq war, the price of oil unexpectedly began to drop in 1983. With the price of a barrel of oil below US$15 for the remainder of the decade, urgently needed revenues never materialized. In the 1980s, Venezuela's oil rents plunged by 51.8 percent in real terms.[17]

Revenues collapsed, but private and public expenditures continued unchecked simply because no political leader was willing to pay the price of controlling the downward spiral. In 1989, Venezuelans elected Carlos Andrés Pérez as President again ten years after finishing his first mandate. Pérez promised the return to the days of *"La Gran Venezuela,"* but they were in for a big disappointment.

Shortly after taking office, Pérez quickly implemented a group of market-oriented decisions that amounted to collapsing the old economic model based on state intervention in the economy, subsidies to the private sector, and welfare programs for the poor. The measures, which the government called the big turnabout, or the *Gran Viraje*, included the decision to dismantle the nationalized structure of the oil industry. The economic measures led to waves of public discontent with the government and the political system represented by the president and Venezuela's political parties. On February 27, 1989, 23 days into the new administration, Caracas exploded into a violent social uprising emanating from the poorest sectors of society. The neoliberal measures implemented by Pérez not only exacerbated the pain of millions of Venezuelans but also eroded the legitimacy of the political system. Three years later, on February 4 and again on November 27 1992, a group of men within the armed forces reacted to the neoliberal policies with two military uprisings against the Pérez government. The rebels, who belonged to a clandestine movement known as the Bolivarian Revolutionary Group, were unable to capture power in either military attempt, but catapulted its leader, Colonel Hugo Chávez, to national politics.

Jailed, and later pardoned, Chávez would run for president in 1998. A fierce nationalist throughout his youth and career in Venezuela's armed forces, Chávez pledged to undo the neoliberal reforms, stop the privatization of the oil sector, and work with OPEC in order to seek better oil prices.

Chávez and OPEC: The Door to the Middle East

Venezuela's role in OPEC opened the Middle East to the new president of Venezuela in 1999. Chávez pledged to reverse Venezuela's past reluctance to

---

17 Karl, *The Paradox of Plenty*, 162.

work with OPEC's quota system. "Venezuela was one of the countries whose past administrations had tried to put an end to OPEC, to sabotage [OPEC]" he emphasized in a television interview several years later.[18] Chávez pledged to adhere to a new strategy that intended to cut production to help sagging oil prices recover some strength. For a decade, oil prices had continuously declined; by the time of his inauguration, the price of a barrel of oil was less than US$10. The strategy succeeded. Oil prices more than doubled within a year, reaching US$28 in early 2000. Chávez's proven commitment to OPEC also elevated Venezuela to a position of leadership within the organization.[19]

Figure 6.2   Iranian President Muhammad Khatami and Saudi Crown Prince Abdullah Ibn Abdul Aziz Al-Saud in Caracas with President Hugo Chávez to commemorate 40th anniversary of OPEC, September 28, 2000

Source: © AFP- Adalberto Roque

18 Hugo Chávez, interview with Al Jazeera TV, March 20, 2009, available at http://redsolsur.blogspot.ae/2009/03/entrevista-del-presidente-Chávez-con_31.html

19 Bernard Mommer, *Petróleo Subversivo*, 7–8 on the Petróleos de Venezuela Website, available at http://www.pdvsa.com/interface.sp/database/fichero/article/524/1.PDF

In 2000, Chávez traveled to the Middle East for his first and most important visit to the region. The purpose of the visit was to invite heads of state to attend the commemoration ceremony of the 40th anniversary of the establishment of OPEC. Recalling the itinerary of the trip that began on August 7 and the learning experience it represented, President Chávez described how he met with King Fahd bin Abdulaziz of Saudi Arabia, and "our good friend," Prince Abdulla, who invited him to "visit the northern and southern oil fields ... all and all to be in contact with Saudi Arabia." He then went to Kuwait to meet Sheikh Jaber Al Sabah, then to Qatar to invite Sheikh Hamad bin Khalifa Al Thani. He finished his tour of the Gulf in the United Arab Emirates, were he was "splendidly" received by Sheikh Zayed Al Nahayan, who confirmed that one of the Sheikhs of the Federation would attend the meeting in Caracas. "One of the Emirs from this country is coming, you know this is a federation," he explained back in Venezuela. From the United Arab Emirates he flew to Iran, where he met president Khatami; and from Iran, he travelled by land to Iraq.[20]

The visit to Iraq was particularly important because it exposed Chávez to the devastation caused by the sanctions imposed by the Security Council on Saddam Hussein's regime after the invasion of Kuwait in 1990. Back in Venezuela, Chávez emerged as one of the few critics of the UN sanctions. Chávez discussed his experience in Iraq in the following manner:

> You know, for the last ten years, there has been a blockade on Iraq. I think this is taking too long. Ten years of blockade! Baghdad is not hell, and Saddam is not the devil. There are children in Baghdad—I saw them—there are children with cancer who cannot be treated because of the blockade ... Infections, cancers, tumours and illnesses of all types, and then, medicines are under ration. I think this is savage, and I call, first to humanism; we first have to remember that we are all sons of God, the children of Baghdad and Iraq are like the children from Venezuela, North America and South America and Africa, they are children of the world ... I call on the United Nations to put an end to the blockade of Iraq. I make this call from the bottom of my heart, because I went there and I have seen [the situation there]. Go there, why do not you go? Go and talk with the people of Iraq? It is of basic justice.[21]

20 Hugo Chávez, "Discurso del Presidente de la República Bolivariana de Venezuela, Hugo Chávez Frías, con motivo de informar al país sobre el viaje a los países de la OPEC," August 16, 2000, in 2000, Año de la legitimación de poderes. Selección de discursos del Presidente de la República Bolivariana de Venezuela, Hugo Chávez Frías, (Caracas: Ediciones Presidencia de la Republica, 2005), 353.

21 Chávez, "Discurso del Presidente de la República Bolivariana de Venezuela, Hugo Chávez Frías, con motivo de informar al país sobre el viaje a los países de la

He was candid regarding his previous "absolute lack of knowledge" of the situation in Iraq, about the region in general and about the importance that the trip had on his own education of the situation in the Arab World.[22]

The trip to Iraq did not sit well with the US State Department, but Chávez would put the criticism aside:

> I did not know, I truly did not know, that since the war between Iraq and Kuwait in 1990, no other head of state had ever visited Baghdad … I found that out after this issue created such uproar. It was never our intention to cause such uproar.

In what would be his first clash with the US, he explicitly referenced the State Department's disappointment with his visit to Iraq. Chávez responded defiantly:

> I found when I was over there that the State Department's spokesman said that they were irritated. What's the name of those creams one puts on when one get a rash? We should send them one of those, so the irritation does not go too far..[23]

On September 20 2000, a month after his trip to Iraq, Chávez inaugurated the Second Meeting of Heads of State and Government of OPEC in Caracas. The first meeting had been held in Algiers in 1975. In his opening remarks, Chávez welcomed his "brothers" from the "powerful Arab, Islamic world."[24] Chávez wanted the meeting to serve as an opportunity for member states to reconnect to the original principles of the organization as envisioned by Juan Pablo Pérez Alfonzo. OPEC, he insisted to the other heads of state, was an instrument of "unity as a strategy towards freedom." Chávez continued reminding his audience that OPEC was the product of the hard work of two Quixote's: the "distinguished Venezuelan", Juan Pablo Pérez Alfonzo, "may

---

OPEC," 354–355. Chávez was not the only person denouncing the humanitarian consequences of the Sanctions. See Geoff Simons, "Targeting the Powerless: Sanctions on Iraq," *Global Dialog*, Summer (2000), 55–67.

22 Al Jazeera, Interview with Hugo Chávez, March 20 2009, available at http://redsolsur.blogspot.ae/2009/03/entrevista-del-presidente-Chávez-con_31.html

23 Chávez, "Discurso del Presidente de la República Bolivariana de Venezuela, Hugo Chávez Frías, con motivo de informar al país sobre el viaje a los países de la OPEC,", 354.

24 Chávez, "Discurso del Presidente de la República Bolivariana de Venezuela, Hugo Chávez Frías, con motivo de la Instalación de la II Cumbre de la Organización de Países Exportadores de Petróleo," , in *"Año de la religitimación de poderes"Selección de Discursos del Presidente de la República Bolivariana de Venezuela Hugo Chávez Frías* (Caracas: Ediciones de la Presidencia de la República, 2005), 510.

God have him in his holy glory", and the Saudi, Abdula Al Tariki.[25] "OPEC," he told his guests, "is without any doubt because of its origins, an instrument in the fight for justice and for liberation." He insisted that all members were obligated to reconnect with OPEC's mission "for [social] transformation, and therefore for peace, for development and harmony." Chávez called for unity as the only response to what he described as the worst political, economic, and cultural crisis that the world had experienced. The only way out of the crisis was through the "union of our efforts, the union of our people, our cultures, our economies, of our sovereign wills".[26] Invoking Simón Bolívar, the founding father of five Latin American republics, Chávez called for unity in the midst of external challenges: "Let us unite, and we will be invincible."[27]

Challenging the US in the Middle East

A year later, following Al Qaeda's terrorist attacks on September 11 2001, the US was on the offensive in Afghanistan in what President George W. Bush had branded as a "war on terrorism." The military response to Al Qaeda began with the invasion of Afghanistan to eradicate the Taliban regime accused of harboring Al Qaeda. Less than a month after the attacks, the US launched a military invasion of Afghanistan. Shortly after the invasion, Chávez emerged as the only head of state that dared to question how the US was operating in Afghanistan. The US could count on Venezuela's solidarity when it came to its fight against terrorism, "nobody should be mistaken about it" Chávez reiterated, but Washington should not consider this to translate into an unconditional authorization to act without any restriction in regards to the local civilian population. "We support the fight against terrorism," Chávez argued, "but do not understand this as a *carte blanche* to do anything." He argued that Venezuela supported chasing terrorists down. However, while showing a photo of an Afghani family killed during an American raid, he accused Washington of "combating terror with terror." Chávez confronted Bush on prime-time television and dared him to: "Find out the terrorists," he said, "but not like this."

---

25   Chávez, "Discurso del Presidente de la República Bolivariana de Venezuela, Hugo Chávez Frías, con motivo de la Instalación de la II Cumbre de la Organización de Países Exportadores de Petróleo," 511.

26   Chávez, "Discurso del Presidente de la República Bolivariana de Venezuela, Hugo Chávez Frías, con motivo del acto de instalación de la II cumbre de la Organización de Países Exportadores de Petróleo," 511.

27   Chávez, "Discurso del Presidente de la República Bolivariana de Venezuela, Hugo Chávez Frías, con motivo del acto de instalación de la II cumbre de la Organización de Países Exportadores de Petróleo," 522.

He showed the photo again: "Look, these kids were alive yesterday, they were having dinner with their father when a bomb—like the ones they are dropping on Afghanistan—was dropped on them."[28]

Afghanistan was only the first step in what was taking shape as a new US foreign policy with a primary focus on the Middle East. Based in part on ideas first expressed by President Woodrow Wilson at the end of the First World War, the Bush administration was discussing the use of force as an effective tool in bringing about political changes in the region in 2002. The use of force intended to transform old dictatorships into liberal democracies. Also known as the "Bush Doctrine," the strategy rested on the principle that democracy would prevail in the world as an inherent human value. Once liberated, the drive for freedom would turn dictatorship into democratic regimes. These new democracies would embrace free trade and, more importantly, would be trusted international partners of other democracies.[29] The doctrine was universal in scope, but it was aimed at the Middle East, and at the Arab world in particular, where there was the utmost urgency of transformation. Regime change, even if it had to come through the use of force, was on the horizon.

As the implementation of the doctrine was taking shape and Iraq was being targeted as the first country to undergo such forcible regime change, Venezuela was hit by political instability and rumors of a coup d'état against President Chávez. The economic and political changes that Chávez had been introducing into the country were expanding the role of the state in the economy. These changes were enlarging the social safety-net with a range of programs that intended to end income disparity and to ease the fate of the poor. With a new Constitution and a mandate to govern with broad powers until 2006, Chávez was not losing any time in transforming Venezuela. Soon, however, his reforms contravened the interests of a political elite and middle class who were afraid of seeing their country transformed overnight into what they considered to be a government that closely resembled that of socialist Cuba. Chávez's supporters and opponents clashed on the streets of Caracas throughout the first months of 2002. The opposition claimed that the protests were infiltrated by supporters of the President who were creating chaos and using snipers to kill innocent people, the government claimed exactly the opposite. Days of confusion and acrimonious discussions ended on April 11 with a successful coup d'état

28 Hugo Chávez "Discurso del Presidente de la República Bolivariana de Venezuela Hugo Chávez Frías con motivo de su gira presidencial por Europa, Asia, África y América," October 29, 2001, in Ministerio de Comunicación e Información (ed.) *2001 Año de las Leyes Habilitantes* (Caracas: Ediciones de la Presidencia de la República, 2005), 543.

29 Tony Smith, *A Pact with the Devil: Washington's Bid fo r World Supremacy and the Betrayal of the American Promise* (New York: Routledge, 2007), 1–23.

organised by elements within the armed forces, the media, and the business elite. The new President Pedro Carmona, from the conservative Venezuelan Federation of Chambers of Commerce, *Fedecámaras*, pledged to undo the changes undertaken by Chávez. The coup lasted only three days. Chávez was returned to power on April 13 2002 after a popular uprising against the coup leaders which counted on the support of members of the Armed Forces that had remained loyal to Chávez.

Back in power, Chávez was convinced that the US was the ultimate mastermind of the April coup and had used the local bourgeoisie as its instrument. Washington, he argued, made his government, not Iraq, the first target of the Bush Doctrine. Chávez was convinced that his failed removal from office was part of a wider military campaign to remove regimes that might contravene Washington's policies, but essentially this operation was a campaign for the political control of oil-producing countries. "They want to expel us from government, they already put us through a coup d'état hatched in Washington."[30]

Chávez was not alone in his conclusions. The Egyptian press noted the similarities of the situation in Venezuela to what they predicted was about to happen across the Arab World. "[B]uilding on the fresh lessons from the Chávez experience," the Egyptian newspaper Al Ahram noted,

> few analysts can fail to see a parallel in the Middle East. CIA-sponsored covert operations have at least one highly visible candidate: President Saddam Hussein of Iraq … [o]ther less visible targets would be Syria and Iran. The two are patrons and supporters of Hezbollah resistance against Israel's transgressions against Lebanon. Both countries refuse to accept the United States' agenda of the "war against terrorism" without raising serious questions.[31]

In April 2003, the US launched a military campaign against Iraq. Chávez stood as a fierce critic of the military intervention in Iraq, and the Bush doctrine that justified the acts. Chávez argued before millions of viewers on the Qatari television news channel Al-Jazeera in December 2004: "We had not hesitated to describe the invasion of Iraq as an aggression against a people. It cannot be

---

30 Hugo Chávez, Discurso del Presidente de la República Bolivariana de Venezuela, Hugo Chávez Frías, con motivo de su intervención en la XXVIII Cumbre del Mercado Común del Sur (MERCOSUR)," *2005 Año del Salto Adelante Hacia la Construcción del Socialismo del Siglo XXI. Selección de discursos del Presidente de la República Bolivariana de Venezuela, Hugo Chávez Frías* (Caracas: Ediciones de la Presidencia de la República, 2005), 352..

31 Eiman Al Amir, *Al Ahram Weekly* online, May 2–8, 2002, available at http://weekly.ahram.org.eg/2002/584/op13.htm

described as a war on terrorism. It is terrorism itself."[32] A year later, at the first meeting of Arab and Latin American heads of state in Brasilia in 2005, Chávez again linked events in Venezuela and Iraq. He called for deep reflection on both sides of the Atlantic regarding how to confront wars that were unleashed not to bring about democracy, but to consolidate imperialist domination through control of the oil reserves of the two regions. According to Chávez,

> Venezuela is under the threat of North American imperialism; we have confronted destabilisation for the last two years, a coup d'état hatched in Washington, and we still continue to endure aggression from the most powerful empire that has ever existed on this planet and I think that in this sense, Arabia and South America are similar: we have the largest reserves of oil in the world, something that unleashes the imperialist voracity. There is a strong smell of oil in these wars![33]

His unequivocal and public rejection of the war in Iraq contrasted sharply with the reaction of Arab leaders across the region. In general, there was a fractured consensus regarding how to respond to the military campaign. There was a general opposition towards the invasion of Iraq across the region, but no state leader dared to confront the United States decision in public. Saudi Arabia rejected the war, fearing that a future Iraq controlled by a Shi'a majority might eventually enhance Iran's role in the region. However, Saudi Arabia was not going to be an obstacle to the military campaign. With economies that rely heavily on US aid, Jordan and Egypt issued timid rejections of the war and refused to adopt a more confrontational stance. Syria voiced its opposition, not much because it was not pleased seeing a long-time enemy being deposed but possibly out of fear that the Al Assad regime might be next.[34] The only

---

32 Hugo Chávez, interview by Faysal Al-Qasim, Al Jazeera TV, Doha, December 3, 2004.

33 Hugo Chávez "Discurso del Presidente de la República Bolivariana de Venezuela Hugo Chávez Frías con motivo de la I Cumbre de la Comunidad Suramericana de Naciones y la Liga Árabe de Naciones," in *2005 "Año del Salto Adelante" Hacia la Construcción del Socialismo del Siglo XXI. Selección de discursos del Presidente de la República Bolivariana de Venezuela, Hugo Chávez Frías*. Brasilia, Brazil, May 10, 2005 (Caracas: Ediciones de la Presidencia de la República, 2005) 340.

34 Robert J. Bookmiller, "Abdullah's Jordan: America's Anxious Ally," *Alternatives: Turkish Journal of International Relations*, 2.2 (2003), 180; Neil MacFarquhar, "A Sense of Gloom Is Felt within the Arab World," *New York Times*, March 19, 2003. Fawaz A. Georges, "Rudderless in the Storm," *Dissent (00123846)*, 51.1 (2004), 9–13; Susan Sachs, "Arab Nations Brace for an Upheaval from a War in Iraq," *New York Times*, March 16, 2003.

vociferous rejection, which in many ways interpreted the feelings of millions across the region, was coming from Caracas.

Nasserism in the Twenty-first Century

Chávez called for a common front uniting Latin Americans and Arabs against imperialism and the world order that had emerged in the last decade of the twentieth century. As he began to articulate a transnational discourse that confronted this new world order, the image of Nasser started to emerge as a constant reference in his demands for unity between Latin Americans and Arabs against imperialism while at the same time placed him within a continuum of global leaders from the South. During the first South American-Arab summit of countries in Brasilia in 2005, Chávez proclaimed himself as a Nasserist. "I am very Nasserist. I wish I could have been at the orders of my colonel, Gamal Abdel Nasser." Later, quoting a passage from Nasser's *The Philosophy of the Revolution*, Chávez called for the Arab world to assume its historical role and recalled Nasser's message for unity, courage, and leadership.

> I don't know exactly why I imagine, constantly, that in this part of the world where we live, there is a role without an actor, a magnificent role constantly in search of someone that knows how to perform it. And I don't know why I imagine this role, this mission, to put it better, is wandering around this huge landscape that surrounds us looking for someone to perform it, until itself collapses near our border, demanding that we perform this role, because no one but us could play this role.[35]

Nasser's historical challenge was now being taken up by Chávez, who demanded that both Arabs and Latin Americans assume "the mission to dignify and lead our peoples to a better world".[36]

Sixty years after Nasser's demand for a common front against colonialism and imperialism in favor of unity, the President of Venezuela called on Arabs and Latin Americans to "retake Nasser's flags." The world they now confronted was unipolar, but the structures of colonialism and exploitation remained intact,

---

35 Chávez, "Discurso del Presidente de la República Bolivariana de Venezuela Hugo Chávez Frías con motivo de la I Cumbre de la Comunidad Suramericana de Naciones y la Liga Árabe de Naciones," 341–342.
36 Chávez, "Discurso del Presidente de la República Bolivariana de Venezuela Hugo Chávez Frías con motivo de la I Cumbre de la Comunidad Suramericana de Naciones y la Liga Árabe de Naciones," 342.

he argued. During an interview on Syrian television years later, Chávez would call for Arabs and Latin Americans to action. They had to

> retake the flags of pan-Arabism, to retake the flags of Arab unity, retake the flags of Arab dignity. Not a single Arab should be crawling to the interests of the American empire that has caused so much damage to the Arab people. Not a single Latin American should be crawling to the interests of the Yankee Empire that has caused us so much damage.

Echoing Nasser, Chávez declared that his opposition to America and its allies in the Arab World and in Latin America was part and parcel of Nasser's anticolonialist call. His fight, quoting Nasser, was, "the battle of destiny." Claiming to be carrying Nasser's flag, Venezuela urged both regions to take action: "Enough of so many defeats, enough of so many divisions."[37]

The 61st General Assembly of the United Nations in 2006 became the perfect world forum for Chávez to "retake the flags of Nasser" and to challenge the actions of the US in Latin America and the Arab world. The theatrics of his speech and the virulence of the attacks helped him claim a position of leadership in the imagination of the Arab world. His speech came at a moment when the situation in the region had destabilized further after the Israeli response to military attacks launched by the militia Hezbollah from Lebanon in the summer of that year. Although the human casualties, the new wave of refugees and the severe damage to Lebanon's infrastructure had enraged the Arab world regardless of sectarian divisions, Arab leaders observed, as in the case of Iraq, what seemed to be an acquiescent silence to the Israeli invasion. Some believed that among the Sunni governments in the region—Saudi Arabia, the Gulf monarchies, Egypt, and Jordan—it was possible to conclude that there was some degree of tacit approval for what could be perceived as the containing Iran's influence in Lebanon.[38]

Chávez never made reference to this complex web of regional political interests. He wanted to use the United Nations forum to indict the Bush administration for the crimes committed in Lebanon by Washington's ally, and in general for the crisis facing the Arab world. At the center of this was the American promotion of democracy through regime change. Chávez was convinced that Venezuela had been the first victim of this policy that was now being applied across the Arab world. "The President of the United States,

---

37 Hugo Chávez, interview by Syrian Television, Syria, September 6, 2009, available at https://www.youtube.com/watch?v=jHqG6xFWH9w

38 Iraqi Prime Minister Denounces Israel's Actions. http://www.nytimes.com/2006/07/20/world/middleeast/20shiites.html?ref=iraq&module=Search&mabReward=relbias%3Ar&_r=0

whom I call 'the devil,' came here talking as if he was the owner of the world," he said in reference to President Bush's speech the day before. Democracy and neoliberal economic models imposed through the use of force were the new face of imperialism, the Venezuelan President argued. The Nasserist of the twenty-first century elaborated further:

> They want to impose a democratic model on us; but according to their own conception of this model: the false democracy of the elites. And also a very original democratic model: imposed through the use of bombs, bombardments, based on invasions and cannons! What a democracy! to that hegemonic drive, the call from Caracas to the Arab world was "insurgence."! [39]

Using the case of the recent Israeli invasion of Lebanon, Chávez continued his attacks on President Bush. "[Bush] spoke to the people of Lebanon: 'Many of you have seen your homes and your communities trapped among cross fire.' How cynical!" he replied. The events of that summer in Lebanon were, according to Chávez,

> Imperialist fire, fascist fire, murderer fire and genocidal fire, from the Empire and Israel against the innocent people of Palestine and the people of Lebanon! That is the truth! However, now they say that they suffer, that we are suffering because we have seen their homes destroyed.

What would the people of Afghanistan, Iran, Lebanon, or Palestine tell Bush if they had the opportunity to talk to him directly? Chávez claimed to have the answer because he knew "most of the souls of those people", and they would have told Bush, "yankee go home." [40]

Arab Popularity

As a vocal critic of the US, Chávez had received media attention in the Arab world since the early years of his administration. Al Jazeera, the leading Arab news channel at the time, echoed the widespread support Chávez was gaining

---

39 Chávez claimed to be basing his speech on Noam's Chomsky's book, *Hegemony and Survival: America's Quest for Global Dominance*, which he had read days before.

40 Hugo Chávez, Address to the 61st General Assembly of the United Nations, September 20, 2006, Petróleos de Venezuela, S.A (PDVSA), available at http://www.pdvsa.com/index.php?tpl=interface.sp/design/biblioteca/readdoc.tpl.html&newsid_obj_id=3010&newsid_temas=110

among Arabs across all countries. In his first interview with Al Jazeera in 2004, the anchor said to Chávez,

> Undoubtedly, you are aware that you are very popular in the Arab world and millions of Arabs support you. I read a commentary some time ago which says if President Chávez were to run in an Arab presidential election he would win more than 90 per cent of the votes—I mean a genuine 90 percent and not falsified.

Chávez's popularity, the anchor stressed, depended on two things: "The first is your care for the poor and the downtrodden in your country, and the second is your defiance of the only superpower in the world, namely, the United States of America."[41]

Chávez began to articulate a close personal identification not only with the politics of the region but also with its people, even claiming over time that he himself was an Arab. Chávez's spirit, he told Algerian President Abdelaziz Bouteflika in 2002, was "like the spirit of those men of the desert. A man of the desert, perhaps because I was born in a huge savannah similar in its extent and in its horizon to those beautiful deserts."[42] Later, at the first Arab-South American summit in Rio in 2005, he expressed how close he felt to Arab culture.

> I have the joy of visiting the deserts of Saudi Arabia, of riding camels; of dancing to the beat of fireworks and the firing of traditional arms in the Arab world. Beyond the language, it is the same soul, the same feelings.[43]

As he radicalized his discourse against the US and Israel, Chávez assumed his Arab persona more assertively. One month before his speech at the General Assembly in 2006, Chávez confessed in a second interview to Al Jazeera that

> My heart beats along with millions of Arab hearts. I could have been an Arab. I have crossed deserts, I have ridden camels, I have sung along with the Bedouins.

---

41 Interview December 6, 2004, Al Jazeera TV, Doha.

42 Hugo Chávez, "Discurso del Presidente de la República Bolivariana de Venezuela Hugo Chávez Frías con motivo de la inauguración del III foro de alto nivel sobre la cooperación África, América Latina, y el Caribe," February 19, 2002, in Ministerio de Comunicación e Información (Ed.) 2002 *Año de la resistencia antiimperialista. Selección de discursos del Presidente de la República Bolivariana de Venezuela, Hugo Chávez Frías.* (Caracas: Ediciones de la Presidencia de la República, 2002), 186.

43 Chávez, "Discurso del Presidente de la República Bolivariana de Venezuela Hugo Chávez Frías con motivo de la I Cumbre de la Comunidad Suramericana de Naciones y la Liga Árabe de Naciones," 2005), 338.

I have learned in those years to love and respect the Arab people. We feel that the Israeli aggression against Palestine and Lebanon is directed against us.[44]

By the end of the decade, his popularity had rocketed in the Arab world, and so has his own personal identification with the region. In one of his lasts visits to the region, he confined to a television host in Damascus that "I humbly say, and you must forgive me, that I consider myself another Arab, another Syrian. I have in my veins Arab blood."[45]

Projection of the Arab–Israeli Conflict onto Latin America

In the months following the Israeli invasion of Lebanon in 2006, Chávez continued redefining himself as an Arab and also began to establish clear parallels between the situation in the Middle East and the growing tensions between Venezuela and its South American neighbor, Colombia. According to Chávez, the ultimate cause of conflict in the world was the influence of the US over countries that acted as proxies for its economic and political interests. In the Middle East, that country clearly was Israel. In South America, Colombia was emerging as "the Israel" of the region. Under this logic, both Israel and Colombia were acting in close coordination to advance the Washington's domination. The countries advanced these interests by using force on behalf of the US and by deepening the divisions among nations that should be united in a common front against the unipolar system. Chávez's Venezuela stood in marked contrast, he argued. Venezuela not only supported the interests of the Arab people but also actively opposed Colombia, the emerging mirror image of Israel in South America.

In March 2008, the pro-American Colombian government of Alvaro Uribe bombarded a cell of communist rebels—the Revolutionary Armed Forces of Colombia, FARC, which was hiding across the border in neighboring Ecuador. The military attack gunned down the second-in-command of FARC, Raúl Reyes, but was widely rejected as an illegal use of force against Ecuadorian territory. Chávez denounced President Uribe's actions and his alliance with the US. Infuriated, Chávez warned that Colombia was acting like an arm of the US, as "the Israel of the region," militarizing their relationship and dividing what should otherwise be one Latin American nation. Chávez warned Uribe that if he had tried the same actions in Venezuela, the response would have been very different. On a television speech to the nation, the Venezuelan president warned:

---

44 Hugo Chávez, interview by Mohamed Kirshan, Al Jazeera TV, Doha, August 4, 2006.

45 Hugo Chávez, interview by Syrian Television, Damascus, September 6, 2009.

This could be the beginning of a war in South America because if you try to do that in Venezuela, President Uribe, I will send you a Sukhoi [Russian armed plane], my friend, just for you to know. We are not going to allow, by anything in the world, that Colombia becomes the Israel of this land. Israel invades Lebanon, bombards, kills … in legitimate defence, they say, Israel invades the Gaza Strip, bombards, to assassinate one Palestinian leader, they bombard a whole neighbourhood and kill one hundred people, they don't care who falls. Israel says this is in legitimate defence; it is the fist of the Empire in the Arab world, in order to prevent Arab unity, to fragment this world, to spread misery and war. Uribe, we are not going to allow you to install here in South America another Israel, no matter what it costs, we are not going to allow you to do that.[46]

Chávez's projection of the Arab-Israeli conflict onto Venezuela's foreign policy in South America intensified with the heightening of the conflict in the Middle East. In Palestine, general elections had brought divisions between the two most important political groups. The winner of Palestine's legislative elections in 2006, the Islamic group Hamas, ended up in a civil conflict the following year with the Palestinian National Authority, which was controlled by the secular organization Fatah. Displaced from power despite having won the elections, Hamas was confined to governing the Gaza Strip from which different factions of the organization launched rocket attacks against Israel in 2008. In December 2008, Israel responded with a major military response in the Gaza Strip that destroyed Gaza's infrastructure and killed more than one thousand people in four weeks. As with the invasion of Lebanon in 2006, Arab leaders were divided and passively ineffective despite widespread public opposition in the streets. In particular, Jordan, Egypt, and Saudi Arabia were understood to have strong reasons to support Israel with their silence against the potentially destabilizing power of Hamas in the region.

From Caracas, Chávez provided his own perspective on the origins and ultimate causes of the Israeli military attack on the Gaza Strip in December 2008. According to Chávez, the crisis was another step in a long strategy that started when "our brother," the Palestinian leader Yasser Arafat was "assassinated" "poisoned" in 2004. "I do not doubt it, I do not have proof, but I do not have any doubts." The operation to assassinate Arafat was launched by the CIA and the Israeli Mossad, Chávez argued, his death was ordained to plant the seeds of the division of the Palestinian movement. The first step in "weakening the Palestinian movement" because Arafat was "the only one who could unite Fatah and Hamas." Chávez continued that the "strategists of Imperial intelligence" knew that there would be a Palestinian "schism" between

---

46 "Chávez compara a Colombia con Israel", available at http://www.youtube.com/watch?v=ZsAUW_GOREk.

the two groups as a direct outcome of the free elections that occurred in 2007. These strategists knew that Hamas would later be elected to government, "branded as a terrorist", and once these events had occurred, they had "the excuse to invade, to kill, [and] bombard." The ultimate goal was to "wipe" the Palestinians "out [of Gaza]." That was the reason, Chávez explained, behind the Israeli withdrawal of Gaza in 2005. The withdrawal cleared the land of Israelis so army could enter later. Once free of "settlers" Israel was "free to act", and expel "more than a million Palestinians". The world was standing by with their "arms crossed", Chávez argued, but "not in Venezuela. Venezuela stands like one united people demanding peace and respect for the Palestinian people."

Chávez warned Israel and the United States of the response from Latin America to the events in Gaza.

> Israel has ended up becoming the assassin arm of the American Empire, and they have tried to create Israelis in Latin America; there would be no assassin arm here in Latin America. In Latin America there would not be an assassin arm of the Empire to hurt our people. Each day Latin America would be more united and therefore more free. We will stand united.

From South America Chávez called Arabs to unite against the empire: "I hope one day the Arab world, the Arab people truly unite!"[47]

On January 5 2009, Venezuela expelled the Israeli Ambassador Shlomo Cohen. Three days later, the streets of Caracas were filled with thousands of government-organized protesters against Israel. Invoking the memory of the founding father of Venezuela, General Simón Bolívar, the marchers chanted, "Alert! Alert! The sword of Bolívar is walking in the land of Palestine!" and "Israel: fascist, assassin, and terrorists." Leading the protests, Venezuelan Foreign Minister Nicolás Maduro declared the actions of Israel in Palestine to be "State terrorism."[48]

A week later, Venezuela broke relations with Israel. The following day, the Venezuelan embassy in Amman received flowers from dozens of protesters chanting Chávez's name and demanding that the Jordanian government break relations with Israel. These protesters provided evidence regarding the inaction

---

47 Hugo Chávez, public rally, January 11, 2009, "Hugo Chávez about the Holocaust in Gaza Palestina, England & German," available at http://www.youtube.com/watch?v=-1W52u3aDsY&feature=related.

48 Venezolana de Televisión, "Pueblo de Venezuela repudia a gobierno de Israel por holocausto en Gaza," January 8, 2009, available at http://www.vtv.gov.ve/noticias-nacionales/13106

of the Kingdom of Jordan and Venezuela's support for the Arab cause.[49] For someone who "had entered the soul of the Arabs", as Chávez claimed, breaking with Israel was "a gesture of responsibility".

> In regard to the fight for the dignity of a people, the respect for the life of a people, and in my very own case in regard to the love of one people, and in regard to the admiration that I feel, and we, the Bolivarians, feel for the Arab people, for the Palestinian people ... I love Arabia. Since I was a kid, I entered in contact with that culture like magic, that people, that magic from the savannah where I was born: the Arabs . I had the opportunity to enter into the soul of the Arab people, so what I did was a gesture of responsibility.[50]

His commitment to the Arab cause was not unnoticed in the Middle East. In Lebanon, Hassan Nasrallah, the leader of the Shi'a militia of Hezbollah, reminded his followers of the importance and transcendence of Chávez's actions.

> [Chávez] dealt a severe blow to those who are now hosting Israeli ambassadors in their capitals and do not have enough courage even to think about telling them to leave their country. Today Arab leaders are required to learn lessons from a leader in Latin America. They have to learn from him how to show support for the people of Palestine.[51]

In Kuwait City, protesters carried posters thanking Chávez for his determination. In the Kuwaiti parliament, there were calls to move the seat of the Arab League from Cairo to Caracas as Chávez had proved that "he was more Arab than some Arabs."[52]

The conflict in Gaza deepened Chávez's conviction regarding the parallels between the Middle East and South America. Tensions between Colombia and Venezuela increased in July 2009, when Colombia announced that it would permit civilian and military personnel from the US to operate in seven military bases around the country.[53] Chávez saw this announcement as further

---

49 http://www.eluniversal.com/2009/01/09/en_ing_esp_venezuela-condemns-a_09A2187285

50 Hugo Chávez, Interview by Dima Khatib, Al Jazeera, Caracas, March 30, 2009.

51 Sayed Hassan Nasrallah, "Ashuraa Gaza Speech," available at http://www.youtube.com/watch?v=CpoGVQLRcOw&feature=related

52 Ahmed Shihab-Eldin, "Competing Meetings on Gaza in Kuwait, Qatar Highlight Divisions in Arab World (Video)," available at http://www.huffingtonpost.com/ahmed-shihabeldin/competing-meetings-in-kuw_b_158801.html

53 "Bases militares estadounidenses en Colombia." El País, 12, November 2009. Available at elpais.com/diario/2009/11/12/opinion/1257980405_850215.html

evidence that Colombia was being transformed by the US into an "Israel in Latin America". Economic and political relations with Colombia would have to be revised.

> We don't want any problems with Colombia, but they [Colombians] go around the rivers, shooting, cross borders, they have Israeli airplanes with Israeli pilots, the same ones that bombard Gaza and kill children. The Yankees and the Israelis are here. Now, they said that we give refuge to terrorist cells from Hezbollah, they are just getting the ground ready for an aggression. They should not try this, because they are going to find the sons of Bolívar ready to defend this holy land![54]

Chávez took his message to Syria as part of a grand tour of the Middle East in September 2009.[55] He was by now the most popular foreign leader in the Arab world, and was basking in his popularity, so he wanted to make the case that Latin America was becoming a mirror image of the conflict between Israel and its neighbors.[56] He argued that

> to the State of Israel we need to ask and demand that it take its hands out of Latin America, because the American Empire, there, is trying to convert Colombia, also our sister nation and daughter of our father Bolívar ... into the Israel of Latin America.

Chávez reaffirmed the connection between the two regions because they were fighting a common enemy: the American Empire. "[L]ook that we are confronting the same enemy, Syria and Venezuela confronting the same enemies: Imperialism and its lackeys here in the Middle East and there in Latin America. That is why we need to unite." This fight against imperialism was nothing new neither in Latin America nor in the Arab World. He, Chávez, claimed to be part of a lineage of fighters against imperialism:

---

54 Hugo Chávez, "Agresiones del gobierno Colombiano obligan a Venezuela a revisar relaciones," Venezolana de televisión, (July 24, 2009) http://www.alopresidente. gob.ve/noticias/2/1310/agresiones_del_gobierno.html

55 The 11-day tour also took him to Libya, Iran, Algeria, Russia, and Belorussia.

56 Shibley Telhami and Zogby International, Arab Public Opinion Surveys, available at http://www.sadat.umd.edu/new%20surveys/surveys.htm; and Hugo Chávez interview, Al Jazeera, March 20, 2009, available at http://redsolsur.blogspot. ae/2009/03/entrevista-del-presidente-Chávez-con_31.html

I am Nasserist . . . I am Nasserist since I was a little kid, I am a soldier of Nasser, I am a soldier of Bolívar, I am a soldier of Fidel Castro. I am from that lineage of revolutionaries like Che!, that is what I am![57]

Unaware of the political turmoil that was soon to engulf Syria and many other countries in the region, Chávez used his visit in 2009 to praise Syrian President Bashar Al Assad and to encourage Syrians to support his regime.

The leadership of Bashar Al Assad, my brother, the President, goes beyond the boundaries of Syria and embraces now the Middle East and the Arab world. I can say that Bashar Al Assad, my brother . . . he is humble, a humble man, adored by his people . . . if I can ask something of the Syrian people, to whom I feel I belong, I feel I belong to this people ... is that every day you support even more your leader, that courageous president who is Bashar Al Assad.[58]

The Arab Spring

In December 2010 events in a small village in Tunisia would shake power structures across the Arab world. Mohammed Bouazizi, a street vendor and the victim of the powerful and omnipresent security services in Tunisia, decided to self-immolate after being denied the right to work on the street by the local police. This personal tragedy soon engulfed the country into a revolt against the regime that had held power for the last 23 years. The revolt exposed the government's authoritarian nature and the income disparity that resulted from years of applying market-oriented reforms to the economy. Ranked by the World Economic Forum Global Competitiveness Report in 2009 as "the Most Competitive Country in Africa", the country was praised for its open and efficient economy, and its social stability.[59] The benefits of the macroeconomic policies benefitted the coffers of President Ben Ali, his family, and entourage, but left the growing number of educated but unemployed youth economically and politically marginalized.[60] After the events of December, fear of the security

---

57 Hugo Chávez in Suwaida, Syria, available at http://www.youtube.com/watch?v=zZO3hVVB5uI; see also his interview with Al Jazeera https://www.youtube.com/watch?v=bKzQfe86K1Y

58 Chávez, interview with Al Jazeera.

59 Anver Versi, "Why Tunisia is Africa's most Competitive Economy," *Middle East*, 404 (2009), 35–42, accessed June 22, 2014.

60 Stephen R. Hurt, Karim Knio, and J. Magnus Ryner, "Social Forces and the Effects of (Post)-Washington Consensus Policy in Africa: Comparing Tunisia and South Africa," *Round Table* 98.402 (2009), 307–308, accessed June 22, 2014.

apparatus gave way to massive protests against the regime and a broad call for political change.

Unable to control the situation, Ben Ali left Tunisia on January 14, 2011 for exile in Saudi Arabia. From Tunisia, the popular uprising spread to Egypt, America's staunchest ally in the region. Two weeks after the events in Tunis, Egyptians turned to the streets demanding that Hosni Mubarak leave. The President had been in power for almost 30 years. No longer afraid of the security apparatus, Egyptians had run out of patience with the nepotism, corruption, and inefficiency of the regime. Over the years, the Egyptian government rejected the people's demands for social justice but willingly accepted economic prescriptions for economic restructuring within the framework of neoliberal market reforms.[61]

Figure 6.3   Hugo Chávez and Mohammed Qaddafi in Tripoli, Libya on October 22, 2010. His last visit to the region.

Source: © AFP/Mahmud Turkia

---

61 Osman Salih, Kamal Eldin. "The Roots and Causes of the 2011 Arab Uprisings," *Arab Studies Quarterly*, 35.2 (2013), 187, accessed June 22, 2014,.

Chávez never had a particularly close relation with either of these two regimes. When he took a stand in either the Lebanese or Palestinian conflicts, he would find himself on the opposite side of Egypt and Tunisia. Chávez hinted at his distance with Egypt during his visit to Qatar to attend the Second South American–Arab Countries' meeting in March 2009. Chávez stated that "relations with the government of Egypt, I would say are normal, contained mainly to a diplomatic level".[62]

From Caracas, the events in the Arab world had a clear explanation. The collapse of these two regimes was the consequence of the contradictions inherent to all neoliberal regimes. These contradictions had previously broken out in Venezuela in 1989 during the uprising against the economic policies of President Carlos Andres Perez. What happened in Tunisia and Egypt, Chávez argued, was part of a global uprising against neoliberalism across the world. This uprising had first began in Venezuela precisely when the capitalist world was celebrating the collapse of communism. Regarding the events in Egypt, Chávez spoke to thousands of followers at a rally commemorating the uprising of February 27, 1989.

> [T]he other night I was hearing some "very clever" analysts, saying that what was going on in Egypt was about to happen here. I said to myself, "what an ignorant gentleman"!! He has not realised that popular rebellion that was taking place in Egypt already happened here 22 years ago!! Compañeros!!![63]

Chávez argued that Hosni Mubarak was a dictator and that the events in Cairo were following the "scientific" steps of a revolutionary process. "There was a dictatorship there, a dictatorship that had more than half of the population living in poverty and extreme poverty, that is the fundamental cause [of the uprising]." This was a social uprising against neoliberalism, and Chávez dismissed the Egyptian uprising as the product of the galvanizing forces of social media. "Some are saying that this is the Twitter revolution." However, according to Chávez, the revolution was an uprising against neoliberalism, and from a Marxist perspective the material causes of the revolution were clearly present on the ground.

> There is no revolution that could be planned out of the blue, or with cellular phones, or by Twitter or whatever, no! This is like a fire . . . revolutions are

---

62 Hugo Chávez, interview by Al Jazeera, Doha, Qatar, March 31, 2009, available at http://www.youtube.com/watch?v=Y0fvCW3_aoc

63 Hugo Chávez, "Conmemoración del Caracazo," Petare, Miranda February 27, 2011. Minutes 24–26, available at https://www.youtube.com/watch?v=saYluyXCZlY

born out of objective and subjective conditions, and these are scientific laws duly proved.[64]

The revolution was both against neoliberalism and against a regime so close to the United States and Israel, and its triumph heralded the beginning of a new era in the Arab world. An official communiqué from Caracas shared "its jubilation with the Egyptian people" and pledged to support the decisions that the country would need to make in the future as "the rightful heirs of the flags of that historical leader Gamal Abdel Nasser."[65]

From Cuba Fidel Castro, who retired from power in 2006 leaving in his place his brother Raúl, joined Chávez in his view of these events. Castro presented his own analysis of the events to his readers across Latin America. According to Castro, the Egypt of Nasser, the country that Latin American revolutionaries so much admired in 1960 as a leader of the anticolonialist movement, disappeared under his successor Anwar Al Sadat. The "Arabs felt outraged," with Sadat's negotiations with Israel in 1979, and many broke diplomatic relations with Cairo, Castro reminded his readers. However, Sadat was rewarded by the US. After Sadat signed its peace treaties with Israel in 1979, Castro explained, "Egypt, an Arab country, was transformed into the second largest recipient of North American armaments. To fight against whom? Against another Arab country? Against its own Egyptian people?" Those arms, Castro argued, were used against the people of Egypt when they rose against their government demanding "respect for their more basic rights." The US, Castro argued, looked the other way with respect to "the privileges and the shameless theft of Mubarak's government." [66]

The Arab uprising corresponded with what Latin American revolutionaries believed was a global uprising against market capitalism and US imperialism.

---

64 Hugo Chávez, transcript from ALÓ, Presidente" No. 370, Ciudad Caribia, terraza B, sector 1, Camino de los Indios, estado Vargas. Domingo, February 13, 2011, available at http://www.alopresidente.gob.ve/materia_alo/25/p--1/tp--32/

65 "Gobierno Venezolano saluda genuina lección de madurez política y democrática de pueblo egipcio," available at http://www.avn.info.ve/contenido/gobierno-venezolano-saluda-genuina-lecci%C3%B3n-madurez-pol%C3%ADtica-y-democr%C3%A1tica-pueblo-egipcio

66 Fidel Castro, "La Rebelion Revolucionaria en Egipto," available at http://www.cubadebate.cu/reflexiones-fidel/2011/02/14/la-rebelion-revolucionaria-en-egipto/#.U6qkfvmSySp. In Ecuador, President Rafael Correa joined Chávez in framing the uprising as a popular revolt against a regime supported by the US and Israel. Correa argued that Mubarak was, "simply the bishop of the United States and Israel in North Africa," and that was the reason he was allowed to govern for 30 years. As long as you are a friend of the US, Correa concluded, "it does not matter if you are the greatest dictator or that you act against human rights."

Nevertheless the uprising soon spread to regimes Caracas and Havana had considered for years as close allies: Libya and Syria. The arguments used to explain the events in Egypt and Tunisia could not be used for these two countries. A new articulation of the reality that was unfolding in front of the world was needed.

Chávez had visited Libya in 2009 and attended both the African Union Meeting and the celebrations of the fortieth anniversary of Qaddafi's coming to power—through a coup d'état against the monarch of the time, King Idris. Addressing the delegation of dignitaries at the African Union , Chávez marked the Libyan revolution and the proclamation of the Great Socialist People's Libyan Arab Jamahiriya as part of a continuum of crucial revolutions that shaped the latter part of the twentieth century. The wonders of numerology, this chain of revolutions has taken place in a year that ended with 9, he argued. These included the Chinese Revolution in 1949, the Algerian—no date provided here for obvious reasons, the Cuban Revolution in 1959, the Libyan Revolution in 1969, and the Islamic Revolution of Iran in 1979. Ten years later, "the revolution began" in 1989 in Venezuela, Chávez noted. In 1999, Venezuela "united itself with those victorious revolutions that end in 9. Ancient philosophers and mathematicians have said that this is the perfect number." The celebration of Libya's revolution called for the unity of all revolutionaries across Latin America and the Arab world against a unipolar world. "[W]e need to be free and leave our sons and grandsons a world living in freedom, and the only way to achieve this is … marching on the path of unity in Africa, in Latin America, in the Caribbean." [67]

Chávez argued that Qaddafi was to the Arabs what Simón Bolívar was to Latin America: the founding father of an independent nation and a regional leader beyond the borders of his own country. "[W]hat Simón Bolívar is to us, Muammar Qaddafi is to the Libyan people; he is the liberator of Libya, the creator of the Arab Socialist Republic." Chávez was convinced that Qaddafi was "one of the greatest leaders of the 20th and 21st centuries".[68]

A year later in October 2010, Chávez visited Qaddafi for the sixth time. In Tripoli, he was given a Doctorate Honoris Causa in Humanistic Economy by the

---

67 Hugo Chávez, African Union Meeting, Tripoli, August 31, 2009 , available at http://www.youtube.com/watch?v=5RnI-zbtEPE

68 Hugo Chávez, Isla Margarita, September 28, 2009, "Welcome to Colonel Muammar Qaddafi," available at https://www.youtube.com/watch?v=S5z52srthwc: on the Afro-South American Meeting in Venezuela, see Government of Venezuela, *II Cumbre Africa America del Sur: Cerrando brechas, abriendo oportunidades. Colección Cuadernos para el debate* (Caracas: Ministerio del Poder Popular para la Comunicación y la Informacion, Marzo 2010). Available at http://uptparia.edu.ve/libros_iut/ii_cumbre_asacompendioweb.pdf

Academy of Postgraduate Studies of Tripoli. In his acceptance speech, Chávez told his audience how his early years were influenced by the events in Africa, from the "socialist and revolutionary" Gamal Abdel Nasser to Qaddafi's Green Book and his calls for direct popular democracy. Chávez contended that it was then when "we began to know the bright mind of Qaddafi", "we began to be influenced by African socialism", and his generation began to look at Africa "with hope". He then connected again Qaddafi to a long historical line beginning with the founding fathers of Latin American nations, "fighters of the human cause, of the human nation", a line of soldiers of freedom that Chávez joined as a young officer. "I soon joined the army … and since then, I became a Nasserist soldier, a socialist soldier, a revolutionary, and since then, Qaddafi, Fidel Castro, el Che Guevara, Omar Torrijos, Juan Velasco Alvarado, soldiers of the people." [69]

Four months after his visit to Tripoli, Chávez could not give credit to the reports coming from Libya. They indicated that there was uncontrolled repression of a growing number of citizens protesting Qaddafi's repression and human rights violations. The crackdown on the opposition conducted by a combination of followers and a foreign militia from neighbouring countries was condemned by both the United Nations Human Rights Council and the United Nations Security Council. On February 26, the Security Council placed Libya under an arms embargo and referred the actions of the Libyan leader and his inner circle to the International Criminal Court.[70] Chávez responded days later that "despite the fact that almost everybody, almost everybody, is today condemning Colonel Mu'ammar al Qaddafi, I don't know why – without knowing for a fact what is happening there, and has happened there [in Libya] – I remember Hugo Chávez on April 11." Chávez was referring to the confusing acts of violence that preceded the coup d'état in his country on April 12, 2002. The opposition blamed Chávez and his supporters for the violence suffered when both sides collided in Caracas that day. Chávez recalled that he was called an "assassin, the murderer of his people, the one that ordered his assassins to murder his peaceful people". Making a historical mistake was too easy and Chávez was not going to succumb to media reports from countries that wanted Qaddafi out. He was not going to condemn Qaddafi, "my friend, our friend", without knowing what was really occurring in Libya. This could be only rumors, Chávez argued. Rumors have been a weapon against regimes that stood against capitalism and imperialism; rumors served to lay the ground for future military actions, he argued. As with Libya, Venezuela had been accused

---

69 Hugo Chávez acceptance of Doctorate Honoris Causa, Tripoli, October 23, 2010, available at https://www.youtube.com/watch?v=hOkWatjddFs

70 Resolution 1970 United Nations Security Council, available at http://daccess-dds-ny.un.org/doc/UNDOC/GEN/N11/245/58/PDF/N1124558.pdf?OpenElement

in the past of being a rogue state. Throughout those years, Venezuela had also been accused by its enemies, Chávez argued, among others of protecting Bin Laden in Venezuela, providing uranium to Iran, having an atomic bomb, financing Colombian guerrillas, narcotrafficking, kidnapping, and harboring Al Qaeda cells and terrorism: and, Chávez indicated, "this is all a global farce". Although the situation in Libya was delicate, Chávez warned that there were other intentions behind the US and Western European concerns regarding the situation in Libya. "[T]he United States is exaggerating and distorting the events in order to justify an invasion and they are already announcing one, in Libya."[71]

The situation in Libya, Chávez argued, was close to a civil war, with the opposition and the government controlling parts of the country. "Let us not succumb to the drums of war." Chávez demanded a negotiated solution to the conflict to prevent military intervention by the West. Libya was a "powder house", according to Chávez, with parts of the territory controlled by forces contrary to Qaddafi, and "there are elements that configure a civil war or the preconditions of a civil war." The problem was to identify the leaders of this opposition movement in Libya. Chávez argued, "there must be a leader there, otherwise this is chaos." Chávez was emphatic: Venezuela "stood for peace" and demanded a negotiated solution to the events unfolding.[72]

It was getting too late for negotiations in Libya. By March 2011, the League of Arab States, the African Union, and the Secretary General of the Organization of the Islamic Conference had all condemned the brutal repression of the opposition and the civilian population by Qaddafi's regime. On March 12, the Arab League called on the Security Council to approve a no-fly zone over the country to prevent Qaddafi's forces from bombarding civilians there. Five days later, the Security Council authorized a no-fly zone. In addition, other measures—short of a military occupation of the country—were authorized to protect civilians caught in the conflict.[73]

The consensus in Cuba and Venezuela was that the conflict was about ending the Arab uprising against neoliberalism, controlling Libya's oil and confiscating its monetary reserves, deposited mostly in Western Europe. "[T]he empire now pretends to turn the table and focus only on whatever Gaddafi has done or not," commented Castro. A "latent" opposition was agitated by the US, "or by Gaddafi's own mistakes", but the clear objective was

---

71 Hugo Chávez, "V Promocion de Licenciados y Licenciadas en Educacion. Mencion: desarrollo cultural II Promocion Bicentenaria," Mision Cultura, February 28, 2011, available at https://www.youtube.com/watch?v=Bn6RzGV5b1Y

72 Chávez, "V Promocion de Licenciados y Licenciadas en Educacion."

73 Resolution 1973 United Nations Security Council, available at http://daccess-dds-ny.un.org/doc/UNDOC/GEN/N11/268/39/PDF/N1126839.pdf?OpenElement

"to hit the revolutionary wave unleashed in the Arab world". By capturing the uprising, the West could control future events in Libya. "Until now, no one was saying a word, everybody was silent making business deals."[74] In Caracas, Chávez added another hypothesis on national television during a meeting of the Political Council of the Bolivarian Alliance for the Peoples of Our America (ALBA),[75] an economic and political organization created as a counterbalance to neoliberal market integration, and expand Venezuela's influence across the region. Chávez began with a question: Why were the countries of Europe that not so long ago were friendly toward Qaddafi and ready to engage in business with Gadaffi now turning their backs on him? Oil was only part of the answer. The other was Libya's incredible international reserves. "Qaddafi told me by phone the other day, 'I am speechless,' Chávez recounts, "governments that not long ago were our friends and were sending business delegations, emissaries, etc., are now all of a sudden against me." Libya's reserves, Chávez was convinced, were the ultimate prize that the West was looking for in Libya. Chávez recalled his 2010 visit to Libya. His staff informed him that Libya had a surprising "one hundred eighty billion in international reserves, six times the reserves of Venezuela for a country with one fifth of the population". Shocked by the numbers, he checked the figures with Libya's Foreign Minister, Moussa Koussa. Koussa told Chávez that the number was wrong, that the real figure was "two hundred billion". With the economic crisis across Europe, Chávez reasoned, they all wanted Libya to invest those reserves in their countries. Not long ago "almost all of them" went to see Qaddafi or invited him to Europe, from the largest to the smallest: Berlusconi, Sarkozy, even the King of Spain. These countries were all competing against one another for investments, "like vampires to see who was able to suck more", Chávez concluded.

Two hundred billion dollars is almost the total amount of four years of oil production in Libya. I would not be surprised if many are rubbing their hands saying, "with this money I will solve the crisis I have here." This is an old story of pillage.[76]

---

74 Fidel Castro Ruz, "la OTAN, la guerra, la mentira y los negocios," March 10, 2011, available at http://www.cubadebate.cu/reflexiones-fidel/2011/03/10/la-otan-la-guerra-la-mentira-y-los-negocios/#.U6-kq_mSySo. See also his previous article, "La Guerra Invitable de la OTAN," March 3, 2011 on Cubadebate, available at http://www.cubadebate.cu/reflexiones-fidel/2011/03/03/la-guerra-inevitable-de-la-otan/#.U6-xsvmSySo.

75 ALBA, Alliance for the Peoples of Our America, which was formed in 2004 by Cuba and Venezuela, is a counter organization created as a response to the market integration of countries exclusively following market prescriptions.

76 Hugo Chávez, "Reunion del Consejo Politico del ALBA," March 4, 2011, available at https://www.youtube.com/watch?v=UerY6TDP8dM, and ALBA's

In its final deliberation, ALBA proposed the creation of a Humanitarian Commission for Peace in Libya attempting to prevent NATO's intervention there. The Commission, accepted by Libya, was rejected due to the opposition of the US and it was never formed. With a Security Council Resolution in hand, a NATO-led air campaign against Qaddafi's armed forces and military installations began on March 19.

Qaddafi was fighting for his own survival and so was Hugo Chávez. On June 30, Chávez announced that he was suffering from cancer and had begun medical treatment in Cuba. On August 1, back in Venezuela after the first round of medical interventions, Chávez announced that Qaddafi was resisting NATO attacks "to the surprise of the world." On national television, Chávez read a letter he had just received from Qaddafi. In this letter addressed to the "Brother combative president, Hugo Chávez", Qaddafi prayed for Chávez's health and pledge to continue the war. In his words to the President, "The Libyan people and I personally pray for your health and we ask God for your swift health recovery." Qaddafi and Chávez both agreed that the war was had been unleashed to control Libya politically, to control its resources, and to prevent South-South integration. "I highly value your noble positions and that of other revolutionary leaders of Latin America in support of the people of Libya, I wish we could continue receiving that support, it gives us courage to continue" the Libyan leader concluded and asked Chávez not to recognize the National Transitional Council as the government of Libya. Chávez thanked Qaddafi for his letter and prayed for him "wherever you might be, resisting another imperialist aggression". Venezuela was not going to recognize any transitional government in Libya. For now they were nothing more than a " group of terrorists". Chávez was clear, "we firmly reject this [the uprising against Qaddafi] with all the strength, with all the force of our revolutionary and Bolivarian morality." The message to Qaddafi was also direct:

Qaddafi, comrade, compañero, *salam aleykum*, live, live, we will live, one day we will meet again and we will give each other a hug larger than Africa and South America ... live, fight brother, we are with you and with Libya. We will overcome.[77]

But it was already too late for Qaddafi. Twenty days later, on August 21 2011, Tripoli fell to the uprising and Colonel Mu'amar Qaddafi was on the run. Two

---

declaration read by Cuba's Minister of Foreign Affairs Bruno Rodriguez, available at https://www.youtube.com/watch?v=UerY6TDP8dM

77 Hugo Chávez, August 1, 2011, "Chávez lee carta de Qadafi y desconoce a rebeldes Libios," available at https://www.youtube.com/watch?v=haDwIY-6buE

months later, Qaddafi was killed, and Chávez vowed to remember him as a "martyr."[78]

Throughout 2011, social uprisings spread beyond North Africa, challenging regimes in countries with dissimilar political structures, such as Bahrain, Yemen. Minor protests were registered also in Jordan, Oman and Saudi Arabia but they did not amount to much. The focus in Venezuela was mostly on the fate of its Arab allies in the region: Libya, and by the end of March, Syria.

"They are now threatening Syria," Chávez lamented. The violent clampdown of civil protests against Bashar Al Assad ended in March with at least 61 people dead across the country. The "supposedly pacific protests" were the beginning of a broader plot against Syria, claimed president Chávez. According to him, the plot was to blame Al Assad for the death of his own people. Assad, "our brother, a humanist, a doctor, educated in London ... clearly not an extremist, a person with the highest human sensibility" was the victim of this strategy that was directed by Washington, Chávez argued. The reading from Caracas intended to explain the events in Syria as part of a US strategy whose objective was to transform Syria into a colony. "[T]he empire comes [to Syria] and wants to bombard that people to save it. So cynical. This is a new format that they have made up: generate an armed conflict so they can ... intervene [in] it, and then transform [the country] ... into a colony."[79]

A year later, what began in Syria as isolated street protests against years of political repression at the hands of the Al Assad family, Hafez al Assad, the father, and Bashar, the son, mutated from an upheaval of an initial secular nature into a mostly sectarian conflict. Shia's and Alawites, a branch of Shia' Islam to which the President and his family belonged, stood firmly behind the regime, whereas a plurality of insurgents identifying mostly with Sunni Islam represented the majority of the Syrian population. In the crossfire, minority religious groups, such as Assyrians, Armenians, Maronites, Greeks, Catholics, and Orthodox Christians, decided, for the most part, to side with the government as they feared that the loss of the protection that they had received for years under the Al Assad regime.[80]

---

78 Hugo Chávez, October 20, 2011, "Chávez lamentó el asesinato de Muammar Al Gaddafi," available at https://www.youtube.com/watch?v=WSCaizga66Q

79 Hugo Chávez, March 26, 2011, available at http://multimedia.telesurtv. net/media/telesur.video.web/telesur-web/#!es/video/Chávez-el-imperio-esta-amenazando-al-gobierno-de-siria/

80 Jonathan Randal, "Syria's Threatened Minorities," *New York Times*, May 4, 2012, available at http://www.nytimes.com/2012/05/05/opinion/syrias-threatened-minorities.html?module=Search&mabReward=relbias%3Ar%2C%5B%22RI%3A9% 22%2C%22RI%3A15%22%5D

As the internal conflict intensified, regional and global powers positioned themselves. On one hand, Iran wanted to preserve Syria as its most important Arab ally in the region and its natural bridge to the Hezbollah militia in Lebanon. China, and Russia in particular, stood behind their old time ally from the time of the Cold War. On the other hand, the opposition counted on the support of the US, the European Union, Turkey, and countries in the Arabian Peninsula, such as Saudi Arabia and Qatar, that sought to counterbalance the growing Iranian influence in the region.[81] The first battles of this international confrontation were fought in the United Nations Security Council where both Russia and China vetoed draft resolutions presented for a vote on October 4 2011 and February 4 2012. The draft resolutions called for the immediate cessation of violence and the resolution of the Syrian conflict by "an inclusive Syrian-led political process conducted in an environment free from violence, fear, intimidation and extremism, and aimed at effectively addressing the legitimate aspirations and concerns of the Syrian people". However, the draft resolutions were taken by Russia as a copy of the same model used in Libya that resulted in justifying the use of force by NATO.[82]

In a news conference after his re-election to a fourth term on October 7 2012, Chávez voiced his support for Syria and praised the Russian Federation for its role in the Security Council. "Yesterday I told Vladimir Vladimirovich [Putin] that I congratulated Russia for its position in regards to Syria, and China's position, which was not the same in the case of Libya, unfortunately." Chávez agreed with Russia that the crisis in Syria was "planned and provoked ... produced from outside"; a new reiteration of the Libyan format. Venezuela stood in support of Assad: "[W]ho else should we support? The terrorists?"[83]

The war in Syria and Libya was being fought in the media across the world. Venezuela's 24-hour news channel, TeleSUR, presented Caracas' perspective on these conflicts. Coincidentally, TeleSUR was founded in 2005 following the example established by the Qatari news channel Al Jazeera. In 2005, during the first Arab-South American Presidential meeting in Brasilia, President Chávez announced his plans to create a similar channel in Venezuela. "What a great success it has been for the Arab world . . . the television channel Al Jazeera," he

---

81 Steven Erlanger, "Syria Poses Risks of a Wider Strike," *New York Times*, February 25, 2012, available at http://www.nytimes.com/2012/02/26/world/middleeast/syrian-conflict-poses-risk-of-regional-strife.html?pagewanted=all&module=Search&mabRew ard=relbias%3As%2C%5B%22RI%3A10%22%2C%22RI%3A17%22%5D

82 Security Council , Department of Public Information, SC 6627th meeting October 4, 2011, and SC 6711th meeting, February 4, 2012, available at http://www.un.org/News/Press/docs/2012/sc10536.doc.htm

83 Hugo Chávez, press interview, October 9, 2012, available at https://www.youtube.com/watch?v=Ue3M6CYUCQw

said. "[W]e in South America have a proposal for a South American news channel. We should think in the framework of our strategic agenda, about having a media alliance between Latin-American and Arab channels".[84] Al Jazeera interviewed Chávez on different occasions throughout his 13 years in power, projecting a favorable image of him throughout the Arab world. When the Arab Spring spread to Libya and Syria, and given Qatar's support for the opposition in both countries, Venezuela's TeleSUR reacted against Doha, signaling the rupture of Venezuela's historically good relationship with Qatar.[85] A case in point was reflected during a TeleSUR insignia program *Dossier*. Without mentioning Al Jazeera, the news analyst Walter Martinez affirmed: "There were some channels that seemed to be doing a pretty good job in the Arab world." While speaking with the TeleSUR correspondent in Damascus, Hisham Wannous,[86] Martinez commented that "[these television channels] were bought and [their] editorial line was changed". Wannous responded that in effect these networks worked for 10 or 15 years to gain the trust of the Syrian people and the Arab world, and they "used this trust to spread false information, thinking that the audience will believe them because they had gained their trust."[87]

The grand strategy, Venezuela insisted, was to punish Syria for its "anti-imperialist stance", a payback for its "support for the resistance in Lebanon and Palestine" and its support for "Iran's right to develop a nuclear program for its own energy needs". Beyond punishing Assad, the geostrategic interests of the superpowers were to "resuscitate old colonialist glories that they had in the Arab world in the past". For example, regarding Turkey's participation in the conflict, TeleSUR argued that the Turks wanted to "reclaim its Ottoman Empire". The Gulf Monarchies, such as Saudi Arabia and Qatar, "have to finance and respond to the objectives of the United States in Syria in order to pay for military assistance that they get from the United States." The first objective in this grand strategy is Syria, followed by Iran, and culminating in the

---

84 Hugo Chávez (10 May 2005), 'Discurso del Presidente de la República Bolivariana de Venezuela Hugo Chávez Frías con motivo de la I Cumbre de la Comunidad Suramericana de Naciones y la Liga Árabe de Naciones', in Ministerio de Comunicación e Información (Ed.) *2005 Año del Salto Adelante* (Caracas: Ediciones de la Presidencia de la República, 2005), 341.

85 See Chávez' comments on Sheikh Hamad bin Khalifa al Thani, ruler of Qatar in Al Jazeera's interview, available at http://redsolsur.blogspot.ae/2009/03/entrevista-del-presidente-Chávez-con_31.html 2009, and later his claims that many of the protests against Qadaffi were staged in a studio in Doha, available at https://www.youtube.com/watch?v=nfRLODcaYdo

86 Wannous worked for Syrian television before joining Al Jazeera.

87 Interview with Hisham Wannous, corresponsal of TeleSUR, November 25, 2012, available at http://juanmartorano.wordpress.com/2012/11/25/periodista-hisham-wannous-en-siria-esta-ocurriendo-una-conspiracion-dirigida-por-eeuu-y-aliados/.

displacement of "Russia from the Mediterranean and the Black Sea in order for the United States to have full control of all access to oil and gas routes".[88] This was the only explanation they could give the events unfolding now in Syria. Their anti-colonialist, anti-imperialist rhetoric did not allow them to contemplate any other alternative response.

There could be no criticism of Al Assad's democratic credentials, that was not the point, Venezuela insisted. Bashar al Assad had begun a series of political reforms since he took power in 2000 and not just since the disturbances began in 2011. Nevertheless, those reforms became entangled because of the obstacles that the "West put in the way in order to involve Syria in a wider conflict: the presence of the Syrian army in Lebanon, and the accusation of its participation in the assassination of Rafik Hariri in 2005, etc." After 2011, the pace of these reforms accelerated, Caracas insisted. The emergency law was eliminated, and a law allowing new parties to participate in politics was enacted. Parliamentary elections, referendums regarding the constitution, and municipal elections were implemented, but armed groups interfered with and prevented implementation of these reforms. These reforms were needed and the government responded to these demands.[89] Venezuela was not going to consider any other interpretation, question Assad's human rights record, or admit the emergence of a sectarian conflict. To its followers across Latin America, TeleSUR insisted that the Syrian Arab Army and Syrian citizens supported President al Assad, there could not be another explanation of the events unfolding. The sectarian war was a foreign element in the internal conflict. It was implanted by external forces in Syria. "They were counting on a sectarian war, but no, the Syrian people are conscious of the trap laid down by the West and its Arab allies." The sectarian divisions, "all fabricated", are not working despite the massacres that had been committed to create a civil war in the country. "Syrians have remained united."[90]

TeleSUR continued articulating Venezuela's view of the events in Syria while Chávez was fighting for his life in the first months of 2013. On March 6 , 2013, Chávez finally succumbed to his illness. The conflict in Syria and Libya would turn much more violent deriving into a confrontation of mostly a sectarian nature. The Arab World they had come to know was collapsing in front of them, as new forces emerged in a climate of sectarian, political, and social confrontation that engulfed their allies in the region in a new chapter of

---

88 Interview with Hisham Wannous, corresponsal of TeleSUR, November 25, 2012, available at http://juanmartorano.wordpress.com/2012/11/25/periodista-hisham-wannous-en-siria-esta-ocurriendo-una-conspiracion-dirigida-por-eeuu-y-aliados/.

89 Interview with Hisham Wannous.

90 Hisham Wannous, *Dossier*, Walter Martinez, November 12, 2012. Available at http://juanmartorano.wordpress.com/2012/11/25/periodista-hisham-wannous-en-siria-esta-ocurriendo-una-consp iracion-dirigida-por-eeuu-y-aliados/

violence no one could have anticipated. Latin American Revolutionaries had no place in this new world emerging in front of them.

Epilogue

For the last 60 years, Latin Americans revolutionaries developed a unique identification with the Arab world. Their connection with the region was both historical and revolutionary. In their own reading of global affairs, Latin American revolutionaries inscribed their own history into the struggles for economic and political independence taking place in the wider Afro-Asian region in general and the Arab world in particular. Progressive Arab regimes were confronting traditional centers of global power with an unparalleled success and an assertiveness in their foreign and national policies not ever seen before in Latin America. Their revolutionary ethos did the rest. At times ignoring or setting aside cultural differences and complex regional power interactions, Latin American revolutionaries were convinced that there was a unique revolutionary partnership, an identical historical call, between them and some Arab countries during and after the Cold War.

They represent a break with a general lack of interests in the affairs of the Middle East and the Arab world in general in Latin America. This lack of interest could be attributed to the fact that most nations of the region had been formally independent for more than a century when the final days of colonialism arrived in the Arab world, mostly in the second half of the twentieth century. It is possible Latin American intellectuals thought that because of cultural and historical differences there was little connection between the two regions that would permit meaningful comparisons. This lack of interest can probably also be attributed to a generalized intellectual dependency on the West. Latin American intellectual and political elites, with very few exceptions, had been brought up believing in the superiority of European cannons of thought and knowledge, and in the conviction that whatever could come from other regions of the world was not only inferior, but potentially dangerous to their own societies. As an example of this view an editorialist of *El Comercio de Lima* depicted the Arab World back in the 1950s as made up of "fanatics who perform solemn and violent oath-taking ceremonies before Saladin's mausoleum in which they pledge to 'wipe out the infidels' from the land of Palestine."[1]

Interest in the Arab world predates the ascendance of revolutionaries to power in Latin America. Intellectuals of the standing of the Venezuelan Juan Pablo Pérez Alfonzo and the Panamanian Eloy Benedetti were the first to alert Latin Americans to the profound changes taking place across the Atlantic in

---

1 "La Acción de la ONU," *El Comercio* (Lima), November 3, 1956, 2.

the 1950s. Theirs is the first call for a direct engagement with Arab countries, Egypt in particular. Pérez Alfonzo and Benedetti were both convinced of the need to act together with Arab leaders in order to counterbalance the economic and political power of stronger nations, and to put an end to surviving colonial structures. Nasser's Egypt emerged as a referent to those intellectuals committed to parallel anticolonialist causes around the Americas. Their writings about the social and political changes taking place in Egypt came at a time when the fear of international communism had led to the clampdown of democratically elected and social-progressive regimes throughout Latin America.

Others further to the left, ostracized after years of autocratic expansion, would focus on the person of Nasser. The Egyptian leader would remind them of the historical Latin American strongman of the nineteen century: the caudillo—a man from the armed forces with no attachments but to his own people, a leader ready to confront conservative elites and predatory foreign interests. By the end of the twentieth century, Hugo Chávez in Venezuela would say he was fulfilling that mission, claiming during his years in power to directly descend from Nasser's lineage.

Something fundamentally different emerged in Latin America with the Cuban revolution. For the first time in more than a century of living as independent nations, a government in the region turned across the Atlantic as a matter of state policy. The Cuban revolutionaries draw parallels between their own colonial and post-colonial experience and that of the emerging nations of the Afro-Asian region and found commonalities that were often disproportionate, and disregarded the particularities of each historical process. Havana had the firm conviction not only that the internal transformations taking place in these countries parallel those taking place in Cuba, but also that there needed to be an alliance with these Arab countries in order to put a final end to the colonial and semi-colonial order.

Despite clear differences in their social and economic projects, Cubans admired Egypt for what it represented to nations across Africa and Asia, the bastion of anti-colonialism. In addition, the emergence of the Afro-Asian bloc represented the perfect alternative to a Cuba increasingly isolated from the inter-American system. With the radicalization of the Cuban revolution, and Cuba's expulsion from the inter-American system, Castro would find in Egypt a referent for its new approach to the world. Cairo was Cuba's point of entry into both the Arab world, Africa, and the emerging nations of the Third World. Nevertheless, it would soon be clear to the Cuban government Cairo was not interested in exploring a military alliance with the Island. In the early 1960s, the particularities of the radicalization of Cuba's revolution and the dynamics of the Cold War took Cuba on a path where a neutral stance in global politics—maintaining good relations with both superpowers in order to have the benefits of their economic aid and political protection was untenable for

Cuba. Cuba's revolution was fundamentally anti-American precisely because it had been the United States, the country regarded as the colonial power, from which they were seeking independence. Cuba needed to bring in the Soviets for its own survival.

Cuba's revolutionary zeal found in the Algerian revolution much of what it did not find in Egypt. Cuba considered Algeria a mirror of its own revolution and Fidel Castro was convinced that Algeria was going through the same revolutionary process, and had the same historical role to play as a new beacon of revolution. The coup d'etat against Ben Bella in June 1965 proved him wrong, but the campaign in Morocco and the misadventures in Africa consolidated the internationalist spirit of the Cuban revolution.

This saga of encounters between Latin American revolutionaries and the Arab world is also an interesting case of diplomatic history and in particular on the power dynamics of the Cold War and the unipolar world that emerged thereafter. Cuba's alliance with Algeria, in the rationale of the Cold War, was an act of defiance against the United States, but it also was an act of independence from the Soviet Union. While the Soviets were attempting to consolidate their own economy and negotiating a more stable international system with the United States, the Cubans pressed hard to export the revolutionary ethos across the global South. Ambassador Jorge Serguera was unequivocal on Cuba's decision to support Algeria during its military confrontation with Morocco:

> We did not consult with the Soviet Union, least of all did we ask for permission of any sort whatsoever. Those were our arms, our soldiers, and our commitment to that revolution. The Soviets were not consulted, we were nobody's lackeys![2]

Although Cuba depended on the Soviet Union for its own survival and continued to receive aid throughout the 1960s, at least in years after the Cuban Missile Crisis fiasco, Havana made sure that the Soviet Union knew that the Cuban revolution could not be treated in the same way as its Eastern European satellites.

The Afro-Asian Solidarity Conference held in Algiers in 1965 served as the forum from which to launch Cuba's complains against the socialist bloc's treatment of the emerging Afro-Asian revolutions. No other Cuban leader was as blunt as Guevara in condemning the Soviet Union, but his speech accurately reflected the official opinion of the Cuban government. The conference in Algeria was used as a platform to launch a foreign policy that was fiercely independent and committed to encouraging the expansion of anticolonial, anti-imperialist regimes regardless of the consequences to the superpower's

---

2 Serguera, interview with the author.

commitment to a peaceful coexistence. Ambassador Serguera recalled Guevara's pointed criticism of fellow socialist nations:

> Che [Guevara] stated that there were socialist countries that needed technology, and that needed arms, and denounced the rich socialist countries selling that technology and arms as if they were gold. Was that a coherent attitude by the socialist states? Of course not, either we all were revolutionaries or we were not.[3]

A rapprochement with the Soviet Union after 1968, and the military defeats in Africa and Latin America forced Cuba to be more selective in its support of Latin American insurgency groups. Militarily defeated in Nicaragua, unable to receive full military support from Cuba, and anxious to give an international projection to their movement of national liberation, the Sandinistas accepted the invitation to train in Jordan and then in Lebanon, over all embracing the Palestinian cause. Once in power, the Sandinistas became the uncompromised supporters of the Palestinian struggle and remained so throughout the 1980s. Notwithstanding the Soviet support for Cuba and Nicaragua in the early years of the 1980s, the encounter between Sandinistas and Palestinians and the subsequent friendship between the two organizations was anything but the Soviet scheme Washington so fiercely denounced. The allegations reinforced, nevertheless, the arguments against the Sandinistas and in favor of the military campaign Washington launched on Nicaragua. If anything, the historical evidence tells another story: two relatively weak movements of National Liberation seeking to expand their international exposure.

Years later, the PLO helped the Sandinistas establish contacts with both Iran, and the leader of Libya, Mohammad al Qaddafi. Since coming to power in 1969 Qaddafi had been interested in branding Libya as a new center of revolutionary struggles across the world. Further investigation is needed on the links between revolutionary groups in Latin America and Libya. The Colombian *Movimiento 19 de Abril* (M-19) and Chile's *Movimiento de Izquierda Revolucionario* (MIR), probably among others, were invited in the late 1980s to receive military training in Libya. In the case of the Colombian M-19, the training, which did not advance their military expertise and might have unnecessarily risked the revelation of their identities to security agencies of other countries, took place in May 1987 lasting throughout the month of Ramadan.[4] Interests to see first-hand what was going on in Libya and the need to establish links with other revolutionary movements might have been the drive behind their acceptance of the invitation to Libya. Nevertheless, by 1990 in part as a sign of the new times,

---

3 Serguera, interview with the author.

4 María Eugenia Vásquez Perdomo, *Escrito para no morir: bitácora de una militancia* (Bogotá: Ministerio de Cultura, 2000), 393–411.

the end of the Cold War and the beginning of new era, the M-19 renounced to its revolutionary activities joining other political parties in Colombia.

Post-Cold War encounters restarted 10 years later with the Venezuelan President Hugo Chávez. After the electoral defeat of the Sandinistas and the inauguration of a new government after 1990, encounters between Latin American revolutionaries and the Arab world seemed definitively closed. Chávez opened a new chapter. Venezuela's presidency of OPEC drove Chávez to the Arab world. His involvement in the affairs in the Arab world increased over time together with his conviction that history had shaped profound parallels to both regions, and that Arabs and Latin Americans were bound to confront the new unipolar international system that emerged after the end of the Cold War.

Chávez developed an identification with the Arab world that had the same referents as those used in the past, but that was original in many ways. Like other revolutionaries before him, Chávez found historical parallels and common current challenges between the Arab world and Latin America. He was a Nasserist of the twenty-first century, convinced that his leadership was part of a chain of anti-imperialist leaders that emerged in world affairs starting with Nasser, continued by Castro, and Qaddafi. The historical parallels between Venezuela and the Arab world were evident to him because of the involvement of the oil industry in the shaping of their states. The coup d'etat against him in 2002 and the invasion of Iraq in 2003 were manifestations of the same neocolonial attempt to control their oil wealth. Emerging as one of the few leaders in Latin America or the Arab world uncompromisingly defending the Palestinian cause, years later Chávez would find parallels between the Israeli military campaigns and his own neighbor Colombia. He accused both Israel and Colombia as being the "armed fist" of the United States, proxies that Venezuela and Palestine had to confront.

Overtime and with his intense involvement in the affairs of the Arab world, Chávez began to develop a personal identification with the Arab World. A parallel "Arab persona" connected him with the region in ways no other Latin American had expressed before. This identification allowed him to speak directly to the Arab masses: his heart was beating alongside "millions of Arab hearts."[5] The connection with "millions of Arab hearts," which accounted for the popularity he enjoyed for years among the Arab public, was made possible by the inability of the region to come to a general consensus to the cataclysmic events of the first decade of the twenty-first century. By confronting the United States over its invasion of Iraq, and Israel for its campaign against Lebanon

---

5   Hugo Chávez, interview by Mohamed Kirshan, Al Jazeera TV, Doha, August 4, 2006.

and Gaza, he could be claiming to understand and speak for millions of Arabs[6] at a time in which it was clear that there was a lack of consensus among Arab leader on how to respond to the military developments taking place in the region. In sum, he developed a populist discourse that connected him directly with millions of frustrated Arab citizens across the region,[7] a variant of the phenomenon of populism but now on a transnational dimension.[8]

By the end of 2010 an unpredicted new phenomenon began to engulf the Arab world. A general uprising against governments in the region began to emerge starting in Tunis. Parallels between both regions were drove again by Latin American Revolutionaries as they tried to explain the new phenomenon: this was at first a clear uprising against neoliberalism and neocolonial control. As such, the events in Tunis and Egypt were explained from Caracas as replicas of the popular uprising in Venezuela in 1989.

Latin American revolutionaries could not understand that their allies of decades could also be oppressive regimes who had controlled the lives of millions of their citizens, and enriched very few. They had been oblivious to the internal sectarian tensions, the gross violation of basic human rights, and in general the repressive nature of these regimes. Initially, the uprisings in Egypt and Tunisia were celebrated as a revolution against neoliberal capitalism, but when the uprisings expanded to Libya and Syria, the explanations from Caracas and Havana changed. This time, the uprisings were not revolts against the economic policies of neoliberalism; they were part of a wider campaign for the economic, military, and political control of the Arab world by the West.

The uprisings were more than a rejection of the neoliberal reforms that had taken place in the last decades in the region. The anti-imperialist discourse was not enough to explain the nature of the social and political uprisings. History proved them right when it came to the feeble commitment of the West to a democratic transition in Libya, and to the civil war Chávez predicted to be looming in the horizon in that country. Chávez, fighting for his own life against a terminal illness, could not see the legitimacy of the demands of those on the

---

6 Francisco Panizza and Romina Miorelli, "Populism and Democracy in Latin America," *Ethics & International Affairs*, 23.1 (2009), 41.

7 Alan Knight, "Populism and Neopopulism in Latin America, Especially Mexico," *Journal of Latin American Studies*, 30.2 (1998), 223.

8 Scholars of Latin America have not been able to arrive at a consensus on how to define the phenomenon of populism. I am using Alan Knight's minimum elements. See also Ignacio Walker, "The Three Lefts of Latin America," *Dissent*, 55.4 (2008), 5–12; Jeremy Adelman, "Post-Populist Argentina," *New Left Review*, 203 (January–February 1994), 65–91. Dodson and Dorraj have compared the phenomenon of populism in Iran and Venezuela, Michael Dodson and Manochehr Dorraj, "Neo-Populism in Comparative Perspective: Iran and Venezuela," *Comparative Studies of South Asia, Africa, and the Middle East*, 291 (2009), 137–151.

streets in Tripoli and Damascus. The football stadium near Benghazi named after Hugo Chávez was now renamed the Martyrs of February in honor of the victims of the uprising against Qaddafi. The Arab World they had in their minds had crumbled and collapsed. Incapable of reading and understand the demands coming from "millions of Arab hearts" Latin American revolutionaries closed the last chapter of their encounters with the Arab world.

Bibliography

Primary Sources

Addiyar. "El Gupo de Habla Hispana en el Estado Palestino," Birzeit: West Bank, Boletín #1. February 1989.

_____."El Grupo de Habla Hispana en el Estado Palestino," Birzeit: West Bank, February 1990.

Departamento de Propaganda y Educación Política del F.S.L.N. *Un Pueblo Alumbra su Historia.* Managua: Centro de Publicaciones "Silvio Mayorga" 1, 1981.

FRUS (Foreign Relations of the United States). 1950, vol. II, *The United Nations; The Western Hemisphere.* Washington, DC: United States Government Printing Office, 1976.

———. 1952–1954, vol. IV, *The American Republics.* Washington, DC: United States Government Printing Office, 1983.

———1958–1960, vol. VI, *Cuba.* Washington, DC: United States Government Printing Office, ,

———. 1955–1957, vol. VII, *American Republics: Central and South America.* Washington, DC: United States Government Printing Office, 1987.

———. 1947, vol. VIII, *The American Republics.* Washington, DC: United States Government Printing Office, 1972.

———. 1948, vol. IX, *Western Hemisphere.* Washington, DC: United States Government Printing Office, 1972.

———. 1945, vol. IX, *The American Republics.* Washington, DC: United States Government Printing Office, 1969.

———. 1961–1963, vol. XI, *Cuba,* October 1962–December 1963. Washington, DC: United States Government Printing Office, 1996.

———. 1955–1957, vol. XVI, *Suez Crisis July 26–December 31, 1956.* Washington, DC: United States Government Printing Office, 1990.

———. 1955–1957, vol. XVII, *Arab–Israeli Dispute 1957.* Washington, DC: United States Government Printing Office, 1987.

———. 1961–1963, vol. XXI, *Africa.* Washington, DC: United States Government Printing Office, 1995.

———. 1952–1954, *Guatemala.* Washington, DC: United States Government Printing Office, 2003.

Ministerio para la Inversión Extranjera y la Colaboración Económica. *Colaboración Cubana a otros países*. Havana: Ministerio para la Inversión Extranjera y la Colaboración Económica, Marzo 2000.

Nasser, Gamal Abdel. *Speeches and Press-Interviews*. Cairo: Information Department. UAR, January–December 1958.

Nasser, Gamal Abdel. *Speeches and Press-Interviews*. Cairo: Information Department. UAR, January–December, 1959.

Nasser, Gamal Abdel. *Speeches and Press-Interviews*. Cairo: Information Department. UAR, January–December, 1960.

Nasser, Gamal Abdel. *Speeches and Press-Interviews*. Cairo: Information Department. UAR, January–December, 1961.

Nasser, Gamal Abdel. *Speeches and Press-Interviews*. Cairo: Information Department. UAR, January–December, 1962.

Republic of Cuba. *Cuba in the Second Conference of Non-aligned Nations*. Havana: The Foreign Ministry Information Department, 1964.

United States District Court for the District of Columbia, *United States of America vs. Oliver L. North*, Criminal No. 88-0080-02 GAG. 1988.

Interviews

Nicaragua

Herrera, Leticia, Sandinista leader trained in Lebanon, interview with author, August 23, 2002, Managua, Nicaragua.

Ortega, Humberto, Former commander of Nicaragua's armed forces, interview with author, August 14, 2002, Managua, Nicaragua.

Salameh, George, PLO ambassador to Nicaragua, interview with author, August 15, 2002, Managua, Nicaragua.

Suarez, Jacinto, Ambassador to the USSR and FSLN international representative in 1978, interview with author, August 12, 2002, Managua, Nicaragua.

Venecco, Raúl, Former Commander of Nicaraguan Air Forces. Interview with author August 21, 2002, Managua, Nicaragua.

Vivas, Rene, member of the group of Sandinistas that traveled to the Middle East, interview with author, August 16, 2002, Managua, Nicaragua.

Cuba

Azugaray, Carlos, Vice-Rector Institute of International Relations, interview with author, Havana, December 16, 2001.

Serguera R, Jorge, Cuba's first Ambassador to Algeria, interview with author, Havana, December 21, 2001.

Entralgo, Armando, Former Ambassador of Cuba to Ghana and Director of the Centro de Estudios de Africa y el Medio Oriente, interview with author, Havana, December 30, 2001.

Palestine

Abu Shariff, Bassam. Former spokesperson of the Popular Front for the Liberation of Palestine, and by 2001, special representative to the United States and Europe of President Arafat. Ramallah, July 22, 2001. Interview conducted in English.

Abu Ali, Mustafa. Leader of the Palestinian Popular Front for the Liberation of Palestine.

Abu-Garbia, Ohtman. President's Deputy for Ideological and Political Affairs. Leader of Al-Fatah, personal witness of the links between the Cuban revolution and the Palestinian revolution. Ramallah, July 26, 2001. Interview conducted in Arabic and Spanish, Ahmad Yacoub translator.

Husseini, Yamila. Colombian-born Palestinian woman who was a popular leader during the first Intifada. Boston, September 2000 and Ramallah July 2001. Interview conducted in Spanish.

Husseini, Zoraida. A Colombian-born Palestinian. Mrs. Husseini was a popular leader during the first Intifada. Ramallah, July 2001. Interview conducted in Spanish.

Malki, Riad. A leader of the first Intifada against Israel and a former student at Javeriana University in Colombia. Ramallah, July 2001. Interview conducted in Spanish.

Soboh, Ahmed. Ministry of Planning and International Cooperation and former PLOAmbassador to Mexico. Al-Birah, July 2001. Interview conducted in Spanish.

Thalhami, Dalwood. Political leader of the Democratic Front for the Liberation of Palestine, member group of the PLO.

Yacoub, Ahmad. Palestinian poet who studied in Cuba and returned to Palestine after the Oslo agreements. Ramallah, July 2001. Interview conducted in Spanish.

Algeria

Ben Bella, Ahmed. Former President of Algeria. Oran, Algeria, October 2005. Interview conducted in Spanish.

Archives

Nicaragua

Centro de Historia Militar Ejército de Nicaragua.
Archivo del Ministerio de Relaciones Exteriores de Nicaragua.
Instituto de Historia de Nicaragua y Centro América Universidad Centroamericana.

Cuba

Biblioteca del Centro de Estudios de Africa y Medio Oriente CEAMO.
Instituto de Amistad con los Pueblos.

Newspapers

Argentina

La Patria, Buenos Aires. 1956, 1957.

Brazil

Impresa Popular, Rio de Janeiro. 1955 – 1957.
Jornal do Comercio, Rio de Janeiro. 1956–1958.
Jornal Israelita, Rio de Janeiro. 1956–1957.
O Estado de São Paulo, São Paulo. 1956–1957.

Chile

Mundo Judío, Santiago. 1956.

Cuba

Revolución, Havana. 1959–1963.
Granma, Havana. 1965–1970.
Bohemia, Havana. 1956–1959.
Verde Olivo, Havana. 1959

England

The Times. 1898–1993.

France

Le Monde Diplomatic, 1997.

Israel

Jerusalem Post, Jerusalem. 1979–1981.
Ha'arest, 1980–1985.

Mexico

El Excelsior

Nicaragua

Novedades, 1969–1972.
Barricada, 1979–1985.
Nuevo Diario, 1982.
Nuevo Amanecer Cultural.

Peru

El Comercio de Lima, 1956.

USA

Washington Post, 1979–1982.
Christian Science Monitor, 1979–1982.
Wall Street Journal, 1979–1982.
New York Times, 1851–1993.

Bibliography for the Main Text

Adelman, Jeremy. "Post-Populist Argentina," *New Left Review*, 203 (Jan–Feb. 1994), 65–91.

Agar, Corbinos Lorenzo, Robledo Antonia, Abdelouahed Akmir, Bartet Leyla, Jiménez Mayda, Marín-Gúzman Roberto, Neuza Neif Nabbhan, Nweihed Aldome, Salhi Mohamed, Yaser Juan, eds. *Mundo. El mundo Arabe y América Latina.* Madrid: UNESCO, 1997.

Ajami, Fouad. *The Arab Predicament: Arab Political Thought and Practice Since 1967.* Cambridge: Cambridge University Press, 1981.

Alexander, Yonah and Sinai Joshua. *Terrorism: The PLO Connection.* New York: Crane Russak, 1989.

Anon. "La Primera Conferencia de Solidaridad de los Pueblos de Africa, Asia y América Latina," *Cuba Socialista,* 54 (February 1966).

Arboleda, Jesús. *The Cuban Counter-Revolution.* Athens, OH: Ohio University Center for International Studies, 2000.

Ageron, Charles-Robert. *Modern Algeria: A History from 1830 to the Present.* London: Hurst & Company, 1991.

Amuchástegui, Domingo. *Cuba in the Middle East: a brief Chronology.* Institute for Cuban & Cuban-American Studies Occasional Paper Series, 1999.

Arciniegas, Germán. *The State of Latin America;* translated from the Spanish by Harriet de Onís. London: Cassell, 1953.

Ball, S.J. *The Cold War: An International History, 1947–1991.* London: Arnold, 1998.

Becker, Jillian. *The PLO: The Rise and Fall of the Palestine Liberation Organization.* New York: St. Martin's Press, 1984.

Benedetti, Eloy. *Tres Ensayos sobre El Canal de Panama.* Panamá: Ministerio de Educación, 1965.

Bethell, Leslie and Ian Roxburgh, eds. *Latin America Between the Second Cold World War and the Cold War 1944–1948.* Cambridge: Cambridge University Press 1992.

———. ed. *Ideas and Ideologies in Twentieth Century Latin America.* Cambridge: Cambridge University Press, 1996.

———. ed. *Latin America: Economy and Society since 1930.* Cambridge: Cambridge University Press, 1998.

Blight, James and Brenner, Philip. *Sad and Luminous Days: Cuba's Struggle with the Superpowers after the Missile Crisis.* New York: Rowman & Littlefield Publishers, 2002.

Bookmiller, Robert J. "Abdullah's Jordan: America's Anxious Ally," *Alternatives: Turkish Journal of International Relations,* 2.2 (2003), 174–195.

Botman, Selma. *Egypt from Independence to Revolution, 1919–1952.* Syracuse, NY: Syracuse University Press, 1991.

Brands, Hall. *Latin America's Cold War.* Cambridge, MA: Harvard University Press, 2010.

Brenner, Philip. "Cuba and the Missile Crisis," *Journal of Latin American Studies,* 22.1–2, (1990), 115–142.

Cain, P.J. and A.G. Hopkins. *British Imperialism: Innovation and expansion 1788–1914.* New York: Longman Publishing, 1993.

Castañeda, Jorge G. *Utopia Unarmed: The Latin American Left after the Cold War.* New York: Vintage Books, 1994.

———. *Compañero: The Life and Death of Che Guevara.* New York: Alfred K. Knopf, 1997.

Castro, Daniel. ed. *Revolution and Revolutionaries: Guerrilla Movements in Latin America*. Wilmington, DE: Jaguar Books on Latin America, 1999.

Castro, Fidel. Ministerio para la Inversión Extranjera y la Colaboración Económica. *Colaboración Cubana a otros países*. Havana: Marzo, 2000.

———. *Obras Escogidas de Fidel Castro Tomo I, (1953–1962)*. Madrid: Editorial Fundamentos, 1976.

———. *Obras Escogidas de Fidel Castro Tomo II, (1962–1968)*. Madrid: Editorial Fundamentos, 1976.

Castro, Josué De. "O Brasil E O Mundo Afro Asiático," *Revista Brasilense* (São Paulo) 36–38 (1961), 9–15.

Chávez, Hugo. "Discurso del Presidente de la República Bolivariana de Venezuela, Hugo Chavez Frias, con motivo de informar al país sobre el viaje a los países de la OPEC," August 16, 2000, in *2000, Año de la legitimación de poderes. Selección de discursos del Presidente de la República Bolivariana de Venezuela, Hugo Chávez Frías*. Caracas: Ediciones Presidencia de la Republica, 2005, 345–380.

———. "Discurso del Presidente de la República Bolivariana de Venezuela Hugo Chávez Frías con motivo de su gira presidencial por Europa, Asia, África y América," October 29, 2001, in Ministerio de Comunicación e Información (ed.) *2001 Año de las Leyes Habilitantes*. Caracas: Ediciones de la Presidencia de la República, 2005, 527–580.

———. "Discurso del Presidente de la República Bolivariana de Venezuela Hugo Chávez Frías con motivo de la I Cumbre de la Comunidad Suramericana de Naciones y la Liga Árabe de Naciones," May 10, 2005, in Ministerio de Comunicación e Información (Ed.) *2005 Año del Salto Adelante*. Caracas: Ediciones de la Presidencia de la República, 2005, 337–342.

———. "Discurso del Presidente de la República Bolivariana de Venezuela, Hugo Chávez Frías, con motivo de su intervención en la XXVIII Cumbre del Mercado Común del Sur (MERCOSUR)," *2005 Año del Salto Adelante Hacia la Construcción del Socialismo del Siglo XXI. Selección de discursos del Presidente de la República Bolivariana de Venezuela, Hugo Chávez Frías*. Caracas: Ediciones de la Presidencia de la República, 2005, 343–358.

———. "Discurso del Presidente de la República Bolivariana de Venezuela Hugo Chávez Frías con motivo de la inauguración del III foro de alto nivel sobre la cooperación África, América Latina, y el Caribe," February 19, 2002, in Ministerio de Comunicación e Información (Ed.) *2002 Año de la resistencia antiimperialista*. Caracas: Ediciones de la Presidencia de la República, 2002, 183–196,

Clark, William P. "Tasking for Central America Public Diplomacy," Memorandum for the Special Planning Group, The White House, July 12, 1980, 2.

Cleveland, William L. *A History of the Modern Middle East*. Boulder, CO: Westview Press, 1994.

Connelly, Matthew. *A Diplomatic Revolution: Algeria's Fight for Independence and the Origins of the Post-Cold War Era*. Oxford: Oxford University Press, 2002.

Dodson, Michael and Manochehr Dorraj. "Neo-populism in Comparative Perspective: Iran and Venezuela," *Comparative Studies of South Asia, Africa, and the Middle East*, 291 (2009), 137–151.

Dobrynin, Anatoly. *In Confidence: Moscow's Ambassador to America's Six Cold War Presidents (1962–1986)*. New York: Times Books, 1995.

Domínguez, Jorge I. *To Make the World Safe for Revolution: Cuba's Foreign Policy*. Cambridge, MA: Harvard University Press, 1989.

Durch, William J. *Revolution from Afar: the Cuban Armed Forces in Africa and the Middle East*. Arlington, VA: Center for Naval Analyses, 1977.

————. *A Talk on Cuban Military Diplomacy in Africa and the Middle East, 1961–1977*. Arlington, VA: Institute of Naval Studies—Center for Naval Analyses, 1977.

————. *The Cuban Military in Africa and the Middle East from Algeria to Angola*. Arlington, VA: Institute of Naval Studies—Center for Naval Analyses, 1977.

Ellner, Steve. "Venezuela," in Leslie Bethell and Ian Roxborough, eds., *Latin America Between the Second World War and the Cold War 1944–1948*. Cambridge: Cambridge University Press, 147–169.

Fanon, Frantz. *A Dying Colonialism*. New York: Grove Press, 1965.

Fernández, Damián. *Cuba's Foreign Policy in the Middle East*. Boulder, CO: Westview, 1988.

————. *Central America and the Middle East: The Internationalization of the Crisis*. Miami, FL: Florida International University Press, 1990.

Fonseca Amador, Carlos. *Un Nicaraguense en Moscú*. Managua: Secretaria Nacional de Propaganda y Educación Política del FSLN, 1980.

García Blanco, Gisela. *La misión internacionalista de Cuba en Argelia (1963–1964)*. Havana: Dirección Política Principal de las FAR, 1990.

Georges, Fawaz A. 'Rudderless in the Storm'. *Dissent* (00123846), 51.1 (2004), 9–13.

Gleason, Abbot. *Totalitarism: The Inner History of the Cold War*. New York, Oxford University Press, 1995.

Gleijeses, Piero. *Conflicting Missions: Havana, Washington, and Africa, 1959–1976*. Chapel Hill, NC: University of North Carolina Press, 2002.

————. "Ships in the Night: The CIA, the White House and the Bay of Pigs," *Journal of Latin American Studies*, 27.1, February (1995), 1–42.

Goldrich, Daniel. *Radical Nationalism: the Political Orientations of Panamanian Law Students*. Bureau of Social and Political Research. East Lansing, MI: Michigan State University, 1962.

Government of Venezuela. *II Cumbre Africa America del Sur: Cerrando brechas, abriendo oportunidades. Colección Cuadernos para el debate*. Caracas: Ministerio del Poder Popular para la Comunicación y la Informacion, Marzo 2010.

Gorst, Anthony and Lewis, Johnman. *The Suez Crisis*. New York: Routledge, 1997.

Gresh, Alain. *The PLO: the Struggle Within: Towards an Independent Palestinian State*. London: Zed Books, c1988.

Guevara, Ernesto Che. 'Desde el Balcón Afro-Asiático,' in E.C. Guevera, *Obras Escogidas: 1957–1967 La transformación Política Económica y Social*. Havana: Casa de las Américas, 1970.

Hahn, Peter L. "Containment and Egyptian Nationalism: The Unsuccessful Effort to Establish the Middle East Command, 1950–1953," *Diplomatic History*, 11.1, Winter (1987), 23–30.

Halperin, Maurice. *The Taming of Fidel Castro*. Berkeley, CA: University of California Press, 1981.

Harding, Earl. *The Untold Story of Panama*. New York: Athene Press Inc., 1959.

Hause, Malcom. "India: Noncommitted and Nonaligned," *The Western Political Quarterly*, 13.1, March (1960), 70–82.

Heikal, Muhammad Hasanayn. *The Cairo Documents: The Inside Story of Nasser and His Relations with World Leaders, Rebels and Statesmen*. Garden City, NY: Doubleday, 1973.

———. *The Road to Ramadan*. New York: New York Times Book Co., 1975.

Hourani, Albert. *A History of the Arab Peoples*. Cambridge, MA: Harvard University Press, 1991.

———. *Arabic Thought in the Liberal Age: 1798–1939*. Royal Institute of International Affairs 1962; reissued by Cambridge: University Press, 1983.

House Select Committee to Investigate Covert Arms Transactions with Iran and Senate Select Committee on Secret Military Assistance to Iran and the Nicaraguan Opposition. *Testimony of Robert McFarlane, Joint Hearings on the Iran-Contra Investigation*, 100th Congress, 1st session, 1988, vol. 100-2, May 13. Washington, DC: United States Government Printing Office, 1987.

Hunter, Jane. *No Simple Proxy, Israel in Central America*. Washington, DC: Middle East Associates, 1987.

Huntington, Samuel. *The Third Way: Democratization in the Late Twentieth Century*. Oklahoma, OK: Oklahoma University Press 1991.

Hurt, Stephen R., Karim Knio and J. Magnus Ryner. "Social Forces and the Effects of (Post)-Washington Consensus Policy in Africa: Comparing Tunisia and South Africa," *Round Table*, 98.402 (2009), 301–308, accessed June 22, 2014.

Ismael, Tareq Y. *The U.A.R. in Africa: Egypt's Policy Under Nasser*. Evanston, IL: Northwestern University Press, 1971.

Jankowski, James. *Nasser's Egypt, Arab Nationalism, and the United Arab Republic*. Boulder, CO: Lynne Rienner Publishers, 2002.

Jassen, Raúl. *Nasser: Soldado de la Revolución Nacional*. Buenos Aires: A. Peña Lillo, 1961.

Jones, Howard and Randall B. Woods. "The Origins of the Cold War in Europe and the Near East: Recent Historiography and the National Security Imperative," *Diplomatic History*, 17.2 (1993), 251–276.

Karl, Terry Lynn. *The Paradox of Plenty: Oil Booms and Petro-states*, vol. 6. Berkeley, CA: University of California Press, 1997.

Khaled, Leila. *My People Shall Live: the Autobiography of a Revolutionary*. Edited by George Hajjar. London: Hodder and Stoughton, 1973.

Klich, Ignacio and Jeffrey Lesser, eds. *Arab and Jewish Immigrants in Latin America*. London: Frank Cass & Co., 1998.

Knight, Alan. "Populism and Neopopulism in Latin America, Especially Mexico," *Journal of Latin American Studies*, 30.2 (1998), 223–248.

Kopilow, David J. *Castro, Israel and the PLO*. Washington, DC: Cuban-American National Foundation Inc. 1984.

Kyle, Keith. *Suez: Britain's End of Empire in the Middle East*. London: I.B. Tauris Publishers, 2003.

Langley, Lester D. "Negotiating New Treaties with Panama: 1936," *The Hispanic American Historical Review*, 48.2, May (1968), 220–233.

Levering, Ralph B., Vladimir O. Pechatnov, Verna Btozenhart-Viehe and Earl Edmondson. *Debating the Origins of the Cold War: American and Russian Perspectives*. Lanham, MD: Rowman & Littlefield Publishers, c. 2002.

Lewis Gaddis, John. *We Now Know: Rethinking Cold War History*. New York: Oxford University Press, 1997.

Livingstone, Neil C. and David Halevy. *Inside the PLO: Covert Units, Secret Funds, and the War against Israel and the United States*. New York: William Morrow and Company, 1990.

Louis, Roger and Roger Owen, eds. *Suez 1956: The Crisis and its Consequences*. New York: Oxford University Press, 1989.

———. *A Revolutionary Year: The Middle East in 1958*. Washington, DC: Woodrow Wilson Center Press, 2002.

Loveman, Brian and Thomas Davies, eds. *Che Guevara: Guerrilla Warfare*, 2nd edn. Wilmington, NC: Scholarly Resources Inc., 1999.

Lucas, Scott. *Britain and Suez: The Lion's Last Roar*. Manchester: Manchester University Press, 1996.

Malik, Mufti. *Sovereign Creations: Pan-Arabism and Political Order in Syria and Iraq*. Ithaca, NY: Cornell University Press, 1996.

Mandouze, André, ed. *La révolution algérienne par les textes: documents du F.L.N.* Paris: Aujourd'hui, 1974.

Márquez, Gabriel García. *El Coronel no tiene quien le escriba*. Madrid: Espasa, 1996.

Mattini, Luis. *Hombres y mujeres del PRT-ERP: la Pasión Militante*. Buenos Aires: Contrapunto, 1990.

May, Ernest R. and Philip Zelikow, eds. *The Kennedy Tapes: Inside the White House During the Cuban Missile Crisis*. Cambridge, MA: Harvard University Press, 1997.

Mesa-Lago, Carmelo. *Cuba in the 1970s: Pragmatism and Institutionalization*. Albuquerque, NM: University of New Mexico Press, 1974.

Moore, Carlos. *Castro, the Blacks, and Africa*. Los Angeles, CA: Center for Afro-American Studies, University of California, 1988.

Ministerio para la Inversión Extranjera y la Colaboración Económica. *Colaboración Cubana a otros países 1960–1999*. Havana: Ministerio para la Inversión Extranjera y la Colaboración Económica, 2000.

Moreira, Neiva. *El Nasserismo y la Revolución del Tercer Mundo*. Montevideo, Uruguay: Ediciones de la Banda Oriental, 1970.

Mortimer, Robert. *The Third World Coalition in International Politics*, 2nd edn. Foreign Relations of the Third World, No 2. Boulder, CO: Westview Press, 1984.

Nasser, Gamal Abdel. *The Philosophy of the Revolution*. Cairo: Dar el-Maaref, 1955. herehere

Office of the Press Secretary, The Vice President's Office, Washington, DC, "Excerpts from Remarks by Vice President George Bush; Austin Council on Foreign Affairs," Austin, Texas, Thursday, February 28, 1985.

Osman Salih, Kamal Eldin. "The Roots and Causes of the 2011 Arab Uprisings," *Arab Studies Quarterly*, 35.2 (2013), 184–206, accessed June 22, 2014.

Ottaway, David and Marina Ottaway. *Algeria: The Politics of a Socialist Revolution*. Berkeley, CA: University of California Press, 1970.

Pan American Union. Inter-American Treaty of Reciprocal Assistance Signed at the Inter-American Conference for the Maintenance of Continental Peace and Security, Rio de Janeiro, August 15–September 2, 1947. Washington, DC: Pan American Union, General Secretariat, Organization of American States.

Panizza, Francisco and Romina Miorelli, "Populism and Democracy in Latin America," *Ethics & International Affairs*, 23.1 (2009), 39–46.

Partos, Gabriel. *The World That Came in From the Cold*. London: Royal Institute of International Affairs, 1993.

Paz, Octavio. *In Light of India*. London: Harcourt Brace & Co, 1997.

Pérez, Louis A. *Cuba Under the Platt Amendment 1902–1934*. Pittsburgh, PA: University of Pittsburgh Press, 1986.

———. *Cuba: Between Reform and Revolution*, 2nd edn. New York: Oxford University Press, 1995.

———. *Essays on Cuban History: Historiography and Research*. Gainsville, FL: University Press of Florida, 1995.

Perez Alfonzo, Juan Pablo. "Organización de Países Exportadores de Petróleo (OPEP)," *Política: Ideas para una América Nueva*, 45, Enero (1966). 7–19.

Pérez Alfonzo, Juan Pablo. "El Camino de Mossadegh," *Política: ideas para una nueva América*, 61.6 (1967), 15–43 .

Pérez-Stable, Marifeli. *The Cuban Revolution: Origins, Course and Legacy*, 2nd edn. New York: Oxford University Press, 1999.

Ramírez, Sergio. *Adiós Muchachos: Una Memoria de la Revolución Sandinista*. Cali, Colombia: Aguilar, 1999.

Roca, Blas. "Las calumnias trostskistas no pueden mandar a la revolución Cubana," *Cuba Socialista*, 56, April (1966) 81–92.

Rock, David, ed. *Latin America in the 1940s: War and Postwar Transitions*. Berkeley, CA: University of California Press, 1994.

Rodríguez Elizondo, Jose. *Crisis y Renovación de las Izquierdas: de la Revolución Cubana a Chiapas, Pasando por "el caso chileno."* Buenos Aires: Andres Bello, 1995.

Rojo, Ricardo. *My Friend Che*. New York: Dial, 1968.

Ruedy, John. *Modern Algeria: The Origins and Development of a Nation*. Bloomington, IN: Indiana University Press, 1992.

Saenz, Vicente. "Los Canales Internacionales," *Cuadernos Americanos*, 16, Mayo–Junio (1957).

———. "Latinoamérica en el proceso actual del mundo," *Cuadernos Américanos*, 4, (Julio–Agosto,1959), 42–60.

Sayigh, Yazid. *Armed Struggle and the Search for State: The Palestinian National Movement*. Oxford: Clarendon Press, 1997.

Schoultz, Lars. *Beneath the United States: A History of U.S. Policy Toward Latin America*. Cambridge, MA: Harvard University Press, 1998.

Scully, Eileen. "The PLO's Growing Latin American Base," *The Heritage Foundation Backgrounder* (August 2, 1983), 1–8.

Serguera Riveri, Jorge. *Caminos del Che: Datos Ineditos de su Vida*. Mexico, DF: Plaza y Valdes, 1997.

Shamir, Shimon, ed. *Egypt from Monarchy to Republic: A Reassessment of Revolution and Change*. Boulder, CO: Westview Press, 1995.

Shapira, Yoram and Edy Kaufman. "Cuba's Israel Policy: The Shift to the Soviet Line," *Cuban Studies*, 8.1 (January 1978), 22–23.

Shaw, Tony. *Eden, Suez and Mass Media: Propaganda and Persuasion during the Suez Crisis*. London: Tauris Academic Studies, 1996.

Simons, Geoff. "Targeting the Powerless: Sanctions on Iraq," *Global Dialog*, Summer (2000), 55–67.

Smith, Tony. *A Pact with the Devil: Washington's Bid for World Supremacy and the Betrayal of the American Promise*. New York: Routledge, 2007.

———. "New Bottles for New Wine: A Pericentric Framework for the Study of the Cold War," *Diplomatic History*, 24, Fall (2000), 567–591.

———. *America's Mission: The United States and the Worldwide Struggle for Democracy in the Twentieth Century*. Princeton, NJ: Princeton University Press, 1994.

Stephen, Schlesinger and Stephen Kinzer. *Bitter Fruit: The Story of the American Coup in Guatemala*. The David Rockefeller Series on Latin American Studies. Cambridge, MA: Harvard University Press, 1999.

Sterling, Claire. *The Terror Network: The Secret War of International Terrorism*, 1st edn. New York: Holt, Rinehart, and Winston, 1981.

———. "Terrorism: Tracing the International Network," *The New York Times Magazine*, 1, March (1981), Section 6.

Stone, Martin. *The Agony of Algeria*. New York: Columbia University Press, 1997.

Stora, Benjamin. *Algeria 1830–2000: A Short Story*. Ithaca, NY: Cornell University Press, 2001.

Somoza, Anastasio. *Nicaragua Betrayed*. Belmont, MA: Western Islands, 1980.

Tablada, Carlos. *Che Guevara: Economics and Politics in the Transition to Socialism*. Sidney: Pathfinder, 1989.

Tareq, Y. Ismael. "The United Arab Republic in Africa," *Canadian Journal of African Studies*, 2.2, Autumn (1968), 175–194.

Trias, Vivian. "Marxismo y Caudillismo," bound with Neiva Moreira, *El Nasserismo y la Revolución del Tercer Mundo*. Montevideo, Uruguay: Ediciones de la Banda Oriental, 1970, 221–254.

United States State Department, Bureau of Intelligence and Research. "Developing Soviet-Nicaraguan Relations," June 24. Washington, DC: United States State Department, 1981.

———. "The Managua Connection: The Sandinistas and Middle Eastern Radicals," *Public Diplomacy Office Review* (467315), 5. Washington, DC: United States State Department, August, 1985.

United States Department of State and Department of Defense, "The Sandinista Military Build-up;" May 1985, Department of State Publications 9432, Washington, DC: Bureau of Public Affairs, 1985.

———. "Background Paper: Central America," May 27, Washington DC: Bureau of Public Affairs, 1983.

———. "Nicaragua Military Build-up and Support for Central American Subversion," July 18, Washington DC: Bureau of Public Affairs, 1984.

Vásquez Perdomo, María Eugenia. *Escrito para no morir: bitácora de una militancia*. Bogotá: Ministerio de Cultura, 2000.

Vatikiotis, P.J. *Egypt since the Revolution*. New York: Frederick A. Praeger, 1968.

———. *The History of Modern Egypt: From Muhammad Ali to Mubarak*, 4th edn. Baltimore, MD: The Johns Hopkins University Press, 1991.

Vega de Uriza, Melania. *Conozcamos nuestros héroes y mártires de la lucha anti-imperialista*, vol. 1. Managua: Instituto de Historia de Nicaragua y Centroamérica, 1982.

Vilas, Carlos Maria. *The Sandinista Revolution: National Liberation and Social Transformation in Central America*. Berkeley, CA: Center for the Studies of the Americas, 1986.

Walker, Ignacio. "The Three Lefts of Latin America," *Dissent*, 55.4 (2008), 5–12.

Wallach, Janet and John Wallach. *Arafat: In the Eyes of the Beholder.* New York: Carol Publishing Group, 1990.

Waterbury, John. "Reflections on the Extent of Egypt's Revolution: Socioeconomic Indicators," in Shimon Shamir, *Egypt from Monarchy to Republic: A Reassessment of Revolution and Change,* Boulder, CO: Westview Press, 1995, 61–65.

———. *The Egypt of Nasser and Sadat: The Political Economy of Two Regimes.* Princeton, NJ: Princeton University Press. 1984.

Wiarda, Howard J. "The Latin American Development Process and the New Developmental Alternatives: Military 'Nasserism' and 'Dictatorship with Popular Support,'" *The Western Political Quarterly,* 25 (1972), 472.

Willetts, Peter. *The Non-aligned Movement: the Origins of a Third World Alliance.* New York: Nichols Publishing Co., 1978.

Yoram, Shapira and Edy Kauman. "Cuba's Israel Policy: The Shift to the Soviet Line," *Cuban Studies,* 8, January (1978), 22–35.

Zimmerman, Matilde. *Sandinista: Carlos Fonseca and the Nicaraguan Revolution.* Durham, NC: Duke University Press, 2000.

Videorecording

Isaacs, Jeremy. *Cold War* [videorecording] production for Turner Original Productions, Inc. Burbank, CA: Warner Home Video; [Atlanta, Ga.]: CNN Productions, 1998. v. 4.

Index